The Complete Idiot's Reference Card

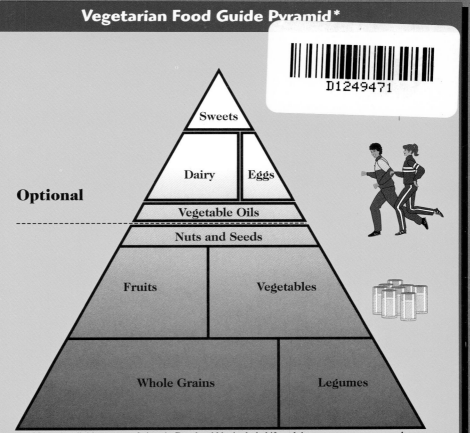

Vegetarian Food Guide Pyramid*

- Sweets
- Dairy | Eggs
- **Optional**
- Vegetable Oils
- Nuts and Seeds
- Fruits | Vegetables
- Whole Grains | Legumes

Note: A reliable source of vitamin B_{12} should be included if no dairy or eggs are consumed.

*Source: Third International Congress on Vegetarian Nutrition and Loma Linda University; reprinted with permission.

For Adults

➤ Aim for at least the minimum number of daily servings from each food group.

➤ Eat according to your appetite. If you need more calories than this meal guide suggests, then eat a greater number of servings from all of the groups to meet your energy needs.

➤ Vegans should be sure to include a reliable source of vitamin B12 in their diets.

alpha books

Description of Food Groups and Recommendations for Food Selection

Food Group	Examples of Food Items	Recommendations
Whole grains	Grains: wheat, corn, oats, rice, millet, etc. Grain products: bread, pasta, tortillas.	Select whole-wheat and whole-grain products.
Legumes	Beans and peas: soy, pinto, kidney, navy, limas, peas, lentils, garbanzos. Soy and soy products: tofu, soy drinks, texturized protein foods.	Select soy-based milk alternatives fortified with calcium, vitamin D, and vitamin B12.
Vegetables	All vegetables.	Emphasize leafy, green and yellow vegetables. Eat both cooked and raw.
Fruits	All fruits.	Emphasize whole fruits rather than juice.
Nuts and seeds	Nuts: almonds, walnuts, peanuts, etc. Seeds: pumpkin, squash, sunflower, etc. Butters: peanut, almond, sesame (tahini).	Eat raw, dry-roasted, or in foods rather than deep-fried.
Vegetable oils	Plant oils: canola, corn, olive, etc.	Emphasize those high in monounsaturates such as olive, sesame, and canola. Limit tropical oils (coconut, palm kernel, palm oil). Avoid hydrogenated fats.
Milk and dairy	Milk, yogurt, cheese.	Emphasize nonfat and low-fat products. If dairy is avoided, must ensure adequate, reliable sources of calcium and vitamin D.
Eggs		Limit eggs or use egg whites only.
Sweets	Honey, syrup (molasses, maple, carob), sugar, sweeteners, jams, jellies, etc.	Eat in moderation.
Vitamin B12	Dietary supplement of fortified foods	A reliable source of B12 (cobalamin) should be included if dairy and eggs are avoided.

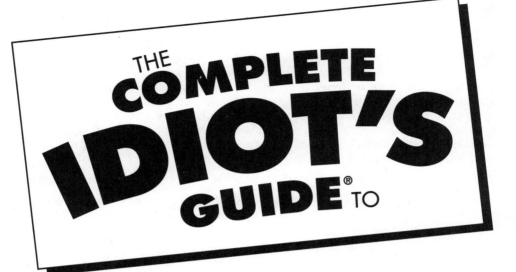

THE **COMPLETE IDIOT'S GUIDE**® TO

Being Vegetarian

by Suzanne Havala, M.S., R.D., F.A.D.A.

alpha books

A Division of Macmillan General Reference
A Pearson Education Macmillan Company
1633 Broadway, New York, NY 10019

For my wonderful parents, Milt and Kay Babich.

Copyright © 1999 by Suzanne Havala

Macmillan Publishing books may be purchased for business or sales promotional use. For information please write: Special Markets Department, Macmillan Publishing USA, 1633 Broadway, New York, NY 10019.

International Standard Book Number: 0-02862879-9
Library of Congress Catalog Card Number: 98-89732

01 00 99   8 7 6 5 4 3 2

Interpretation of the printing code: the rightmost number of the first series of numbers is the year of the book's printing; the rightmost number of the second series of numbers is the number of the book's printing. For example, a printing code of 99-1 shows that the first printing occurred in 1999.

Printed in the United States of America

Development Team

Publisher
Susan Clarey

Executive Editor
Anne Ficklen

Managing Editor
Cindy Kitchel

Marketing Brand Manager
Felice Primeau

Editor
Jim Willhite

Production Team

Production Editor
Christy Wagner

Copy Editor
Susan Aufheimer

Cover Designer
Mike Freeland

Photo Editor
Richard H. Fox

Illustrator
Kevin Spear

Book Designers
Scott Cook and Amy Adams of DesignLab

Indexer
Sandra Henselmeier

Layout/Proofreading
Angela Calvert
Natalie Evans
Daniela Raderstorf
Julie Trippetti

Contents at a Glance

Contents

Appendices

Foreword

The fourth edition of the *Dietary Guidelines for Americans* acknowledged for the first time what nutrition scientists had been saying for years. A vegetarian diet can be a healthy way to eat. Medical science has yet to record a single case of someone dying from an overdose of vegetables. On the contrary, medical evidence consistently shows that people who regularly eat more fruits and vegetables than the average experience significantly reduced risks of obesity, breast cancer, diabetes, heart disease, and stroke. But I'm telling you what you already know. Most Americans know they should be eating more fruits and vegetables. Knowing what to do is not enough; we need to know better how to do it.

At the Pritikin Longevity Centers we have, through trial and error, learned a great deal about effective ways to get former steak lovers to eat more servings of fruits and vegetables. Although our methods are not identical to those you will read about in this book, they are motivated by the same principle: In the long run people can only eat what they enjoy. In this book, Suzanne Havala has distilled years of personal experience and a wealth of expert knowledge to share with you some of the most effective ways to make the transition from the standard American diet (SAD) to the vegetarian way of life. Like the engineer that my father was, Suzanne knows how to modify people's current, unhealthful eating practices ever so subtly in the direction of more healthful eating. She shows readers some excellent ways in which to substitute various plant-based foods for the meat dishes currently consumed. She shows the reader that vegetarianism need not entail the wholesale abandonment of ways of eating to which they have become accustomed. She shows, instead, that small, easily tolerated changes can lead to significant health benefits with no appreciable decrease in eating enjoyment. I salute Suzanne for writing this very much-needed how-to guide to more healthful eating.

Robert Pritikin
Director
Pritikin Longevity Centers
Santa Monica, California

Introduction

When I was a mere sprout—not yet a fully actualized, deviant, nonmeat eater—I wore a button that said, "Real People Wear Fake Fur," which I had picked up at the Ann Arbor street fair where my older sister was in school at the University of Michigan. It was the late '60s, and it was at about that same time that my mother announced to the family that from then on she would be a vegetarian. She never said why, but for the next several years, the former Wisconsinite ate cheese omelets or cheddar-cheese-on-whole-wheat-toast-and-pickle sandwiches for dinner while the rest of us ate the meat that she prepared for us. That is, of course, until one by one, the kids followed her lead and, without fanfare, went vegetarian ourselves.

My dad worried that we'd miss vital nutrients. He chided my mother for planting the idea. Mom was pegged as "unusual" at the hospital where she worked. By now, it was the early 1970s, and vegetarians either lived on communes or wore Birkies and had long hair on college campuses. They weren't kids and middle-aged working moms.

I was a high-school athlete—a competitive swimmer—and I hoped that a vegetarian diet would boost my endurance and athletic performance, as it had for record-holder Murray Rose. It didn't help enough, but it did pique my interest in nutrition and set me on the path to a career in dietetics. It would be many years, however, before the scientific community would come around to the idea that a diet based on grains, fruits, vegetables, legumes, seeds, and nuts could be adequate, never mind superior, to one based on animal products.

In college, I learned about vegetarianism in the unit on fad diets. At that time, a blood cholesterol level of 300 milligrams per deciliter was considered normal, and patients in the coronary care unit in the hospital got bacon and eggs and white toast for breakfast.

My grandmother worried that I wouldn't get enough iron without eating red meat, and she thought that my slender body wasn't "healthy" enough in size to meet her old-world, Eastern-European standards. Years later, when I married and my husband decided to go meatless, *his* mother would phone me, worried that her son wasn't getting enough protein and that her daughter-in-law the dietitian might be leading him into malnutrition.

Such were the trials and tribulations of being a vegetarian, until now.

What's changed? Just about everything.

The American Dietetic Association—generally the conservative holdout on such matters—has gone from cautious at first, later tentative at best, to now clearly stating in its position paper that vegetarian diets confer health advantages. The federal government has given the thumbs-up to vegetarian diets and now recommends that Americans should start basing their meals on fruits, vegetables, grains, and legumes—a thinly veiled way of saying, "Okay, we give. Plant-based diets are healthier," without stepping on the toes of the meat and dairy industries with whose interests the government is charged with protecting and promoting. The trend is strong, and with the volume of research confirming the advantages of a vegetarian-style diet, there's no going back. Now the task is to help a society make the transition to an eating style that is outside the cultural norm.

Vegetarian diets are no longer an oddity—they're converging with mainstream dietary recommendations. This book, then, is for everyone who wants a peek into the future of preventive nutrition and a leg up on making the switch.

What You'll Find in This Book

This book is divided into seven parts. Each part focuses on a different aspect of vegetarianism, from the basic "who, what, and why" to the nutritional underpinnings of a diet without meat, how to make the transition, and how to maintain the changes after you've made them. Together, the seven parts of this book lay the foundation for understanding the vegetarian lifestyle and building the skills necessary to successfully adapt.

Part 1, "Vegetarianism 101: The Basics Before We Begin," peels away the first layer of mystery around issues of vegetarianism. We'll get to the bottom of the various definitions of vegetarian diets, revealing once and for all what the word "vegan" means (and how to pronounce it). We'll look at what vegetarians *do* eat, including vegetarian traditions around the world, rather than stopping at what they *don't* eat. This part also discusses the reasons that motivate people to adopt a vegetarian diet.

Part 2, "Nutshell Nutrition," gets to the nitty-gritty of all of the questions you've ever had about where vegetarians get such nutrients as protein, calcium, iron, and vitamin B12. "If you don't eat meat, where do you get your protein?" and "If I don't drink milk, will I get enough calcium?" These questions are explored in detail. This section also covers the issue of vitamin and mineral supplements and whether or not you should take them.

Part 3, "You're Special," takes you on a stroll through the stages of life and describes how you can adapt a vegetarian diet to meet nutritional needs at all ages and how to deal with some of the special challenges that accompany each stage. We'll start with vegetarian diets during pregnancy and through birth and infancy. Then we'll take baby steps through toddlerhood and beyond, discussing vegetarian diets for older children as well as the challenges of teenage vegetarians. We'll look at vegetarian diets for athletes of all ages, and we'll also discuss the merits of a vegetarian diet for older adults.

Part 4, "Making the Switch," is packed with good-sense advice and strategies for making the transition to a more plant-based diet. This is the practical stuff, which is what I have found that people need help with the most. "Should I make the switch gradually or all at once?" "How can I manage this if I'm the only one in my household who eats this way?" "What staples should I start out with, and do I have to shop at a health food store?" We'll cover all these issues and more.

Part 5, "Meal Planning Made Easy," continues to help you with the practical matters by discussing how to plan tasty, nutritious, satisfying vegetarian meals with a minimum of fuss. A daily food guide is presented in this section, as well as directions for choosing foods. You'll get sample menus and ideas for quick and easy meals and snacks. There are great fix-and-freeze ideas and make-ahead meals for the Sunday cook, as well as advice for dealing with holidays and entertaining. There's also a terrific section on recipe substitutions, with ideas that go beyond the ordinary. You'll amaze your friends with some of the versatile and practical suggestions presented here.

Part 6, "Taking the Show on the Road," discusses how to do the vegetarian thing when you're not at home, from restaurants and dinner parties to air travel and at the office. We'll look at the social side and how not to lose your friends, as well as veggie etiquette, so that you'll know how to handle eating away from home with grace and charm. We'll also troubleshoot the most common situations you'll run into when you're not in the comforts of your own kitchen.

Part 7, "Veggie Survival Strategies," is a final shot of gumption for aspiring vegetarians. Before you start on your merry way, we'll fortify you with yet more smart ideas for honing your new skills and challenging your increasingly sophisticated taste buds. Simply stated, this part is about getting support for your lifestyle choice.

At the end of book, you'll also find two appendices: one a reference for recommended nutrient intakes; the other a glossary of terms.

But Wait, There's More!

Throughout the book, you'll run across the following sidebars. These boxes are nuggets of information that help to reinforce ideas presented in the text or little extras that I thought you'd be interested in knowing.

The Last Bite

These boxes contain some interesting facts and other information that, while not vital to your understanding of the subject, might be fun to know.

Heads Up!

You'll definitely want to read these words to the wise. They'll help you avoid pitfalls or mistakes that you might otherwise stumble into.

Helpful Hint

These are tips and bits of advice to smooth the way and help you understand some of the fine points of vegetarian lifestyles.

Veggie Talk

Check these boxes for definitions of new or important terms.

Acknowledgments

My heartfelt thanks to the following people for making this book possible: to Jennifer Griffin, senior editor at Macmillan, with whom I was especially delighted to have had the opportunity to work on another book; to Jim Willhite, Development Editor, who so expertly guided this book to completion; to the talented editorial, design, and production crew at Alpha Books and Macmillan; to my agent, Patti Breitman; and to Robert Pritikin for his enthusiasm, support, and kindness in writing the foreword. Very special thanks to my mom and dad, Milt and Kay Babich, who far exceed the call of duty. They literally ran my household for me, inside and out, for four months, including getting my old farmhouse in the city ready to sell and moving me across the state, while I did little else but sit suspended in front of my computer, tapping out chapters, and barking out orders. I have the most wonderful parents in the whole wide world.

Trademarks

All terms mentioned in this book that are known to be or are suspected of being trademarks or service marks have been appropriately capitalized. Alpha Books and Macmillan General Reference cannot attest to the accuracy of this information. Use of a term in this book should not be regarded as affecting the validity of any trademark or service mark. The following trademarks or service marks have been mentioned in this book:

Barbara's®

Beano®

Better Than Milk? Dairy-Free Tofu Beverage Mix™

Birkies®

Coke®

Contandina™

Del Monte™

Dippity Do™

Dr. Pepper®

EdenSoy® Extra™

Elsie the Cow™

Ener-G® Egg Replacer™

Fig Newtons®

Geritol®

Grape-Nuts®

Green Giant® Harvest Burger®

Green Giant® Harvest Burger® for Recipes™

Health Valley Fiber 7 Flakes®

Isomil®

Jell-O®

Kellogg's Just Right®

Kellogg's Mueslix®

Kellogg's Nutri-Grain®

Kellogg's Product 19®

Kellogg's Raisin Bran®

Lact-Aid®

Minute Maid®

Miracle Whip®

Morningstar Farms® Breakfast Links®

Morningstar Farms® Breakfast Patties®

Morningstar Farms® Breakfast Strips®

Morningstar Farms® BurgerBeaters®

Morningstar Farms® Chik Patties®

Morningstar Farms® Grillers®

Prosobee®

Red Star® T-6635+™

Smokey the Bear™

Soyalac®

Styrofoam™

Total®

Twinkies®

Twizzler®

Vegelicious®

Westsoy®

Woodsy Owl™

Part 1
Vegetarianism 101: The Basics Before We Begin

If you are going to get to where you want to be, then there's no getting around it: You've got to have a plan. And when it comes to making diet and lifestyle changes, that's especially true. In order to change the way you eat, you not only have to develop and practice new skills and a new mindset, but you have to replace old traditions with new ones. That's the fun of it, and that's the challenge of it as well.

What better place to start than understanding the basics? The chapters that follow reveal the who, what, and why of the vegetarian way.

Veggie   NOT Veggie

Chapter 1

What's a Vegetarian?

In This Chapter

➤ Who's who and what they will and won't eat

➤ About labels and why they really don't matter

➤ If you don't eat meat, what *do* you eat?

Are vegetarians members of a secret club? Seems like it. To gain admission, you have to shop at natural foods stores and eat strange foods such as tempeh and nutritional yeast. It helps if you're a celebrity. Maybe a rock star or an actor. They're into weird lifestyle alternatives. The rules are complicated and somewhat mysterious. Some people are lacto, and some are lacto ovo. Worse yet, some are vegans. What the heck is a vegan?

Not to worry. Sit back, relax, and read on. It'll all be very clear in just a few pages. And it's pretty simple and straightforward too.

In this chapter, you'll learn what the term "vegetarian" means and what different types of vegetarians eat.

Try This Label on for Size

Most of us are pretty good at describing the essence of a person in three words or less:

"He's a liberal Democrat."

"They're yuppie boomers."

"She's a white, Anglo-Saxon Protestant."

It's like the saying goes: One picture (or label) says a thousand words.

We use other labels too. When people use labels to describe vegetarians, different terms correspond to different sets of eating habits. A lacto ovo vegetarian eats differently than a vegan eats. In some cases, the term used to describe a type of vegetarian refers to a whole range of lifestyle preferences, rather than to the diet alone. In general, though, the specific term used to describe a vegetarian has to do with the extent to which that person avoids foods of animal origin.

Label Lingo

In 1992, *Vegetarian Times* magazine sponsored a survey of vegetarianism in the United States. The results showed that almost 7 percent of the American public considered themselves vegetarians. At that time, that figure equated to about 12.4 million adults.

However, a closer look at the eating habits of those "vegetarians" found that most of them were eating chicken and fish occasionally, and many were eating red meat at least a few times each month. That finding prompted many of the more strident vegetarians—those who never ate meat, fish, or poultry—to pose the question, "Since when do chicken, fish, and cows grow in a garden?"

The fact is, many people today use the term "vegetarian" loosely to mean that they are consciously reducing their intake of animal products. The term has a positive connotation, especially among those who know that vegetarian diets confer health benefits.

What about the "real" vegetarians? Who are they and what do they eat (or not eat)?

According to a Roper Poll sponsored by the nonprofit Vegetarian Resource Group in 1994, the actual number of people who never eat meat, fish, or poultry is about 1 percent of the adult population. The poll was repeated in 1997, and the number remained the same.

Veggie Talk

A **vegetarian** is a person who eats no meat, fish, or poultry and no by-products from those sources.

The definition of a vegetarian most widely accepted by fellow vegetarians is this:

A *vegetarian* is a person who eats no meat, fish, or poultry. Not "I eat turkey only for Thanksgiving," or "I eat fish once in a while." A vegetarian consistently avoids all flesh foods as well as by-products of meat, fish, and poultry. A vegetarian avoids refried beans made with lard, soups made with meat stock, and foods made with gelatin (such as Jell-O), some kinds of candy, and most marshmallows.

Of course, vegetarian diets vary in the extent to which they exclude animal products. The major types are:

Lacto Ovo Vegetarian Diet

A *lacto ovo vegetarian* diet excludes meat, fish, and poultry but includes dairy products and eggs. Most vegetarians in the United States, Canada, and Western Europe fall into this category. Lacto ovo vegetarians eat such foods as cheese, ice cream, yogurt, milk, and eggs and foods made with these ingredients.

Lacto Vegetarian Diet

A *lacto vegetarian* diet excludes meat, fish, and poultry, as well as eggs and any foods containing eggs. So, a lacto vegetarian, for instance, would not eat the pancakes at most restaurants, because they contain eggs. Some veggie burger patties are made with egg whites, and many brands of ice cream contain eggs. A lacto vegetarian would not eat these foods. A lacto vegetarian would, however, eat other dairy products such as milk, yogurt, and cheese.

Vegan

Technically, the term *vegan* refers to more than just the diet alone. A vegan is a vegetarian who avoids eating or using all animal products, including meat, fish, poultry, eggs, dairy products, any foods containing by-products of these ingredients, wool, silk, leather, and any nonfood items made with animal by-products. Some vegans avoid honey.

So in addition to avoiding foods containing animal products, vegans also avoid animal products in all other areas of their lives.

Are vegans from the planet Vegan? No, but they'll think *you're* from another planet if you don't pronounce the word correctly. It's pronounced *VEE-gun*. Never mind what *Webster's* says. This is the accepted pronunciation within the vegetarian community.

Veggie Talk

A **lacto ovo vegetarian** eats no meat, fish, or poultry but does include dairy products and eggs to some extent in the diet.

Veggie Talk

A **lacto vegetarian** eats no meat, fish, poultry, or eggs but does include dairy products to some extent in the diet.

Veggie Talk

A **vegan** is someone who eats no meat, fish, poultry, eggs, or dairy products and who also avoids the use of other animal products, including wool, silk, leather, and any nonfood items made with animal by-products.

The term *strict vegetarian* is the correct term to use to mean those who avoid all animal products in their diet but who don't carry animal product avoidance into other areas of their lives. In practice, however, the term vegan is usually used by both strict vegetarians as well as vegans, even among those in the know. Call it a bad habit. Rather than calling themselves vegans, though, strict vegetarians will often say that they "eat a vegan diet."

So, a vegan, for instance, would not use hand lotion that contains lanolin, a by-product of wool. A vegan would not use margarine that contains casein, a milk protein, and a vegan would not carry luggage trimmed in leather. Vegans (as well as many other vegetarians) also avoid products that have been tested on animals, such as many cosmetics and personal care products. Many vegans avoid using regular, white granulated sugar, since much of it has been processed using char from animal bones (for whitening).

It can be difficult to maintain a vegan lifestyle in our culture. Most vegans are strongly motivated by ethics, however, and rise to the challenge. It's not as difficult as you might think, either, once you get the hang of it. A large part of maintaining a vegan lifestyle has to do with being aware of where animals products are used and knowing about alternatives. Vegetarian and animal-rights organizations have many materials to help people maintain a vegan lifestyle. Sometimes vegans unwittingly use a product or eat a food that contains an animal by-product. There are times when it's hard to know if a product is free of all animal ingredients. However, the intention is to strive for the vegan ideal.

Those are the three primary types of vegetarian diets. Of course, we could go on from there.

Question: What do you call a person who generally avoids red meat but eats chicken and fish, though less frequently than most people?

Answer: A *semi-vegetarian*. ("Why not a semi-omnivore?" you might ask, but we're talking about the vegetarian lifestyle here.)

Question: What do you call a person who avoids red meat and poultry but eats fish or seafood?

Answer: A *pesco vegetarian*.

Question: What do you call a person who avoids red meat but eats poultry and fish or seafood?

Answer: A *pesco pollo vegetarian*.

More Lingo

The list actually goes even further. One adaptation of a vegetarian diet is a *raw foods diet*, in which adherents eat a diet that consists primarily of uncooked foods. Practitioners of a raw foods diet believe that cooking causes undesirable changes in foods and that humans were designed to eat foods in their natural, raw state. Another adaptation, the *fruitarian diet*, consists only of fruits; vegetables that are botanically classified as fruits, such as tomatoes, eggplant, zucchini, and avocados; and seeds and nuts. Planning a nutritionally adequate fruitarian diet is difficult, and the diet is not recommended for children.

This book will focus on the most common forms of vegetarian diets—vegan, lacto, and lacto ovo vegetarian diets. These types of vegetarian diets are nutritionally adequate and are associated with health advantages.

As you can see, there's a label to suit practically everyone.

Veggie Talk

A **raw foods diet** consists primarily of uncooked foods, and a **fruitarian** diet consists only of fruits, vegetables that are botanically classified as fruits, and seeds and nuts.

The Last Bite

Macrobiotic diets are often lumped into the general category of "vegetarian" diets, even though they may include seafood. The diet excludes all other animal products, however, as well as refined sugars, tropical fruits, and "nightshade vegetables" (potatoes, eggplant, and peppers). The diet is related to principles of Buddhism and is based on the Chinese principles of yin and yang. Therefore, macrobiotic diets include foods common to the Asian culture, such as sea vegetables (kelp, nori, arame), root vegetables (such as daikon), miso soup, and others. Many people follow a macrobiotic diet as part of a life philosophy. Others follow the diet because they believe it to be effective in curing cancer and other illnesses, an idea for which there is currently little scientific support.

The Vegetarian Continuum (Or Why Labels Have Limitations)

Now that you know the criteria for the different types of vegetarian diets, which label would you affix to your own eating style?

What would you call a person who avoids all flesh foods and only occasionally eats eggs and dairy products, and then usually as a minor ingredient in a baked good or dish, such as a muffin, cookie, or veggie burger?

Helpful Hint

If you are new to vegetarianism, you might begin to notice a bit of peer pressure from some longtime vegetarians who have moved down the continuum closer to the vegan end of the spectrum and are encouraging you to "move along." You may get this sense from materials that you may read or from people that you'll meet. Ignore it, and compare yourself to no one but yourself. Adopting a vegetarian or partly vegetarian diet is a highly personal decision. Do what's right for you, and move at a pace that's comfortable for you.

Technically, the person is a lacto ovo vegetarian, right? But that person's diet seems as though it's leaning toward the vegan end of the spectrum.

As a nutritionist, I see this kind of variation—even within the same category of vegetarian diet—all the time. One lacto ovo vegetarian may eat heaping helpings of cheese and eggs and have a high intake of saturated fat and cholesterol as a result. In fact, this type of vegetarian may have a nutrient intake similar to the typical nonvegetarian American's—not so hot. Another lacto ovo vegetarian may use eggs and dairy products but only in a very limited fashion—as a condiment or minor ingredient in foods. This person's nutrient intake could more closely resemble that of a vegan's. That is, of course, assuming that the vegan isn't a Coke and French fries vegetarian.

What am I getting at? That labels **are** only a starting point, and they have their **limitations**. Even if you know what type of vegetarian a person **is**, there can be a lot of variation in the degree to which **he** or she includes or avoids animal products.

Many new vegetarians find that their diets evolve over time. At the start, for example, many vegetarians rely heavily on cheese and eggs to replace meat. Over time, they learn to cook with grains, beans, and vegetables, and they experiment with cuisines of other cultures. They decrease their reliance on foods of animal origin. Gradually, they consume fewer eggs and dairy products. One day, they might even find themselves eating a mostly vegan (or strict vegetarian) diet.

You might say that vegetarian diets are on a continuum, starting from the typical American, meat-centered diet, to the vegan ideal. Most vegetarians fall somewhere in between. Some may be content with wherever they land on the continuum. For others, their diets will continue to evolve as they hone their skills and develop new traditions, moving from semi-vegetarian, or lacto ovo vegetarian, closer and closer to the vegan end of the spectrum.

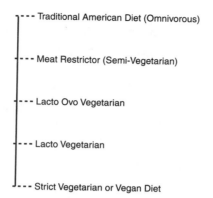

The vegetarian continuum.

- - - Traditional American Diet (Omnivorous)

- - - Meat Restrictor (Semi-Vegetarian)

- - - Lacto Ovo Vegetarian

- - - Lacto Vegetarian

- - - Strict Vegetarian or Vegan Diet

If You Don't Eat Meat...What's Left to Eat?

Your eating style is a mindset. Here's proof:

Ask your neighbor or coworker what he's having for dinner tonight. The chances are good he's going to say...

"We're grilling steaks tonight."

"I'm having fish tonight."

"Chicken."

Or he might be going out to eat at a restaurant that serves a Western-style, meat-centered meal, such as a 32-ounce steak, for example.

Ever notice how no one mentions the rice, the potato, or the salad, vegetables, bread, or anything else besides the meat? Those are the incidentals, the "side dishes." They're less important than the "main course." We live in a society in which meals revolve around meat as the focal point of the plate. It's just a habit. Our tradition.

A semi-vegetarian might push the meat to the side of the plate, move the vegetables and grains and legumes to the center, and double their portion sizes. They might eat more meatless meals more often. Other vegetarians push the meat off the plate altogether and build an entirely different kind of meal.

Veggie Talk

The term **legumes** refers to dried beans and peas, such as pinto beans, black beans, kidney beans, garbanzo beans, lentils, split peas, adzuki beans, black-eyed peas, navy beans, and so on. You can buy them dry, canned, frozen, and sometimes even as flakes and flour.

Helpful Hint

If you are expecting a bona fide vegetarian to come to your house for dinner, you'll want to be sure to leave the chicken stock out of the vegetables or rice and the ground meat or meat flavoring out of the pasta sauce. Worcestershire sauce contains anchovies, and many stir-fry sauces contain oyster sauce. Check the labels. Your guest will appreciate your thoughtfulness.

When people think of vegetarian diets, they often visualize a plate with a big hole in the center—a gaping bare spot where the meat used to be. They get a little hungry.

"What's left to eat?" they wonder.

"Rabbit food," they figure, thinking about the stuff that is usually relegated to the side of the plate, or maybe the little bit of fruit garnish teetering on the edge.

And they get a little hungrier.

Just the opposite is true, however.

That's because the variety is actually in the plant world. The abundant, colorful, flavorful, fragrant, delicious, and nutritious varied plant world.

When you think about it, most people really only eat a few types of meat. They cook it in a bunch of different ways, and they usually doctor it up with spices and condiments to give it some variation in flavor. The lament I hear most often from people trying to improve their diets is "Chicken and fish, chicken and fish. I know a 1,001 ways to cook chicken and fish. I'm going to overdose on chicken and fish."

Because our diet traditionally centers on meat (and puts heavy reliance on eggs and dairy products too), the diet can be fairly monotonous. Once you make the switch to a vegetarian diet, however, lots of options open up. There are hundreds of different types of fruits, vegetables, grains and grain products, *legumes*, and other vegetarian foods. There is an endless number of ways that you can fix them. Many of those dishes originated in cultures other than our own. Some examples are listed in the table that follows. Some of them may be familiar to you; you'll find that others will open a window to the world.

Vegetarian Traditions Around the World

Food	Country or Origin
Fried plantains	West Africa
Yogurt and tomato soup	Afghanistan
Spring rolls	China
Stir-fried tempeh	Indonesia
Samosas	Malaysia
Pumpkin soup	Brazil
Cream of watercress soup	Dominican Republic

Food	Country or Origin
Bean soup	El Salvador
Corn soup	Guatemala
Pigeon pea soup	Jamaica
Spaghetti with marinara sauce	Italy
Garbanzo bean dip or hummus	Middle East
Lentil soup	Syria
Spiced beans in coconut milk	East Africa
Lentil stew	Ethiopia
Black-eyed pea stew	Ghana
Soybean and spinach stew	Ghana
Beans with cassava	Rwanda
Corn meal with pumpkin	Zimbabwe
Stir-fry with noodles	Cambodia
Vegetables stir-fried with spices	Bangladesh
Lentils and curried vegetables	Nepal
Red kidney beans in sauce	Pakistan
Bean burritos	Mexico
Pigeon peas and rice	Bahamas
Squash or pumpkin stew	Bolivia
Fried beans	Brazil
Spanakopita or spinach pie	Greece
Bean and pumpkin stew	Chile
Coconut rice and beans	Colombia
Potato cakes with peanut sauce	Ecuador
Stuffed eggplant	Haiti
Lima bean casserole	Peru
Brown bean casserole	Egypt
Yogurt and spinach soup	Egypt
Couscous	Morocco
Apple beanpot	Saudi Arabia

The bottom line: There's a tendency to think of vegetarian diets in terms of what they exclude and that the number of food choices has been reduced. Just the opposite is generally true. Once you adopt a vegetarian diet, more options open up, and your diet is likely to have greater variety than it did before.

The Least You Need to Know

➤ A true vegetarian is a person who eats no meat, fish, or poultry and no foods that contain by-products of these ingredients.

➤ Many people today use the term "vegetarian" loosely to mean that they are cutting back on their intake of animal products.

➤ There are several different styles of vegetarian diets, and even within categories, there can be considerable variation in the amounts of animal products eaten.

➤ Vegans eat no foods of animal origin or foods containing animal by-products, and they also avoid the use of nonfood animal products such as wool, silk, leather, personal care products made with animal by-products, and so on.

➤ Adopting a vegetarian eating style is a personal choice, and you should make the transition at a pace that is comfortable for you.

➤ Vegetarian diets generally include a wider range of foods than the typical American, meat-centered diet.

Chapter 2

Why Go Vegetarian?

In This Chapter

➤ The smart way to get fit and stay healthy

➤ Saving the planet with your knife and fork

➤ Be a hero for hunger

➤ Speaking up for the voiceless

➤ When meat's not your cup of tea

➤ The spiritual side

What's all the excitement over tofu and bean sprouts?

In some ways in life, what you don't know won't hurt you. On the other hand, there are times when what you *do* know can help you…a lot. Vegetarian diets are like that. There are some compelling reasons to go vegetarian. Many people find that one of those reasons will pique their interest. Then, once they learn more, the other reasons reinforce their original reason for being interested. Vegetarianism is that way. Once you think about it from all of the various angles, a vegetarian diet makes a whole lot of sense.

In this chapter, we'll take a look at the most common reasons that people decide to go vegetarian.

The Health Connection

Many people view their health (or lack thereof) as something that just sort of happens to them. Bad habits "catch up." They've got bad genes. Their doctor had just given them a clean bill of health, then they had a heart attack out of the blue. (Well, we all have to die of *something*.) Who could have foreseen it? They lived reasonably. Everything in moderation, right? What more could they have done?

Heads Up!

"The average age (life expectancy) of a meat eater is 63. I am on the verge of 85 and still work as hard as ever. I have lived quite long enough and I am trying to die; but I simply cannot do it. A single beef steak would finish me; but I cannot bring myself to swallow it. I am oppressed with a dread of living forever. That is the only disadvantage of vegetarianism."

—George Bernard Shaw
(1856–1950)

Veggie Talk

Saturated fat is found in large amounts in foods of animal origin, particularly red meats, the skin on poultry, and in dairy products. Saturated fats raise the body's blood cholesterol level.

A lot, most likely.

You'd be surprised to learn how much power you wield with your knife and fork.

The fact is, vegetarians enjoy better health than nonvegetarians. The fewer animal products a vegetarian consumes, the better his or her health.

In comparison with nonvegetarians, vegetarians have lower rates of cancer, coronary artery disease, diabetes, high blood pressure, gallstones, and kidney stones. They're less likely to be obese too. In general, a vegetarian diet is "good for what ails you," and it helps prevent the onset of many ailments in the first place. That's because a diet that is composed primarily of plant matter has protective qualities.

Trimming the Fat

In general, vegetarians get less total fat in their diets as compared to nonvegetarians. The fewer animal products the diet contains, the less fat it usually contains. Vegan diets, for instance, tend to be lower in fat than lacto vegetarian or lacto ovo vegetarian diets. Fat is a concentrated source of calories, so diets that are low in fat tend to be lower in calories. No wonder vegetarians tend to be leaner than nonvegetarians.

Vegetarian diets also tend to be lower in *saturated fat* than nonvegetarian diets. Although there are plant sources of saturated fat, saturated fats come primarily from animal products, particularly high-fat dairy foods and meats. In fact, two thirds of the fat in dairy products is saturated fat. Even so-called low-fat dairy products contain a substantial amount of saturated fat. Saturated fats are usually firm at room temperature, like a stick of butter. Foods that are high in saturated fat include red meats, the skin on poultry, butter, sour cream, ice cream, cheese, yogurt made with whole milk, 2 percent milk, and 4 percent whole milk.

Saturated fats stimulate the body to produce more *cholesterol*. Cholesterol is a waxy substance that is found in the plaques of arteries that are diseased. Everyone needs some cholesterol, but our bodies manufacture what we need. We don't need more from outside sources, and for people with a predisposition for heart disease, too much cholesterol can contribute to hardening of the arteries.

Cholesterol is produced in the liver, so it's found only in animal products. Foods of plant origin contain no cholesterol. (Have you ever seen a lima bean with a liver?)

Even though chicken and fish contain less saturated fat than red meat, they contain just as much cholesterol. Vegetarian diets are not only lower in saturated fats than nonvegetarian diets, they're lower in cholesterol too. Diets that are low in total fat, saturated fats, and cholesterol are the healthiest. They are associated with a reduced risk of cancer, coronary artery disease, diabetes, high blood pressure, and obesity.

The Fiber Factor

Dietary fiber is the part of a plant that is only partially digested in our bodies, or it's not digested at all. It's our lack of ability to digest fiber that gives us the health benefits. Fiber can bind with environmental contaminants and help them pass out of the body. Fiber also decreases the amount of time that it takes for waste material to pass out of the body so that potentially harmful substances have less time to be in contact with the lining of the intestines.

Foods that are high in fiber are bulky. They have a tendency to fill you up before you can "fill out." In that way, foods that are rich in fiber help to control your weight. When you eat foods that are fiber rich, you tend to get full before you take in too many calories.

Veggie Talk

Cholesterol is a waxy substance that is a major component of the plaques that form in diseased arteries. Cholesterol is only found in animal products. There is no cholesterol in foods of plant origin.

Heads Up!

Lacto ovo vegetarian diets have the potential to be high in total fat, saturated fats, and cholesterol if care is not taken to limit the amount of eggs and high-fat dairy products consumed. If you switch to a lacto ovo vegetarian diet, be careful not to rely too heavily on these foods to replace the meat that you once ate.

Veggie Talk

Dietary fiber is the part of a plant that is only partially digested in our bodies, or it's not digested at all.

Veggie Talk

Diverticulosis is a condition in which there are herniations or small outpouchings in the large intestine. These pouches can become filled with debris and inflamed, a painful disease known as **diverticulitis**. Diverticular disease is caused in large part by not having enough fiber in the diet.

Helpful Hint

There shouldn't be a need for a magazine rack in the bathroom (unless the reading material is for use in the bathtub). If you have enough time to read an article, then you probably aren't getting enough fiber and water in your diet.

Fiber has other benefits too. People who get plenty of fiber in their diets are less likely to have trouble with constipation, hemorrhoids, varicose veins, and *diverticulosis*. Getting plenty of fiber (and water) in your diet keeps your stools large and soft and easy to pass. You shouldn't have to strain and exert a lot of pressure to have a bowel movement.

Diets that are high in fiber are associated with less obesity and lower rates of cancer and coronary artery disease. Blood sugar levels in diabetics are also controlled better when the diet is high in fiber.

Most Americans get only 12 grams of fiber in their diets each day. Vegetarians get at least twice that much or more. One cup of oatmeal contains 8 grams of fiber, a medium pear with skin has 4 grams of fiber, 1 cup of vegetarian chili has 14 grams of fiber, a slice of whole-wheat bread contains 2 grams of fiber, and 1 cup of chopped, steamed broccoli provides 6 grams of fiber.

Current dietary recommendations call for fiber intakes of at least 30 grams per day, but 40 or 50 grams is even better. Vegetarians can easily reach the higher figures. It's also important to drink plenty of fluids when your fiber intake is high, and water is an especially good choice.

Keeping the Lid on the Protein

Most vegetarians get enough protein, but they don't overdo it. There are benefits to that.

The Last Bite

"Nothing will benefit human health and increase the chances for survival of life on earth as much as the evolution to a vegetarian diet."

—Albert Einstein (1879–1955)

When you moderate your protein intake, you help to conserve your body's stores of calcium. Diets that are too high in protein, especially protein from animal sources, cause the kidneys to let more calcium pass into the urine. That's part of the reason that standard recommendations for calcium intake for Americans are so high. The recommendations are jacked up to compensate for calcium losses that are caused by Flintstones-sized standing rib roasts and 16-ounce steaks that cover the plate. Americans love meat, and they pay for it with calcium loss.

Speaking of your kidneys...when you moderate your protein intake by eating a vegetarian diet, you also cause less wear and tear on your kidneys. Vegetarians have fewer kidney stones and less kidney disease than nonvegetarians. High intakes of animal protein are also linked to higher blood cholesterol levels and more coronary artery disease, as well as a greater incidence of some types of cancer.

The Last Bite

One of the problems that astronauts face upon returning to Earth after a mission in space is an increased incidence of kidney stones. As part of NASA's space station program, preparations are underway to serve a vegetarian diet to astronauts on long missions. There are several practical reasons for this, but NASA hopes that one of the benefits will be a lesser incidence of kidney stones due to a lower intake of animal protein.

Phytochemical Soup

It wasn't long ago that news of the health benefits of *beta-carotene* got people running to the drugstore for supplements. Then, studies found that supplements of beta-carotene didn't provide the same health benefits as did *whole foods* that were high in beta-carotene. Whole plant foods, that is.

Now we know that there are over 600 different carotenoids, and beta-carotene is only one of them. In fact, we know that there are probably thousands of other *phytochemicals* such as these. Phytochemicals are substances found in foods of plant origin that have biological activity for humans and help protect our health. Since it's the consumption of whole foods, rather than individual nutrients, that seems to be associated with good health, it's possible that phytochemicals work in synergy with each other. It's also a sure thing that scientists haven't identified all of the beneficial phytochemicals in foods yet. So, taking supplements of individual, isolated nutrients isn't as good as getting these substances directly from the foods that you eat. The less processed a food is, the richer it is likely to be in phytochemicals.

Phytochemicals such as beta-carotene, other carotenoids, vitamins E and C, and the mineral selenium, are all examples of *antioxidant nutrients*. These nutrients are abundant in foods of plant origin. They are thought to help reduce the risk of cancer, coronary artery disease, lung disease, cataracts, and other diseases by their ability to rid the body of *free radicals*.

Free radicals are molecules that are produced as a by-product of your body's normal metabolism. They are also produced when you are exposed to environmental contaminates such as air pollution and ozone, sunlight and X rays, and certain dietary components such as fat and the form of iron found in meat. Free radicals speed up the aging process by damaging your cells. They can impair your immune system and cause numerous diseases and illnesses.

The bottom line: Vegetarian diets are rich in the phytochemicals that promote and protect our health. The more animal products you include in your diet, the more plant matter you displace. Whether you make the transition to a fully vegetarian diet or not, you could benefit greatly from radically increasing the ratio of plant to animal products in your diet.

Veggie Talk

Beta-carotene is a substance found in abundance in deep yellow or deep orange and red fruits and vegetables and is believed to help protect against cancer and coronary artery disease. **Whole foods** are foods that are as close to their natural state as possible, or the least processed as compared to other foods in the same category. For instance, whole-wheat flour is a whole food; white flour is not. A baking potato is a whole food; a potato chip is not.

You are here.

Most Americans eat too many animal products and not enough plant matter.

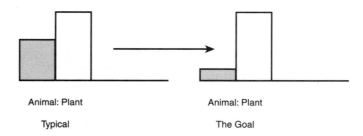

Animal: Plant

Typical

Animal: Plant

The Goal

Keeping Our Planet Fit

Smokey the Bear taught us that "Only *you* can prevent forest fires." And Woodsy Owl urged us to "Give a hoot, don't pollute." Neither of them were vegetarians, but *you* can go one giant step further toward keeping the planet clean and healthy by adopting a vegetarian diet.

"How so?" you ask.

A disproportionate amount of our Earth's natural resources is used to produce meat and other animal products.

For starters:

➤ It takes about 25 gallons of water to grow 1 pound of wheat, but it takes about 390 gallons of water to produce 1 pound of beef.

➤ A cow has to eat 7 pounds of protein from grain and soybeans to produce 1 pound of beef. With that kind of return on investment, most businesses would be closing up shop for good.

Veggie Talk

Phytochemicals are substances found in plants that protect our health. **Antioxidant nutrients** are phytochemicals that are present in abundance in plant products and help rid the body of free radicals.

Animal agriculture—the production of meat, eggs, and dairy products—places heavy demands on our land, water, and fuel supplies.

This Land Is Your Land, This Land Is My Land...

"...This land was made for you and me."

As it turns out, though, it doesn't take kindly to the degree of animal agriculture to which it's being subjected.

Livestock grazing causes *desertification* of the land by causing erosion of the topsoil and drying out the land. Our topsoil is being depleted faster than it can be created. Healthy, abundant supplies of topsoil help ensure that we'll have enough arable land to grow the food that we need to survive. Unfortunately, the amount of land resources needed to raise animals for their meat is exponentially greater than the amount needed to grow enough plant matter to feed the same number of people directly. Satisfying a big national appetite for meat means paying with our precious land.

Our national appetite for meat and other animal products also costs us our trees and forests. These trees may not be the ones in your own backyard or your neighbor's. Much of the deforestation happens in Latin America, Central America, and South America, where the number of acres of tropical rain forest cleared to make way for grazing cattle is so big that most of us would have a hard time comprehending its enormity.

Veggie Talk

Free radicals aren't renegades from the '60s. They're molecules that damage your cells. Meat is high in the oxidants that cause your body to produce free radicals, and low in the antioxidants that help your body get rid of them.

Our tropical rain forests are sort of like our planet's lungs. One of the many ways that trees help keep our world healthy is by exchanging the Earth's carbon dioxide for fresh oxygen. The trees take our waste and convert it into a product (oxygen) that we need to survive. If we didn't have our trees, we'd all be huffing and puffing as though we had reached the summit of Everest. "Breathing through a straw" is how mountain climbers describe the feeling of thinning oxygen. Losing a large percentage of the Earth's rainforests has repercussions for every corner of our planet.

In the wake of deforestation, many species of plants and animals are also wiped out. These plants and animals hold the keys to many scientific discoveries that may benefit mankind. The plants and animals of the rainforests are on the "front line," but eventually the assault on them will reach all of us.

Veggie Talk

Desertification is the slow death of the land caused by the overgrazing of cattle. The topsoil erodes and the land dries out, preventing it from supporting the growth of plant life.

Water World

When you look at a map of the Earth, you sure see a lot of blue. It's hard to believe that we could be short of that stuff anytime soon.

Actually, one of the greatest threats of animal agriculture is to our supplies of *fresh* water. There's lots of the salty kind. The aquifers that lie deep below the Earth's surface, however, hold the kind of water that we need to irrigate our land and to drink. Those giant pools of fresh water are dwindling rapidly because we're sucking up great quantities of the stuff to irrigate the great quantities of land needed to graze the animals from which we get a relatively small amount of food. A very inefficient use of a very precious resource.

Furthermore, whether fresh or salt, all of our water is being polluted, and animal agriculture is a major contributor to that problem. Pesticides, herbicides, and fertilizers used to grow feed for animals are contaminating our water supplies, in addition to the nitrogenous fecal waste that is produced by the animals themselves and washed into our streams, rivers, lakes, and bays. We have less clean water, and the creatures that live in that water become contaminated or are killed off by the pollution as well.

Filching Our Fossil Fuels

Webster's defines *filching* as "appropriating furtively or casually," as in "snitching a doughnut from the platter." It's synonymous with "steal." Steal sounds a little more serious. In that context, animal agriculture is not only stealing, it's ransacking our planet's fossil fuels.

The production of meat, eggs, and dairy products requires the intensive use of fossil fuels, including petroleum, for everything from transporting animal feed and the animals themselves to running farm machinery and operating the factory farms where the animals are raised.

The Last Bite

If the true cost to society of producing animal products for human consumption were passed on to consumers, few of us could afford to put these foods on the dinner table. At least we wouldn't be able to afford the amount that we presently consume. Fortunately for those who have a hankering for ham and eggs, the government subsidizes many of these foods to keep producers in business and consumers satisfied. Of course, the costs don't go away, they just get deferred. We'll have to pay eventually. Sound familiar? It's sort of like the cost of tobacco to society, which has been divvied up among all of us in dollars spent for health care. As someone once said, "You can pay me now, or you can pay me later."

Hunger Hurts

Hunger for me and you and most of the United States is skipping a meal because we were in too much of a rush to fix breakfast. When we get the midnight munchies, we pop a bag of popcorn or grab a bowl of cereal.

For the rest of the world, hunger is a state of slow starvation with no next meal or snack in sight.

World hunger is a problem of epic proportions and is equally complicated in terms of ethics, politics, and economics. However, many people choose a vegetarian lifestyle as a way of making a contribution to the fight against world hunger. While it may seem as if one, lone vote will hardly count, fortunately, many people choose to cast their votes in favor of a diet and lifestyle that can sustain the most people.

In the simplest sense, when we eat foods directly from the soil—fruits, vegetables, grains, legumes, nuts, and seeds—we can nourish many more people than the number that could be fed if the plant matter was fed to animals first and we, in turn, ate the animals.

Other issues that relate to the problem of world hunger include:

➤ The appetite of the affluent nations for meat and other animal products creates a market in poor countries for the resources needed to produce those foods. The result is that in developing nations, those with the power often opt to grow cash crops or feed for livestock for export, rather than growing less profitable crops that might feed the local people.

➤ Another result of the market for meat in affluent nations is the choice of those in power in poor countries to raise animals for export to the wealthy overseas. The losers: again, the locals who might have benefited from less profitable plant foods grown to feed the masses. Another downside to this practice: In some of these developing nations, natural resources such as land and forest are depleted and are no longer suitable for growing the crops of grain and legumes that could feed the masses.

A Voice for the Voiceless

Albert Schweitzer said, "Until he extends his circle of compassion to all living things, man will not himself find peace."

Some people step on spiders, and some people pick them up with a piece of tissue and set them outdoors.

Some people feed the squirrels corn on the cob and peanuts in their backyards, and some people shoot them.

Some people leave their dogs outdoors in subfreezing weather, and some people bring them into their own beds to snuggle under a warm blanket.

Some people eat animals, and some people wouldn't think of it.

It's all a matter of sensitivities, reverence for life, and respect for an animal's rights, according to those who choose a vegetarian lifestyle.

Slaughterhouses and Such

Ever wonder why your Cub Scout troop never took a field trip to a slaughterhouse?

Most of us could well imagine the horrors of the slaughterhouse and meat-packing plants if we allowed ourselves to think about it. Those who share their lives with dogs or cats know that animals have feelings, and you probably also know that cows, chickens, and pigs don't live in idyllic pastures and barnyards anymore. They live and die in factory farms and slaughterhouses the likes of which would rival any horror movie. The part we see is the neat and tidy packages of legs and shoulders in little Styrofoam plates wrapped in plastic.

Suffice it to say that some people do allow themselves to think about how animals are treated. They put themselves into the hooves and claws and take a stand for nonviolence.

The Last Bite

"I have from an early age abjured the use of meat, and the time will come when men such as I will look on the murder of animals as they now look on the murder of men."

—Leonardo da Vinci (1452–1519)

Virtual Vegan Reality

In addition to avoiding meat, fish, and poultry, vegans avoid the use of all other animal products. In part, that's because many animal by-products, such as leather and wool, subsidize the meat industry. The production of other animal products, such as eggs, milk, and other dairy products, are also seen by vegans as exploiting those animals, subjecting them to inhumane conditions and treatment, and supporting the meat industry. Male calves that are born to dairy cows, for instance, are typically taken from their mothers and raised for veal. Chickens that are raised for their eggs generally live in factory farm conditions in which they are routinely subjected to such practices

as *debeaking*. When a chicken is debeaked, a machine is used to cut off the end of the chicken's beak in an effort to reduce the pecking damage caused when chickens that are crowded together in tight quarters lash out at each other.

Inhumane treatment of animals leads many people to adopt a vegetarian lifestyle. Vegetarians of all persuasions see their lifestyle choice as being the ethical and compassionate choice.

For more information about animal rights, including sources of cruelty-free products, contact People for the Ethical Treatment of Animals (PETA) at 501 Front Street, Norfolk, VA 23510, (757) 622-7382, or visit their web site at www.peta-online.org.

Veggie Talk

Debeaking is the poultry industry's practice of snapping off the end of a chicken's beak with a machine. Think of it this way: It's what would happen if you took the saying "Cutting off your nose to spite your face" literally.

Meat's Too Tough to Chew and Other Complaints

Some people go vegetarian for the simple reason that they don't like meat. They chew and chew and chew, and still there's a glob of flesh in their mouth. Aesthetically, it's just not pleasant.

Some people are turned off by thoughts of *Listeria* and *Salmonella* and *Mad Cow Disease*. After all, a sizable number of the cases of the "24-hour flu bug" are really a good dose of a food-borne pathogen, usually carried in an animal product. Turkey, anyone?

Mad Cow Disease, also known as *Creutzfeldt-Jakob Disease* (CJD), is a progressive and fatal disease characterized by the brain tissue becoming spongy and porous, and the animal (or person) literally losing its mind. The disease is probably not caused by a bacterium or virus, however. The best guess at the present time is that it may be caused by an infectious protein. In England, the practice of feeding ground bone meal from dead cows to cows that were then marketed as food for people is thought to have spread the disease. The practice, now stopped in England, was commonplace in the United States as well, until just recently, when recognition of the risks (and the public's disgust at finding this out) forced meat producers to halt the practice.

Veggie Talk

Listeria and **Salmonella** are types of bacteria found on meats and in other animal products. A good dose of either can cause severe illness at best and death at worst, though a small dose of Salmonella poisoning may be passed off as the "24-hour flu." **Mad Cow Disease** is the popular name for **Creutzfeldt-Jakob Disease** or CJD. Mad Cow Disease is characterized by a progressive and fatal deterioration of the brain tissue, literally causing the animal (or person) to lose its mind.

Despite assurances from American cattle producers that "there has never been a case of CJD in this country," viewers of *The Oprah Winfrey Show* heard Oprah swear off cheeseburgers and then saw her get into major legal trouble with the cattle ranchers in Texas, who wanted her tried for libeling beef. The case against Oprah was thrown out of court.

Mad Cow Disease happened in England, but it couldn't happen here, could it? Does this remind anyone of the 1973 movie *Soylent Green* in which people were fed wafers made out of *people*!?

Some people find meat hard to digest. Some people just like rice and potatoes and vegetables better.

Miso Soup for the Spirit

Some of the world's greatest thinkers and philosophers have chosen or advocated a vegetarian lifestyle, including Pythagoras, Socrates, Plato, Leonardo da Vinci, Albert Einstein, Ben Franklin, and Mahatma Ghandi, among others.

For still others, their vegetarian lifestyle stems from religious or spiritual teachings.

Some Christians interpret a passage from the Old Testament to mean that humans should eat a vegetarian diet:

> "And God said, behold, I have given you every herb-bearing seed, which is upon the face of all the earth, and every tree, in the which is the fruit of a tree yielding seed; to you it shall be for meat."
>
> —Genesis 1:29

Members of the Seventh-day Adventist Church are encouraged to follow a vegetarian diet, and about half of its members do so. The Trappist monks, who are Catholic, also follow a vegetarian diet.

Numerous Eastern religions or philosophies also advocate a vegetarian diet, including Buddhism, Jainism, and Hinduism.

See the following table for a list of people throughout the centuries who have been advocates of a vegetarian lifestyle.

Vegetarians Are in Good Company

Yesterday
Louisa May Alcott, writer
Clara Barton, nurse and first president of the American Red Cross
Cesar Chavez, activist and leader of the United Farm Workers
Charles Darwin, naturalist and author
Leonardo da Vinci, artist
Isadora Duncan, dancer
Thomas Edison, inventor
Albert Einstein, physicist
Ben Franklin, scientist, statesman, and philosopher
Mahatma Gandhi, spiritual leader
Jerry Garcia, musician with the Grateful Dead
Sylvester Graham, inventor
Horace Greeley, journalist
John Harvey Kellogg, physician and food scientist
Linda McCartney, photographer and vegetarian activist
John Milton, writer
Malcolm Muggeridge, writer
Sir Isaac Newton, physicist
Plato, writer and philosopher
Pythagoras, Greek philosopher

continues

Vegetarians Are in Good Company   (continued)

Yesterday

Swami Satchidananda, spiritual teacher and yoga master

Albert Schweitzer, musician, physician, Nobel Peace Prize winner

George Bernard Shaw, writer and Nobel Prize Laureate in Literature

Mary Wollstonecraft Shelley, English novelist

Percy Bysshe Shelley, English poet

Upton Sinclair, author

Isaac Bashevis Singer, writer and Nobel Prize winner

Socrates, Greek philosopher

Benjamin Spock, author and pediatrician

Henry David Thoreau, writer

Leo Tolstoy, author

Voltaire, French writer

H. G. Wells, author

John Wesley, religious leader

Ellen G. White, religious leader

Today

Hank Aaron, home-run record-setting baseball player

Bryan Adams, rock musician

Maxine Andrews, singer with the Andrews Sisters

Bob Barker, TV personality

Kim Basinger, actress

Jeff Beck, rock musician

Cindy Blum, opera singer

Surya Bonaly, Olympic figure skater

Lisa Bonet, actress

David Bowie, rock musician

Boy George, rock singer

Berke Breathed, cartoonist

Christie Brinkley, model

Roger Brown, professional football player

Ellen Burstyn, actress

Peter Burwash, Davis Cup winner, tennis pro

Kate Bush, rock singer

Andreas Cahling, champion bodybuilder

Chris Campbell, Olympic medalist in wrestling

Today

Benjamin Carson, M.D., neurosurgeon

Deepak Chopra, M.D., author

Phil Collen, rock guitarist with Def Leppard

James Cromwell, actor

Jeff Dahl, rock musician

Ray and Dave Davies, rock musicians with the Kinks

Patti Davis, author

Skeeter Davis, country singer

Harvey and Marilyn Diamond, cookbook authors

Ani DiFranco, singer

Joe Elliot, guitarist with Def Leppard

Elvira, actress and TV personality

Melissa Etheridge, rock singer

Peter Falk, actor

Michael W. Fox, author

Michael Franks, jazz singer

Peter Gabriel, rock musician

Jennie Garth, actress

Sara Gilbert, actress

Philip Glass, composer

Bobcat Goldthwaite, comedian and actor

Elliot Gould, actor

Dick Gregory, comedian

Richie Havens, folk-rock musician

Henry Heimlich, M.D., inventor of the Heimlich maneuver

Doug Henning, magician

Dustin Hoffman, actor

Desmond Howard, professional football player and Heisman trophy winner

Steve Howe, guitarist with the rock group Yes

Chrissie Hynde, rock musician with the Pretenders

Janet Jackson, rock musician

Michael Jackson, rock musician

Andrew Jacobs, U.S. Congressman from Indiana

Steve Jobs, CEO, Apple Computer

Casey Kasem, TV and radio personality

Billie Jean King, tennis champion

k.d. lang, country-rock singer

continues

Vegetarians Are in Good Company   (continued)

Today

Frances Moore Lappé, author and world-hunger activist

Tony La Russa, manager of the Oakland A's

Cloris Leachman, actress

Sabrina LeBeauf, actress

Annie Lennox, rock singer

Phil Lesh, musician with the Grateful Dead

Marv Levy, head coach of the Buffalo Bills

Carl Lewis, Olympic runner

Peggy Lipton, actress

Patrick Macnee, actor

Catherine Malfitano, opera singer

Bill Manetti, power-lifting champion

Steve Martin, actor and comedian

Colman McCarthy, syndicated columnist

Paul McCartney, rock musician and vegetarian activist

Michael Medved, author and film critic

Natalie Merchant, rock singer

Donna Mills, actress

Hayley Mills, actress

Matthew Modine, actor

Edwin Moses, Olympic gold medallist in track

Martina Navratilova, tennis champion

Kevin Nealon, comedian

Olivia Newton-John, rock singer

Stevie Nicks, rock singer with Fleetwood Mac

Paavo Nurmi, long-distance runner with 20 world records

Dean Ornish, M.D., author

Bill Pearl, bodybuilder and four-time Mr. Universe

Kate Pierson, rock singer with the B-52s

Tracy Pollan, actress

Raffi, children's musician

Phylicia Rashad, actress

Jeremy Rifkin, author and activist

Anthony Robbins, author and motivational speaker

Fred Rogers, TV's "Mister Rogers"

Murray Rose, Olympic gold medalist and world-record holder in swimming

Today

Todd Rundgren, rock musician

Boz Scaggs, rock musician

Fred Schneider, rock singer with the B-52s

Dave Scott, six-time Ironman triathlon winner

Jerry Seinfeld, actor and comedian

Grace Slick, founding member of the Jefferson Starship

Rick Springfield, rock musician

Michael Stipe, rock musician with R.E.M.

Larry Storch, actor

John Tesh, composer and TV personality

Cicely Tyson, actor

Eddie Vedder, rock singer with Pearl Jam

Lindsay Wagner, actress

Robert James Waller, author

Lesley Ann Warren, actress

Dennis Weaver, actor

Forrest Whitaker, actor

Vanessa Williams, singer and actress

Wendy O. Williams, rock singer

The Least You Need to Know

➤ Vegetarian diets are generally more healthful than nonvegetarian diets.

➤ Vegetarian diets make more efficient use of our land, water, and fossil fuel resources than diets that give prominence to meat, eggs, and dairy products.

➤ More people can be fed on a vegetarian diet than can be fed on a nonvegetarian diet.

➤ Many vegetarians believe a meatless diet is a more humane and compassionate choice in consideration of animals and other humans.

➤ Many of the world's religious leaders and great thinkers have advocated a vegetarian diet.

Part 2
Nutshell Nutrition

"If you don't eat meat, then where do you get your protein?"

Most vegetarians have heard that one more than once.

"...and your iron, calcium, vitamin B12?" and this list goes on.

Let's face it, every one of us has the Basic Four Food Groups branded on our frontal lobes. We will forever conjure up pictures of Swiss and Gouda, rib-eye steaks, 12-ounce glasses of frothy white milk, hamburger patties, and Elsie the Cow every time someone asks us to name the foods that provide us with protein, calcium, and iron.

Even though you may be savvy enough to know that there are other food sources of key nutrients such as these, it's hard to change the mindset of a culture in which animal products have held center stage for generations.

That's why I'm devoting this part of the book to some basic nutrition issues. The chapters that follow should help clear up any questions or concerns you might have about the nutritional adequacy of a diet that limits or excludes foods of animal origin.

Protein Power

Many vegetarians worry too much about whether or not they are getting enough protein, and if they aren't worried, then it's a good bet that their mother or their spouse or another family member *is*.

There's rarely a need to worry about the protein intake of vegetarians, but it's not hard to understand why people do. In the first grade, our teachers made us cut out pictures of protein-containing foods from magazines and paste them on a cardboard poster of the Basic Four Food Groups. We cut out pictures of hamburgers, hotdogs, pot roasts, and ham and cheese sandwiches. We got extra credit if we included peanut butter—a tricky and unexpected choice because it didn't come from an animal.

It's hard to shed ideas that have been wired into your brain, but this chapter will help you loosen your grip on some of them and will teach you all you need to know about protein in meatless diets.

Plant Proteins Reign Supreme

The fact is that animal products are concentrated sources of protein. That's why diets in which animal products play a prominent role are often *too high* in protein. Rather than relying on animal products, we can get plenty of protein from plant foods. It's easy to do, and it's healthier too. Vegetables, grains, legumes, seeds, and nuts all contain protein. The following is a list of some vegetarian foods that are good sources of protein.

Primo Protein Sources

Bean burritos

Tofu lasagna

Lentil soup

Bean soup

Vegetarian chili

Falafel (garbanzo bean balls)

Pasta primavera

Red beans and rice

Vegetarian pizza

Oatmeal

Cereal and soymilk

Barbecued tempeh

Vegetable stir-fry

Veggie burgers

Veggie Talk

Protein is a vital part of all living tissues. On a more technical level, proteins are nitrogen-containing compounds that break down into amino acids during digestion.

A Protein Primer

The word *protein* comes from a Greek word meaning "of first importance." It was the first material identified as being a vital part of all living organisms. Proteins make up the basic structure of all living cells, and they are a component of hormones, enzymes, and antibodies.

Most of the protein in our bodies is found in our muscles, but there's also protein in our bones, teeth, blood, and other body fluids. The collagen in connective tissue is a protein, and so is the keratin in your hair. The casein in milk, albumin in eggs, blood albumin, and hemoglobin are all examples of proteins as well.

Anatomy of a Protein

The building blocks of protein are *amino acids*. There are 20 amino acids found in most proteins. Linked together, amino acids form proteins, but individual amino acids have specialized functions in the body as well. The amino acid tryptophan, for instance, plays a role in the creation of the vitamin niacin. The amino acid glycine combines with toxic substances and converts them into harmless forms that are then excreted from the body. Histidine is involved in the formation of the vasodilator histamine, a substance that you've probably had experience with if you've ever had a stuffy nose from hay fever or another allergy. Individual amino acids can also combine with other nonprotein substances to perform still other functions in the body.

Your body can manufacture most of the amino acids that it needs to build proteins. It does this by using parts from carbohydrates, fats, and other amino acids. However, there are nine amino acids that the body cannot manufacture, and these have to come from the food that you eat. These nine amino acids are called *essential amino acids* or indispensable amino acids.

You may recognize the names of some of the essential amino acids. The "big nine" are:

➤ Histidine

➤ Isoleucine

➤ Leucine

➤ Lysine

➤ Methionine

➤ Phenylalanine

➤ Threonine

➤ Tryptophan

➤ Valine

Veggie Talk

Amino acids are the building blocks of proteins and have other functions in the body as well.

Veggie Talk

Essential amino acids are amino acids that cannot be manufactured by the body. There are nine of them, and you have to get them from your food.

Plants Provide Enough

Plants contain all of the essential amino acids in varying amounts. Some plants are higher in certain essential amino acids and lower in others. Even though some plants contain less of one or more of the essential amino acids, it's easy to get enough of what you need, even if you eat nothing but plant products and your diet contains no meat, eggs, or dairy products at all.

In fact, as long as you get enough calories to meet your energy needs, it's nearly impossible to be deficient in protein. If you ate nothing but potatoes but got enough potatoes to meet your energy needs, you'd get all of the essential amino acids that you need.

Now, I'd never suggest that you should eat nothing but potatoes. There are other nutrients that you need from foods besides protein, and no one food has it all. That's why it's important to include a reasonable variety of foods in your diet. However, the practical matter about protein and essential amino acids is that if you eat enough vegetables, grains, legumes, nuts, and seeds (or a reasonable variety of most of those foods), you'll be sure to meet or exceed your need for all of the essential amino acids.

The Last Bite

You may have memories from many years back of magazine photos of starving children in Biafra, with their big, distended bellies and hollow, sad eyes. These children were suffering from protein-calorie malnutrition, a condition known as kwashiorkor. In real life, this is how protein deficiencies are seen. Protein deficiency goes hand in hand with calorie deprivation. These children were probably deficient in plenty of other nutrients too, since they simply did not have enough food. When you get enough calories in your diet, and your diet contains a reasonable variety of foods, it's nearly impossible to be protein deficient.

No "Combining" Necessary

The only combination you have to worry about is the one on your locker at the gym. You don't have to consciously combine foods in your diet so that their amino acid profiles complement each other in any particular way.

This may be different from what you've heard in the past. The idea that vegetarians have to carefully combine foods in a certain way is actually still being perpetuated by some health professionals and writers who don't realize that the recommendations have changed. The next time you read a magazine article that says that vegetarians have to "complement their proteins," you can smile smugly to yourself, knowing that you know better. Write a letter to the editor too.

What gave people the idea that vegetarians had to be careful about combining foods in the first place?

Those of you who are old enough to remember know: It was a book from the early 1970s, Frances Moore Lappé's *Diet for a Small Planet* (Twentieth Anniversary Edition, Ballantine Books, 1991). This classic raised awareness about the relationships between food choices and the efficient use of our natural resources, and it advocated a vegetarian diet. But the book also made generations of vegetarians aware of the concept of "protein complementarity." Unfortunately, it was this idea that made it seem as though it may be difficult or risky to eat a vegetarian diet.

"Hey You! Nice Proteins You've Got There"

When I open the front cover of my old, dog-eared, 1972 copy of *Diet for a Small Planet*—the one with the crunchy, yellowing pages—the very first thing that appears is the following:

"What is protein complementarity?"

[It is] the combination, in the proper proportions, of nonmeat foods, that produces high-grade protein nutrition equivalent to—*or better than*—meat proteins.

"And that is what this book is all about."

The idea was that since plant foods are limited in one or more of the essential amino acids, we should combine a food that is limited in a particular amino acid with a food that has an abundance of that same amino acid. The concept was to complement one plant food's amino acid profile with another's, fitting two foods together like puzzle pieces. That way, you'd have a "complete protein," with adequate amounts of all of the essential amino acids present and available to the body at the same time.

Complex protein complementarity charts detailed the manner in which foods should be combined. Conscientious vegetarians were careful to eat their beans with rice or corn and to add milk or cheese to their grains (macaroni and cheese being a perennial favorite). They wistfully acknowledged that they should have taken better notes in organic chemistry.

Veggie Talk

Complementary proteins are not nutrients that say nice things about you. The concept of complementing proteins was that foods were combined in such a way that the essential amino acid profile of one food made up for limited supplies of one or more essential amino acids in another food. Together, the foods formed a complete, or high-quality, protein. This practice is no longer considered necessary.

Stopping the Insanity

Frances Moore Lappé did us all a big favor by raising public awareness of the need for responsible food choices. In recent years, however, nutrition scientists have given the issue of protein complementarity a little more thought, and the verdict is that we might have gone a wee bit overboard.

Suffice it to say, the facts upon which the complementary protein concept were based were accurate and are still accurate. It's just that the conclusion that was drawn was wrong.

Thousands of nutrient interactions take place in your body every day without your knowledge or conscious participation. It's just like the normal functioning of every cell and every organ. You breathe without consciously inhaling and exhaling, and your kidneys do their thing without instructions from you. If you had to consciously orchestrate these and other body functions—including the interactions of amino acids—it's likely that you wouldn't be here to read this book today.

The idea that proteins had to be complemented was also supported by some very early lab data from studies of protein-deprived rats. The rats were fed diets that were deficient in individual essential amino acids. Without these essential amino acids, they couldn't build complete proteins and became protein deficient. Of course, those were laboratory conditions. In real life, we eat whole foods that contain an array of amino acids, including all of the essential amino acids. We don't eat specially developed, amino acid deficient, laboratory rat chow. So, these studies had little relevance for free-living human beings.

Your body can complement its proteins without much help from you. Your job is to do two things:

➤ Make sure you get enough calories to meet your energy needs.

➤ Eat a reasonable variety of foods over the course of the day.

That's really all there is to it.

The Last Bite

Protein is the least likely nutrient to be deficient in a vegetarian diet, but it's interesting to note that soybeans are a rich source of all of the essential amino acids. Soybeans could actually serve as the sole source of protein in a person's diet if that was necessary for some reason.

So How Much Protein Is Enough?

Really, you don't have to worry about your protein intake. Okay, if you live on Twinkies and Dr. Pepper, then maybe you could end up protein deficient. But you'd be lacking in many vitamins and minerals and other phytochemicals too. Nevertheless, I know that some of you want to know precisely how much protein you need, so here's the way to figure it out:

The rule of thumb for determining your protein needs is to aim for 0.8 gram of protein for every kilogram of your body weight. One kilogram is equal to 2.2 pounds.

So, for example, if you weigh 120 pounds, that's about 54.5 kilograms (120 pounds divided by 2.2 pounds per kilogram). Multiply 54.5 kilograms by 0.8 gram of protein per kilogram of body weight, and you get 43.6 grams of protein, or approximately 44 grams of protein.

Forty-four grams of protein isn't much, and the formula I've used has a generous margin of error worked into it.

To give you an idea of how easy it is to get the protein you need, take a look at the list of foods and their protein content below. Think about what you eat in the course of a day and the size of the portions you take. Calculate your own protein requirement using the formula I gave earlier, then compare that to the amount of protein you eat in a typical day.

How Much Protein Do You Eat?

Food	Grams of Protein
If You Eat Animal Products	
1 oz. any type of meat	7
1 oz. cheese	7
1 egg	7
1 cup milk	8
Quarter-pound hamburger (no bun)	28
4-oz. chicken breast	28
10-oz. rib-eye steak	70
3-egg omelet with 2 oz. cheese	35
If You Eat Vegetarian Meat Alternatives	
1 typical veggie burger patty	5–25
1 typical veggie hotdog (1 link)	8
4 oz. tempeh	20
4 oz. tofu, depending on type	5–9
8 oz. soymilk (plain)	10

continues

How Much Protein Do You Eat? (continued)

Food	Grams of Protein
Legumes (Dried Beans and Peas)	
½ cup most legumes, depending on type	5–9
½ cup bean burrito filling	6
1 cup black bean soup	16
1 cup vegetarian chili	24
½ cup vegetarian baked beans	6
½ cup garbanzo beans on a salad	6
Nuts and Seeds	
1 oz. nuts, depending on type	4–7
1 oz. seeds, depending on type	4–11
2 Tbsp. tahini (sesame seed butter)	6
2 Tbsp. cashew, almond, or peanut butter	8
Grains and Grain Products	
1 slice whole-wheat bread (firm style)	2–3
1 bran muffin	3
½ cup whole-grain flake cereal	2
½ cup cooked oatmeal	3
1 whole bagel	6
½ cup cooked pasta	7
½ cup cooked rice	4
1 flour tortilla	2
1 peanut butter sandwich with 2 Tbsp. peanut butter	20+
1 cup spaghetti, before sauce	14
1 bean burrito	8
Vegetables	
1 cup most vegetables (green beans, tomatoes, cabbage, broccoli, for example)	4
1 cup pasta mixed with 1 cup assorted vegetables	18
Fruits	
Most fruits have only a trace of protein	

Take a look at the sample day's vegan menu that follows:

Breakfast

1 cup cooked oatmeal with cinnamon and raisins and 1 cup plain soymilk

1 slice whole-wheat toast with margarine and jelly

6 oz. fresh orange juice

Lunch

Mixed green salad with vinaigrette dressing

1 cup lentil soup

1 chunk corn bread

½ cup fresh fruit salad

Water

Dinner

4 oz. bean curd mixed with Chinese vegetables and brown sauce

1 cup steamed rice

½ cup cooked greens with sesame

Orange wedges

Herbal tea

Snack

Bagel with tofu cream cheese

Herbal iced tea mixed with fruit juice

Heads Up!

A message to body builders: Listen up! Flooding yourself with protein from powders, egg-white shakes, and big steaks doesn't build muscle. *Work* builds muscle, and your body can make those muscles from pasta and vegetables. Eating more meat doesn't help you build more muscle. Any extra calories from meat will just be converted into body fat.

This menu provides about 1,600 calories and 53 grams of protein. You can see that even if no animal products are included at all, it's easy to get all the protein you need.

Technically, vegetarians may actually need a smidgen more protein than nonvegetarians. That's because many plant sources of protein are somewhat less digestible than animal sources or processed plant protein products, such as soymilk, tofu, some veggie burger patties, and so forth. Elite athletes also need slightly more protein than the average person, but they easily get that protein in the extra calories they consume due to their high activity level. Practically speaking, the formula given earlier should cover virtually everybody's protein needs.

Too Much of a Good Thing?

It bears repeating that, as I mentioned in Chapter 1, "What's a Vegetarian?" there really is such a thing as too much protein. Excessively high protein intakes—a habit that many people are guilty of—causes you to lose calcium. It increases your blood cholesterol level as well as your risk of heart disease and cancer. Vegetarian diets typically contain enough protein without providing too much.

The Least You Need to Know

➤ Protein is made up of amino acids, nine of which you have to get from your food.

➤ Plants contain all nine essential amino acids.

➤ You'll get enough protein and essential amino acids if you get enough calories to meet your energy needs and eat a reasonable variety of foods.

➤ There's no need to consciously combine foods within meals as the old "complementary protein" idea recommended.

➤ Vegetarians typically get enough protein but not too much. Avoiding excessive amounts of protein in your diet has health advantages.

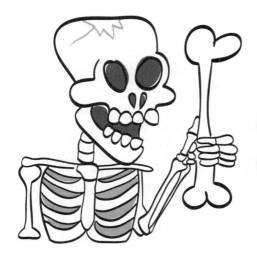

Chapter 4

Boning Up on Calcium

> ## In This Chapter
>
> ➤ Who drinks milk and why
>
> ➤ If you don't drink milk, where do you get calcium?
>
> ➤ Why recommendations are sky-high
>
> ➤ How to hang on to what you've got
>
> ➤ Getting enough

Dogs do it.

Deer do it.

Even chipmunks and raccoons do it.

They all produce milk for their babies.

Cows do it too. So do humans. Fifty percent of them, anyway.

But dogs don't drink chipmunk's milk. And deer don't drink raccoon's milk.

That's because milk is species specific. Each species' milk is tailor-made for its own kind. So how on Earth did people start drinking milk from cows? Even adult cows don't drink cow's milk. And if we drink cow's milk, why stop there? Why not drink dog's milk? Or bear's milk?

Strange business, this diet thing, when you stop to think about it.

Doesn't Everyone Drink Cow's Milk?

If you don't drink milk, you're not the oddball. In fact, you've got lots of company.

You might be surprised to learn that most of the world's people do not drink cow's milk. The reason? Most of them can't digest it.

During infancy, your body produces an enzyme called *lactase*. Lactase helps the body digest *lactose*, the form of sugar found in milk. As a baby becomes a toddler, she needs less of her mother's milk, so the body's production of lactase also begins to decline. By the time a human child is three to five years of age, she has stopped breast-feeding and doesn't naturally need milk in her diet anymore. At that time, the body has stopped or nearly stopped producing lactase. That's natural too.

That explains why most of the adult people in the world don't drink milk. They stopped producing the lactase needed to digest the milk. They don't need human milk anymore, so there's no need for their bodies to produce the lactase, either. They lost the ability to digest milk from their own species, and they certainly can't digest milk from another species. If they tried, they'd have symptoms of *lactose intolerance*.

Lactose intolerance is the normal condition of adults who try to drink milk. Since they can't digest the milk sugar, the sugar moves into the intestines without having been completely digested. The result is the symptoms that characterize lactose intolerance: gas, bloating, abdominal cramps, and diarrhea.

Among your friends and family members, those who are of Asian, African, Mediterranean, Native American, or South American descent are probably lactose intolerant to some degree. Most Hispanics and Jews are at least somewhat lactose intolerant. Who's not? People of Northern European descent. That's thought to be due to a genetic mutation that occurred some time in generations past that allowed those people to continue to produce lactase into adulthood.

Veggie Talk

Lactase is an enzyme produced by infants and very young children. It allows babies to digest **lactose**, the form of sugar found in milk.

Veggie Talk

Lactose intolerance is the normal condition of most of the adults in the world. They can't digest the milk sugar, lactose, because their bodies no longer produce the enzyme lactase.

So, people of English and Scandinavian descent, for instance, are not as likely to have problems digesting milk. Since people of Northern European descent colonized the United States, Canada, Australia, and New Zealand, dairy products were a cultural tradition brought over to those countries from Northern Europe. Cultural diversity is increasing in the United States as more people from other countries move here, and with it, the prevalence of lactose intolerance is also increasing.

Why Drink Cow's Milk?

If so many people can't tolerate it, why is cow's milk promoted by health professionals as an important part of a "balanced" diet? The answer is partially as simple as the fact that it was a cultural tradition brought over to this country by people for whom it was a staple food for generations. But once that tradition took root, economic and political forces maintained it.

The Politics of Your Plate

The United States Department of Agriculture is in the business of protecting and promoting agriculture in our country. In large part, that means advocating for the meat and dairy industries. However, the Department is also charged with issuing dietary recommendations for the American public. A conflict of interest? You bet. Even when research into the connections between diet and disease began to implicate dairy products and meats and it became clear that we need to limit our intake of these foods, the Department of Agriculture was reluctant to pointedly say so. Today's guidelines make note of the fact that we need to eat more plant products and that vegetarian diets can be an acceptable alternative, but they are less clear in acknowledging that this means that people also need to reduce their consumption of animal products.

So for generations we've had the Basic Four Food Groups, a model for meal planning that had meat and dairy products forming two of the four pillars of the diet. Never mind that there was never a human requirement for any of those foods. Fruits and vegetables? Squashed together in one group of their own. Breads and cereals formed the fourth group.

The Basic Four has finally been retired and replaced with a different model—the Food Guide Pyramid. The Pyramid has its own set of problems, but it's an improvement on the old Basic Four. In the meantime, the dairy industry continues its marketing efforts to get more people to drink milk.

Helpful Hint

Need a replacement for cow's milk? Try soymilk. You can find it in any natural foods store and in most supermarkets. Many brands are calcium-fortified. You'll also see rice milks and soy/rice blends, but they aren't as nutritious as soy. Soymilks vary in flavor from brand to brand, so experiment to find the one you like the best.

Helpful Hint

"Where's your milk mustache?" the billboards ask. Many of the faces sporting them are African, Hispanic, and Asian—faces of people that are probably lactose intolerant. Enzyme products such as Lact-Aid, that are either taken by mouth, added to food, or have already been added to the milk, work with varying degrees of success. If you are lactose intolerant, consider sporting a soymilk mustache instead.

The dairy industry has historically been aggressive about providing nutrition education for the public. For decades, the industry has produced its own versions of meal planning guides and distributed them free of charge to schools, hospitals, and doctors' offices. For many of us, these were the only nutrition education materials we ever saw while we were in school.

I remember the guides showing that good sources of calcium included milk, cheese, and ice cream. If you didn't want these, well…there were always the dreaded *sardines with bones*. Or voluminous quantities of broccoli. The choice seemed obvious at the time. After all, how much broccoli can a person eat?

Facts About Femurs

Then there's all the fuss about your bones.

We associate calcium intake with the health of our bones and teeth, but as you'll see in the next section of this chapter, bone health isn't just about getting enough calcium. In fact, there are more important factors relating to bone health than how much calcium you have in your diet.

But for the record, vegetarians around the world tend to have rates of *osteoporosis* that are the same as or lower than those of nonvegetarians. Unfortunately, there isn't enough reliable research data about the bone health of Western vegetarians, particularly vegans. And it often isn't possible to apply standards for calcium intakes, which are based on studies from other parts of the world, to Western vegetarians. In cultures where a plant-based diet is the norm, data about bone health is more widely available. In the United States and Canada, efforts are now underway to collect more data about the bone health of vegans and other vegetarians, now that more people are moving away from a traditional Western eating style.

In the meantime, nutritionists have to hedge a little bit when asked to make specific recommendations about calcium intake for Western vegans and other vegetarians. You might guess that recommendations for calcium intake for Western vegetarians would be similar to those for vegetarians in other countries, but lifestyle differences among cultures (such as physical activity levels, alcohol intake, smoking patterns, sunlight exposure, salt use, etc.) can make it difficult to apply one culture's recommendations to another's.

Veggie Talk

Osteoporosis is the condition that results when the bones begin to waste away and become porous and brittle. Bones in this condition are susceptible to fractures. In the most severe cases, the bones can break with the slightest stress, such as a sneeze or a cough. Osteoporosis is a major health problem affecting 15 to 20 million Americans, often with life-threatening consequences.

What? No Milk Mustache?

Cow's milk is a concentrated source of several nutrients. It's rich in calcium, riboflavin, fat, protein, and calories. It has to be, because it has to enable a calf to grow into a several-hundred-pound cow with a massive skeleton in a matter of months. It's made to meet the special needs of a baby cow. And like all mammals, including humans, after infancy the cow doesn't need milk anymore. From that point on, the cow gets the calcium and other nutrients it needs from the plants on which it grazes.

Like grown cows, human vegetarians who don't drink cow's milk or eat dairy products can get calcium from plants. Okay, so our choices might be a little different. We eat at our kitchen tables rather than standing up in a field.

A sampling of calcium-rich plant foods for humans includes:

➤ Dark green, leafy vegetables such as kale, Swiss chard, collards, and mustard and turnip greens

➤ Broccoli

➤ Chinese cabbage

➤ Tofu processed with calcium

➤ Legumes such as pinto beans, black beans, and garbanzo beans

➤ Almonds and sesame seeds

➤ Dried figs

➤ Calcium-fortified orange juice or soymilk

There are many others. Don't worry—you don't have to eat sardines with bones. And there are lots of delicious ways to work high-calcium foods into your meals:

➤ Bean chili over rice with steamed broccoli and a chunk of cornbread

➤ Stir-fried Chinese vegetables with bean curd (tofu) over rice

➤ Falafel (garbanzo bean balls) served in pita pockets and a glass of orange juice

➤ Steamed kale with garlic and sesame seeds

➤ Fig cookies with a glass of fortified soymilk

➤ Green beans with slivered almonds

➤ Black bean dip served with broccoli and cauliflower florets and carrot sticks

Bushels and Bushels of Broccoli

"So, how much calcium do I need?"

Translation: "Do I have to eat a truckload of broccoli to get it?"

Probably not. It's most likely that vegetarians need less dietary calcium than non-vegetarians need because they absorb and retain calcium better than nonvegetarians. So, intakes of calcium below current recommendations are probably not a problem for most vegetarians.

But determining calcium requirements is more complicated than you may realize.

The recommendations for calcium intake for Americans vary by age and sex. They are also based on certain assumptions, some of which are relevant to the culture in which we live.

Calculating Calcium

American recommendations for calcium intake take several factors into consideration. First, scientists know that our bodies normally lose a certain amount of calcium every day through our feces, sweat, and urine. Scientists can also estimate the amount of calcium that is typically absorbed from the food that you eat. With these two figures, they can estimate how much calcium you need to take in each day in order to break even. Then they add a margin of safety—a "fudge factor"—just to be on the safe side. The latest set of recommendations, issued in 1997 by the National Academy of Sciences, are higher than previous recommendations for people in certain age groups (see the following figure).

When it comes to vegetarians, though, the amount of calcium that is actually absorbed and retained from food is probably a good deal higher than the amount absorbed by most Americans, so recommended intakes could theoretically be lower. How much lower depends on a few factors.

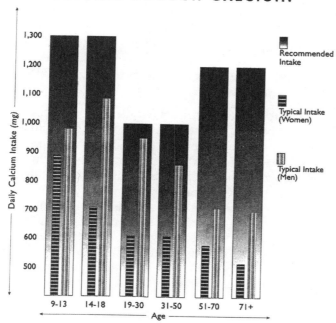

GETTING ENOUGH CALCIUM?

"Getting Enough Calcium?" Source: Nutrition Action Healthletter, *April, 1998.*

Both men ⊞ and—especially—women ▦ report consuming far less calcium than the new National Academy of Sciences report recommends ▬ . However, most people eat more food than they report, so actual intakes are somewhat higher than those shown here.

The Protein Factor

As I mentioned in Chapter 1, "What's a Vegetarian?" Americans have a penchant for meat and other high-protein foods, and they pay for it with calcium.

When you eat meat and other forms of animal protein, your blood becomes more acidic. In order to neutralize the acid in the blood, your body draws calcium from your bones and sends it into the bloodstream. This calcium is eventually lost through your urine as your kidneys filter your blood.

Helpful Hint

It's best for most people to limit their protein intake to 70 grams per day. Most people who eat diets that center on meat or lots of dairy products exceed this level.

Protein from plant sources doesn't have the same effect as protein from animal sources. That's because protein from animal sources have more *sulfur-containing amino acids*. Now we're getting a little more technical. Suffice it to say that the sulfur in animal products contributes greatly to the acid condition of the blood, which makes the bones lose more calcium. The sulfur also has an effect on the kidneys that causes more calcium to be lost in the urine.

The amount of protein in your diet probably has a greater bearing on the health of your bones than the amount of calcium in your diet. Scientists think that the ideal ratio of calcium to protein is about 16:1. In other words, you should get about 16 milligrams of calcium in your diet for every gram of protein that your diet contains. So if your protein intake is about 45 grams a day (a typical intake for many vegetarians), your calcium intake should be at least 720 milligrams. If you were a meat eater getting 90 grams of protein in your diet (and many meat eaters get more), then you would need 1,440 milligrams of calcium each day.

Veggie Talk

Sulfur is an element found in certain amino acids. **Sulfur-containing amino acids** are found in the greatest quantities in meat and other animal proteins, and they increase the loss of calcium from your body.

The Last Bite

The countries with the highest intakes of dairy products and animal protein also have the highest rates of hip fracture.

The Sodium Factor

Sodium also has a profound calcium-losing effect on the body. Table salt and processed foods contain lots of sodium, as do canned foods and condiments such as ketchup, mustard, and pickles. Imagine how much protein and sodium a junk food junkie gets in his bacon-double-cheeseburger and fries, sausage biscuit with gravy, and cold cuts such as ham and bologna. Imagine how much more calcium is needed to compensate for what is lost due to foods like these.

It's a good idea for everyone to limit high-sodium foods. Even vegetarians, who typically moderate their protein intakes, need to be aware that too much sodium in the diet can increase their calcium losses. We all need sodium, but we can get what we need in what is naturally found in our food supply. We don't have to add sodium to foods. Read the labels on the packaged foods that you buy, and try to limit your sodium intake to not more than about 2,000 milligrams each day—good advice for vegetarians and nonvegetarians alike.

Other Factors

There are many other factors that affect your body's calcium balance too. Too much phosphorus (found in red meats and soft drinks) causes the body to lose calcium, as does the caffeine found in such places as cola drinks, other soft drinks, coffee, and tea. These have a lesser effect than protein and sodium, though.

Substances such as *phytates* and *oxalates*, found in plant foods, also affect calcium by binding with it and diminishing its absorption. Whole grains are high in phytates, and spinach is high in oxalates, making most of the calcium it contains unavailable to your body. Overall, though, plant foods contain plenty of calcium that can be well-absorbed. In fact, some research shows that the calcium in such plant foods as kale, Chinese cabbage, and broccoli is absorbed better than the calcium found in cow's milk.

Your level of physical activity matters too. The more weight-bearing exercise you include in your daily routine, the more calcium you'll hang onto. People who walk regularly or engage in strength-training by using a weight set at home or at the gym have denser bones than people who are couch potatoes.

Heads Up!

Vegetarians who eat lots of salty snack chips, condiments such as ketchup and soy sauce, and processed foods such as many soups and meat substitutes may be sacrificing calcium as a result. If this sounds like you, you can improve your diet by limiting foods such as these.

Veggie Talk

Phytates and **oxalates** are substances found in plant foods that inhibit your body's ability to absorb the calcium in the foods that contain them. Overall, however, the calcium from plants is absorbed well and sometimes even better than the calcium found in cow's milk.

Even your exposure to sunshine makes a difference in how much calcium your bones absorb. Your body manufactures vitamin D when you are exposed to sunlight. Vitamin D helps your body absorb calcium. (More about vitamin D in Chapter 7, "The Other Suspects: Riboflavin, Vitamin D, and Zinc.")

There's one more factor that people often forget. That is, your body adjusts the absorption of many nutrients, including calcium, according to its needs. In other words, when you need more calcium, your body magically becomes more efficient at absorbing what is present in your food. When you need less calcium, your body absorbs less, even if you flood yourself with calcium from dairy products or supplements.

Getting Enough

Generally, it's a good idea for adult vegetarians, particularly vegans, to try to include two or more servings of calcium-rich foods in their diets each day. Teens and young adults should get an extra serving. It's important for everyone to limit their protein intakes to moderate levels (not more than 70 grams per day) and that sodium intakes are also limited (not more than 2,000 milligrams per day). Chapters 8 through 11 explain how you can ensure that vegetarian diets are meeting the needs of people at different ages.

The following table shows a comparison of the calcium content of some familiar foods.

Calcium Comparisons

Source	Food	Calcium Content (mg)
Dairy	Milk, skim, 1 cup	350
	Mozzarella cheese, part skim, 1 oz.	183
	Yogurt, nonfat plain, 1 cup	274
Plant	Almond butter, 1 Tbsp.	43
	Blackstrap molasses, 1 Tbsp.	172
	Bok choy, cooked, 1 cup	160
	Broccoli, cooked, 1 cup	70
	Collard greens, cooked, 1 cup	360
	Figs, dried, ½ cup	143
	Garbanzo beans, canned, 1 cup	77
	Kale, cooked, 1 cup	180
	Kidney beans, canned, 1 cup	69
	Lentils, cooked, 1 cup	38
	Mustard greens, chopped, cooked, 1 cup	104
	Navy beans, canned, 1 cup	123
	Orange, fresh, 1 medium	61
	Orange juice, Minute Maid, fortified with calcium	300
	Pinto beans, canned, 1 cup	103
	Soymilk, EdenSoy Extra, vanilla, 1 cup	200
	Tofu, firm, processed with calcium sulfate, ½ cup	861
	Turnip greens, chopped, cooked, 1 cup	197
	Whole-wheat bread, 2 slices	40

Sources: USDA Nutrient Database for Standard Reference (www.nal.usda.gov/fnic/foodcomp).

The Least You Need to Know

➤ Milk is species specific. There is no human requirement for milk from a cow.

➤ Most of the world's people drink little or no cow's milk, and most adults are lactose intolerant to some degree.

➤ Good plant sources of calcium include dark green, leafy vegetables, broccoli, legumes, figs, almonds, tofu processed with calcium, fortified soymilk or orange juice, and many others.

➤ Vegetarian adults should try to include at least two servings of calcium-rich plant foods in the diet each day.

➤ Moderate your protein intake and limit sodium to not more than 2,000 milligrams each day to help conserve calcium.

Chapter 5

What About Iron?

In This Chapter

➤ Where to mine for iron

➤ About the two types

➤ How to ensure you get enough

➤ Why too much is not a good thing

"List three good food sources of iron."

When I ask most people that question, they say "Red meat," and draw a blank after that.

Like protein and calcium, most people associate iron with an animal product, but, like protein and calcium, iron is also widely available in foods of plant origin.

You may also associate having enough iron with having enough energy. Do you remember the old Geritol commercials from the late 1960s? People with "iron poor blood" were tired all of the time—lethargic and groggy. Iron is a mineral that forms part of the hemoglobin of red blood cells and helps carry oxygen to the body's cells. Iron is also part of the myoglobin that provides oxygen to the muscles in your body. When your iron stores are low or depleted, you can't get enough oxygen to the cells of your body. A form of anemia results, and you may feel very tired.

Before you begin yawning, you might like to know that vegetarians are not more prone to iron deficiency than nonvegetarians. *Iron deficiency anemia* happens to be one of the most common nutritional deficiencies around the world, but most of it occurs in developing countries, rather than in affluent countries, and the cause is more likely to be parasites than to be diet. In developed countries, iron deficiency is most likely to affect children and young people as well as pregnant or premenopausal women.

Iron Is Everywhere

Iron is available everywhere you look in the plant world. Rich sources include whole or enriched breads and cereals, legumes, nuts and seeds, dark green, leafy vegetables, and some dried fruits. Vegetarians typically don't have trouble getting enough, as you'll learn in this chapter.

The Nuts and Bolts About Iron in Plants

You may have heard that the iron in plant foods isn't absorbed as well as the iron that comes from meat. That's true, but it really doesn't matter for most vegetarians.

Iron is found in foods in two forms: *heme* and *nonheme iron*. It pays to understand the differences between the two types because it will help you understand the issues surrounding iron in the vegetarian diet. You'll be ready with the answers the next time someone asks you, "If you're a vegetarian, where do you get your iron?"

Heme Who?

The iron found in meat, poultry, and fish is the heme form. Heme iron is found in meat (including poultry and fish) and is easily absorbed by the body—more easily absorbed than iron obtained from plant sources. In fact, when meat is present in the diet, it increases the amount of iron that you absorb from plant foods as well. As you'll learn in a few minutes, though, this characteristic doesn't necessarily make heme iron a better source of iron, and it may even have drawbacks.

Nonheme What?

Vegetarians don't eat meat, but that's generally not an issue when it comes to getting enough iron.

Veggie Talk

Iron deficiency anemia *is a condition that results when the iron stores in your blood are depleted and you can't get enough oxygen delivered to the cells of your body. Fatigue is one symptom. Vegetarians are not more prone to iron deficiency than are nonvegetarians.*

Veggie Talk

Heme iron *is the form of iron found in meat, poultry, and fish. It's more readily absorbed by the body than iron that comes from plant sources.*

Veggie Talk

Nonheme iron *is the form of iron found in plant foods. Other substances in plant foods help the body absorb the iron found in plants.*

The form of iron found in plant foods is called nonheme iron. Nonheme iron is absorbed less efficiently than heme iron. However, certain other food components can radically improve the body's absorption of nonheme iron. It's these other enhancers of iron absorption in plant foods that help vegetarians absorb the iron they need.

The Tug of War Over Iron

There's actually a little game of tug-of-war over iron going on in your body. That's because in addition to enhancers of iron absorption, foods also contain substances that inhibit iron absorption.

We've already said that meat is an iron absorption enhancer. But vegetarians don't eat meat, so what are some plant substances that improve the absorption of nonheme iron?

The most potent enhancer of iron absorption from a plant source is vitamin C. When vegetarians eat a rich food source of vitamin C with a meal, they can enhance the absorption of the iron present in the meal by as much as 20 times.

Fruits and vegetables are good sources of vitamin C. Some examples include:

➤ Broccoli

➤ Brussels sprouts

➤ Cabbage

➤ Cantaloupe

➤ Cauliflower

➤ Citrus fruits such as grapefruits, lemons, and oranges, and their juices

➤ Green peppers

➤ Honeydew melons

➤ Kiwi fruit

➤ Kohlrabi

➤ Papaya

➤ Potatoes

➤ Strawberries

➤ Tomatoes

You probably eat vitamin C–rich foods with many of your favorite meals and don't even realize it. In each of the vegetarian meals below, a vitamin C–rich food helps the body absorb the iron that is present at that meal:

➤ Bowl of cooked oatmeal with fresh strawberry slices and soymilk

➤ Pasta tossed with steamed broccoli, cauliflower, carrots, green peppers, and onions with marinara (tomato) sauce or garlic and olive oil

➤ Veggie burger with tomato and lettuce and a side of home fries

➤ Tempeh sloppy Joe with side of coleslaw

➤ Peanut butter and jelly sandwich on whole-wheat bread with orange quarters

➤ Bowl of black bean soup with sourdough roll, mixed green salad with tomatoes, green peppers, and onions, and a slice of cantaloupe

➤ Vegetarian chili over brown rice with steamed broccoli or Brussels sprouts

There are other plant components that improve iron absorption, but vitamin C is the most powerful. Using cast-iron cookware such as skillets, pots, and pans can also increase the amount of iron you absorb, especially when you use them to cook acidic foods, such as tomatoes or tomato sauce.

Heads Up!

If you are an avid tea-drinker, be careful. More than coffee, tea impairs your body's ability to absorb dietary iron. In some areas of the country, it's commonplace for people to drink a half gallon of iced tea or more each day, and quantities of tannins that large may be problematic for some people. Consider switching to herbal tea, since most do not contain tannins.

It All Works Out in the End

Other substances in your food have the opposite effect and can inhibit your body's ability to absorb iron. One of those is the tannic acid in tea. In poor countries where diets are low in vitamin C–rich fruits and vegetables and low in iron, a tradition of tea-drinking can tip the scales and cause iron deficiency. That doesn't commonly happen in Western countries, where people generally eat a wider variety of foods and have access to plenty of fruits and vegetables.

Just as there are many substances that enhance iron absorption, there are many that inhibit it as well. Certain spices, the phytates found in whole grains, the calcium in dairy products, and coffee all decrease the availability of dietary iron. The reality is, however, that if you eat a reasonable mix of foods, these inhibitors and enhancers of iron absorption offset each other.

Ironing Out the Facts

So your iron status depends upon the mix of foods that you eat. The enhancers and inhibitors of iron absorption that occur naturally in foods usually offset each other, assuming that your diet contains a reasonable amount of variety.

Your body's ability to absorb iron also depends upon the degree to which you need the iron in the first place. Never underestimate your body's ability to adapt to varying dietary conditions. When you need more, your body becomes more efficient at absorbing the iron that is present in your food. When you need less, your body absorbs less. Pretty neat, huh?

Getting Enough

Vegetarians need more iron in their diets than nonvegetarians, since the iron in plant foods is not absorbed as efficiently as the iron in meat. However, you might be surprised to learn that on average, vegetarians tend to get substantially more iron in their diets as compared to nonvegetarians. Vegans get the most, since the dairy products that other vegetarians eat contain virtually no iron and tend to displace iron-containing plant foods.

Iron Is Everywhere

Food Type	Food	Iron Content (mg)
Breads and cereals	Bran flakes, ¾ cup	8.1
	Whole-wheat bread, 1 slice	0.9
	Oatmeal, 1 cup cooked	1.6
	Brown rice, 1 cup steamed	1.0
Legumes	Black beans, 1 cup cooked	3.6
	Garbanzo beans, 1 cup cooked	4.7
	Lentil soup, 1 cup	2.7
	Navy beans, 1 cup cooked	4.5
	Pinto beans, 1 cup cooked	4.5
	Soybeans, 1 cup cooked	8.8
	Tempeh, 4 oz.	1.9
	Tofu, firm, 4 oz.	1.8
	Vegetarian chili, 1 cup	3.5
Nuts and seeds	Peanut butter, 2 Tbsp.	0.6
	Almond butter, 2 Tbsp.	1.2
	Sunflower seeds, ¼ cup	1.0
Fruits	Apricots, dried, ¼ cup	1.5
	Cantaloupe, 1 large wedge (¼ of large)	0.4
	Prunes, ¼ cup	1.1
	Prune juice, 1 cup	3.0
	Raisins, 1 small box (1.5 oz.)	0.9
	Watermelon, 1 cup diced	0.3
Vegetables (1 cup cooked unless otherwise noted)	Bok choy	0.4
	Broccoli, chopped	1.3
	Brussels sprouts	1.9

continues

Iron Is Everywhere   (continued)

Food Type	Food	Iron Content (mg)
	Collard greens, chopped	0.9
	Kale, chopped	1.2
	Kelp (seaweed), 2 Tbsp.	0.3
	Mustard greens, chopped	1.0
	Swiss chard, chopped	4.0
	Turnip greens, chopped	1.2
Other	Blackstrap molasses, 2 Tbsp.	7.0

Source: USDA Nutrient Database for Standard Reference (www.nal.usda.gov/fnic/foodcomp).

How Much Do I Need?

The Recommended Dietary Allowances for iron vary by age and sex (see Appendix A, "Recommended Dietary Allowances and Dietary Reference Intakes"). Generally, the recommendations are higher for premenopausal women than for men and postmenopausal women, since women who menstruate lose more iron than people who do not. So the recommendations for adult men and postmenopausal women are only 10 mg per day as compared to 15 mg per day for premenopausal women.

It's not practical, though, for most people to count the milligrams of iron in their diets. Rather than living life with a calculator in the palm of your hand, it's far more enjoyable to just keep a few key points in mind.

Heads Up!

A primary reason that some people don't get the nutrition they need is that they let the junk push the good stuff out of their diets. If you load up on soft drinks, snack chips, and desserts, you'll end up displacing the healthier foods that you need. A small piece of cake or a few pieces of candy can add up to 300 calories or more. For 300 calories, you can eat a lot of broccoli, beans, and rice. Be honest with yourself about how much junk your diet contains, and when you want a snack, reach for a piece of fruit.

A Few Key Points

Be aware of which foods are particularly good sources of iron, and include them in your diet regularly. Be sure to get plenty of vitamin C–rich fruits and vegetables in your diet, as well. You can't go wrong with fruits and vegetables. That's a common theme nowadays in any discussions about nutrition. One national campaign urges everyone to eat "five a day"—five servings of fruits or vegetables. Of course, they're talking about small, ½-cup servings. For most vegetarians, a goal of five ½-cup servings would mean cutting *back*! When we're talking servings for vegetarians, we're talking heaping helpings—1 cup or more. It's a health-wise goal for anyone—vegetarian or not.

...But Not Getting Too Much

Recently, nutrition scientists have been speculating that it may be healthier to get the bulk of your iron from plant sources rather than from meat. The fact that iron from meat is so readily absorbed can pose a problem for people with *hemachromatosis*, a condition in which the body stores an excessive amount of iron and which is associated with increased rates of coronary artery disease. But there's much more to the picture than that.

In Chapter 2, "Why Go Vegetarian?" we talked about dietary factors such as fat and the iron in meat that can cause the production of free radicals which, in turn, can damage the cells in the body and lead to disease. Iron is a potent oxidant. Scientists believe that when sufficient quantities of heme iron are present, such as in diets that center on meat, cholesterol is oxidized into a form that is more readily absorbed by the arteries. This leads to increased rates of coronary artery disease.

Plant sources of iron, on the other hand, are not absorbed as easily. In the case of nonheme iron, the body absorbs only what it needs. This helps to minimize the body's exposure to oxidants such as iron. As we also mentioned in Chapter 2, the additional antioxidants found in plant foods also help to offset the effects of free radicals.

Veggie Talk

Hemachromatosis is a condition in which the body stores excessive amounts of iron. Too much readily absorbed iron from meat can exacerbate the condition.

So it's easy enough to get plenty of iron on a vegetarian diet, and it's probably also healthier too.

The Least You Need to Know

➤ Vegetarians are not more prone to iron deficiency than are nonvegetarians.

➤ Vegetarians should be sure to eat plenty of iron-rich plant products such as green, leafy vegetables, whole and enriched grain products, and legumes.

➤ To enhance iron absorption, vegetarians should eat plenty of vitamin C–rich fruits and vegetables.

➤ Vegetarians should avoid excessive amounts of tea, especially when the diet is low in fruits and vegetables, because its tannin depletes iron.

➤ Vegetarians and nonvegetarians alike should limit junk foods, which in excess can displace more nutrient-dense foods.

And Vitamin B12?

The science of nutrition is in its infancy, and the issues surrounding vitamin B12 in the vegetarian diet are evidence of this fact. For all we know about the nutrients that are essential to human health, there is often even more that we don't know. In the case of vitamin B12, some mysteries and unanswered questions about sources of the vitamin and how the body utilizes it have created controversy over recommendations for vegetarians and, in particular, for vegans.

Much Ado About So Little

The Recommended Dietary Allowance for vitamin B12 is teeny tiny—just 2 micrograms (µg) per day. Just a fraction of a pinch would be enough to last your entire life.

So what's the big deal about vitamin B12?

The issue is this: Vitamin B12 is only found in animal products. As far as anyone knows, plants contain none. So, vegans could theoretically risk a vitamin B12 deficiency if their diets didn't contain a source of it. Vitamin B12 deficiency can lead to severe and irreversible nerve damage. Despite the need for such a miniscule amount of the vitamin, the stakes are high if you don't get what you need.

Vitamin B12 Factories

Vitamin B12 is being manufactured all around us and inside of us as well. The vitamin is produced by microorganisms—bacteria that exist in the soil, in ponds, streams and rivers, and in the guts of animals, including humans.

Busybodies in Your Intestines

Bacteria are busy making vitamin B12 in the guts of all animals, including yourself. So if you eat any animal products at all, you're getting vitamin B12 from them. If you are a vegetarian that includes eggs, cheese, yogurt, cow's milk, or other dairy products in your diet, then you have a source of vitamin B12. Nonvegetarians get even more vitamin B12 from meat, poultry, and seafood.

In your own body, the vitamin B12 is produced in your intestines, but the current thinking is that it's produced beyond the site of absorption. In other words, bacteria in your intestines produce vitamin B12, but you can't reliably use what they produce.

Some scientists think there's something wrong with that assessment of the matter. They say that humans must be able to use the vitamin B12 that's produced in their own bodies. After all, why would the human body evolve in such a way that an essential substance is produced but can't be utilized? Mother Nature would have weeded that inefficient creature out of the pack—pronto.

We do know that the body recycles much of the vitamin B12 that we have. The body also hoards it. Most of us have at least a three-year supply of vitamin B12 stored in our livers and other tissues, and some people can go without vitamin B12 as long as 20 years before depleting their body stores and developing deficiency symptoms. In fact, the most common cause of vitamin B12 deficiency isn't a lack of the vitamin in the diet. It's the diminished ability of the body to absorb the vitamin. This problem occurs in the general omnivorous public, and is not a vegetarian issue, per se. It's thought that older adults are at the greatest risk, since the body's ability to produce the substance needed to absorb vitamin B12 diminishes with age. In fact, recommendations for adults over the age of 50 years have recently been increased to 2.4 micrograms per day.

Factories on the Outside

Vitamin B12 is also being produced all around us outside of our bodies. For instance, it's produced by microorganisms living in and around rivers, streams, and ponds. So if you were living in the wild, drinking from a mountain stream, you'd have a natural source of vitamin B12 in the water. These days, it isn't safe for most of us to drink from these sources. Instead, we drink chlorinated tap water and hope there are no microorganisms or other forms of bacteria living in it. Of course, that means that city tap water doesn't contain any vitamin B12, either.

The other place you'll find vitamin B12 is in the soil. Vitamin B12–producing microorganisms live in the soil in your garden and everywhere outdoors. If you raise vegetables, pick them, and eat them without first thoroughly washing them, it's possible that you might ingest some particles of soil still clinging to the food. The soil harbors vitamin B12–producing microorganisms—another natural source of the vitamin! I have childhood memories of raiding my family's carrot patch like one of the neighborhood rabbits. I'd look at the green tops poking out of the ground and try to guess where the biggest carrot was hiding. Then I'd pull it out of the ground, rinse it off a little with the garden hose (*little* being the operative word here) and munch away. No doubt there was dirt on that carrot, and no doubt I ate it. Voilà! Vitamin B12 the natural way.

Of course, most of us don't eat food that we pick from our backyard gardens. We eat fruits and vegetables that we "picked" from bins at the grocery store, shiny and clean without a hint of soil clinging to them. There's no vitamin B12 there, either.

Who Needs to Care?

Our need for vitamin B12 is truly miniscule, but the tiny bit that we might have gotten in years past via contamination of our food or water described above isn't available to most of us now. If you eat animal products regularly, you've got a source of vitamin B12. If you don't, then you need to find an alternate source. That means that vegans, or people who eat a near-vegan diet, need to pay attention to getting a reliable source of vitamin B12 in their diets.

What about the fact that your body recycles vitamin B12, that it takes years to develop a deficiency, that lack of vitamin B12 in the diet is not a likely reason for people to be deficient, and so on?

All of that is true. It's also true that, despite the theoretical risk, few cases of vitamin B12 deficiency in vegans have been reported. There may be several reasons for that, including the fact that the anemia caused by vitamin B12 deficiency can be masked by folic acid. Folic acid is found in plant foods, especially green, leafy vegetables. Vegetarians, especially vegans, tend to get a lot of folic acid in their diets, so it's possible that a vitamin B12 deficiency could go undetected.

This is part of the controversy. Some scientists think that vitamin B12 deficiency is rare in vegans, and others think that it's there but is being disguised or underreported.

What's a Vegan to Do?

Take the conservative approach on this one. It's easy to find reliable sources of vitamin B12, such as fortified soymilk and rice milk, fortified breakfast cereals, or even a vitamin tablet (more about sources further on in this chapter). Include them in your diet regularly, just to be on the safe side. It's really very little trouble.

More About Sources of Vitamin B12

Now on to the finer points about vitamin B12 sources.

There is vitamin B12, and there's vitamin B12. Or you could say, vitamin B12 by any other name may not be the kind of vitamin B12 that you need.

Helpful Hint

If you've been eating a vegan or near-vegan diet for at least three years and have not been supplementing your diet with a source of vitamin B12, consider seeing your health care provider for a blood test to measure your stores of the vitamin. One of the first symptoms of deficiency is tingling or numbness in your hands, fingers, or toes, although these symptoms can be caused by conditions other than vitamin B12 deficiency too.

Veggie Talk

Cyanocobalamin is the form of vitamin B12 that the human body is able to utilize.

There are many forms of vitamin B12. The form that you need is called *cyanocobalamin*. Other forms of vitamin B12 are known as analogs. The analogs are inactive in the human body. It's the cyanocobalamin that has biological or physiological activity in the human body.

Why would I burden you with this information?

The reason is that there is often some confusion over which foods are reliable sources of vitamin B12 for vegans. In the past, foods such as sea vegetables, tempeh, miso, and nutritional yeast were touted as being good sources of vitamin B12. When those foods were tested for vitamin B12 content for purposes of labeling the food packages, the labs used a microbial assay that measured for all forms of vitamin B12, rather than for cyanocobalamin. So, people bought those foods, thinking that they were getting the amount of vitamin B12 that the labeled listed, when, in fact, much of what was listed may have been an analog.

Now, scientists say that up to 94 percent of the vitamin B12 in these foods is actually analogs rather than cyanocobalamin. There is some fear that analogs might compete for absorption with cyanocobalamin and promote a deficiency. Of course, there are other people who think that idea is phooey.

However, the current consensus among nutritionists is that it's better to be safe than sorry. For that reason, vegans are advised to get a *reliable* source of vitamin B12 in their diets.

Don't be fooled into thinking that these foods are reliable sources of vitamin B12. They contain mostly analogs of vitamin B12, rather than the cyanocobalamin needed by humans:

Vitamin B12 Imposters
Tempeh
Miso (a fermented soy product used as a soup base or condiment)
Tamari (a fermented soy sauce product)
Nutritional yeast
Sea vegetables such as kombu, kelp, nori, spirulina, and other forms of algae
Bean sprouts

Reliable Vegan Sources of Vitamin B12

The most reliable sources of vitamin B12 for vegans are vitamin B12 supplements or fortified foods. Vegans should include one or the other in their diets every day.

Fortified Foods

When you read food packages, be sure to look for the word *cyanocobalamin* to be sure that the food you are eating contains the right form of the vitamin. You shouldn't have any trouble finding lots of products that have been fortified with cyanocobalamin.

Many cyanocobalamin-fortified food products are mainstream brands that you can find in any supermarket, such as breakfast cereals and meat substitutes. Other fortified products that are easy to find are soymilk and other milk substitutes. If you can't find them in your neighborhood supermarket, you'll find lots of choices at a natural foods store.

When you read food labels for information about vitamin B12, don't let the new labeling format confuse you. The Recommended Dietary Allowance (RDA) for vitamin B12 is 2 micrograms per day for adults. That figure has a safety margin worked in and is an amount that covers the needs of most people. But food labels now list nutrients in products as a percentage of the *Daily Value* (DV). The Daily Value is a goal based on a reference diet of 2,000 calories per day. Your own needs may be more or less, depending upon your individual calorie needs. The Daily Value used for vitamin B12 is 6 micrograms per day, which is three times the RDA. So if a food label says that one serving of the item provides 50 percent of the DV for vitamin B12, then it provides 3 micrograms of vitamin B12. Just aim for the RDA for vitamin B12 (2 micrograms), and you should be fine, but realize that the numbers listed on food labels are a percentage of a higher number (6 micrograms).

Helpful Hint

Make it a habit to check food labels regularly, because food manufacturers have been known to change the formulation of products from time to time.

Another product that many vegans enjoy using is nutritional yeast. It has a savory flavor similar to that of Parmesan cheese, and many people use it the same way. You can sprinkle it over salads, baked potatoes, pasta, casseroles, cooked vegetables, and popcorn. The trick is making sure that you are getting the right brand, since most forms of nutritional yeast in natural foods stores contain vitamin B12 analog. The brand you need is Red Star T-6635+. This product has been specially formulated to contain cyanocobalamin.

Heads Up!

If you are using nutritional yeast, look for Red Star T-6635+ at your natural foods store. If they don't have it, ask the manager to order some for you. You can also order it by mail through The Mail Order Catalog, PO Box 180, Summertown, TN, 38483; phone (800) 695-2241 or fax (615) 964-3518.

About Vitamin B12 Supplements

Using a vitamin B12 supplement is a fool-proof way to go. You can use a supplement instead of or in addition to eating fortified foods.

Buy the lowest dose of vitamin B12 supplement that you can find. You only need 2 micrograms per day, but you'll probably find that most of the supplements supply much more. Remember that your body adapts its level of absorption according to its needs and the amount in your diet. If you take a 50 microgram supplement of vitamin B12, your body will probably only absorb about 2 micrograms of it.

If you flood yourself with vitamin B12, your body is going to absorb only what it needs and you'll waste the rest. So there's no point in taking megadoses of the vitamin.

Vegetarian Food Sources of Vitamin B12

Food Group	Food	Vitamin B12 (μg)
Cereals	Wheat Chex, 1 cup*	2.4
	Fiber 7 Flakes, ¾ cup (Health Valley)*	0.6
	Grape Nuts, ¼ cup (Post)*	1.5
	Just Right, Fruit and Nut, 1 cup (Kellogg's)*	1.4
	Mueslix, Apple and Almond Crunch, ¾ cup (Kellogg's)*	1.3
	Nutri-Grain, Wheat, ¾ cup (Kellogg's)*	1.5
	Product 19, 1 cup (Kellogg's)*	6.0
	Raisin Bran, 1 cup (Kellogg's)*	1.6
	Total, 1 cup (General Mills)*	7.7

Food Group	Food	Vitamin B12 (µg)
Meat substitutes	Harvest Burger, 1 patty (Green Giant)*	1.5
	Harvest Burger for Recipes (protein crumbles), ⅔ cup (Green Giant)*	1.0
	Breakfast Links, 2 links (Morningstar Farms)	3.6
	Breakfast Patties, 1 patty (Morningstar Farms)	1.5
	Breakfast Strips, 2 strips (Morningstar Farms)	0.1
	BurgerBeaters, 1 patty (Morningstar Farms)*	2.4
	Chik Patties, 1 patty (Morningstar Farms)	0.9
	Grillers, 1 patty (Morningstar Farms)	6.7
Milk substitutes	Dairy-Free Tofu Beverage Mix, 2 Tbsp. Better Than Milk?*	0.6
	Potato milk, 1 cup (Vegelicious)*	3.0
	Soy beverage, 1 cup (EdenSoy Extra)	3.0
Nutritional yeast	Red Star T-6635+, 1 Tbsp. flakes*	2.0
Eggs	Wholeegg, one large	0.5
	Egg white, one large	0.1
Dairy products	Cheese, mozzarella, part skim, 1 oz.	0.2
	Ice cream, ½ cup	0.3
	Skim milk, 1 cup	1.0
	Yogurt, plain, nonfat, 1 cup	1.5

Sources: USDA Nutrient Database for Standard Reference (www.nal.usda.gov/fnic/foodcomp) or Manufacturer.

*Note: Vegan choices are marked by an *.*

The Least You Need to Know

➤ Vegans and near-vegans are the only vegetarians who have to worry about the vitamin B12 content of their diets.

➤ The human body hoards vitamin B12. We recycle it within our own bodies, we need very little from outside sources, and we hang onto it once we get it.

➤ In a "natural" world, vegans would get the little bit of vitamin B12 they need through contamination of their food and water supplies.

➤ Certain foods once thought to be good sources of vitamin B12 are not reliable sources because they contain mostly analogs of vitamin B12.

➤ Vegans need a reliable source of cyanocobalamin, the form of vitamin B12 that is biologically active in humans.

Chapter 7

The Other Suspects: Riboflavin, Vitamin D, and Zinc

> ## In This Chapter
>
> ➤ Getting your riboflavin
>
> ➤ Fueling your own vitamin D factory
>
> ➤ About zinc
>
> ➤ Do you need supplements?

Riboflavin, vitamin D, and zinc merit discussion because, like the other nutrients we've covered so far, they too are generally thought of in association with animal products. Dairy products are rich sources of riboflavin and vitamin D, and zinc is found in meat, eggs, liver, and dairy products.

Where do vegetarians—especially vegans—get these nutrients?

Riboflavin Round-Up

Riboflavin (B2) is present in small amounts in many foods, and many of the foods that are the most concentrated in riboflavin come from animals. Among the richest sources are milk, cheddar cheese, and cottage cheese. Other animal sources include organ meats, other meats, and eggs. Sea vegetables, such as some forms of seaweed, are even more concentrated in riboflavin, although most Americans haven't yet developed a

Veggie Talk

Another name for **riboflavin** is **vitamin B2**. Riboflavin has multiple functions in the body, many related to enzyme activity. Our requirements for riboflavin are related to our energy intake, so the recommended intakes vary according to a person's calorie needs.

taste for them. Green leafy vegetables, enriched breads and cereals, legumes, and several other plant foods also contain some riboflavin.

So vegetarians who eat dairy products and seaweed have options, but what about those poor vegans? Isn't it a challenge for vegans to get enough riboflavin? After all, we're back to truckloads of broccoli and kale, right?

Not necessarily.

It's a logical question but one based on an important assumption: that the current recommendations for riboflavin intake are accurate. In fact, it may be that vegans, and anyone else who avoids dairy products, may have an easier time meeting their riboflavin needs than was once thought.

A Clue from China

The *New York Times* once called the China Project the "Grand Prix of Epidemiology." The China Project is a huge population study taking place throughout The Peoples' Republic of China and, presently, Taiwan as well. It's a collaborative effort between Cornell University, Oxford University, and the Chinese government, and its purpose is to study the relationships between peoples' diets and disease rates.

The China Project began in 1983, and in the early years of the study, the Chinese people still largely ate a diet that could be described as "nearly vegan," though the diet has become more Westernized since then. With rare exceptions, dairy products were not a part of the diet. Despite riboflavin intakes well below the Recommended Dietary Allowance, no cases of riboflavinosis, or riboflavin deficiency, were seen.

The Last Bite

Many nutritionists have concerns that when recommendations for nutrients such as those for riboflavin are set too high, people might be encouraged to consume more animal products in order to meet them. As a result, they may put themselves at risk for the diseases and conditions that result from diets rich in animal products and the low intakes of dietary fiber and high intakes of animal protein, saturated fat, and cholesterol that follow.

Dr. T. Colin Campbell, the principal American investigator in this study, and his associates have speculated that human riboflavin needs are actually much lower than that specified by the current RDA. Other studies have also shown that intakes of riboflavin below the RDA do not result in symptoms of riboflavin deficiency.

How Much Riboflavin Do Vegetarians Need?

It's very likely that recommended riboflavin levels have been set too high. However, until there is scientific consensus on the issue, it makes sense for vegetarians to strive to meet the present RDA. The recommended intake for adult men is 1.7 milligrams per day and 1.3 milligrams per day for women.

That doesn't mean mountains of mustard greens, however. Riboflavin is truly spread widely throughout the plant world, and there are many choices. As always, one of the chief strategies for ensuring that anyone's diet is adequate is to limit the junk foods and to pack your meals with as many nutrient-dense foods as you can.

Riboflavin Content of Vegetarian Foods

Food Group	Food	Riboflavin (mg)
Dairy	Cheddar cheese, 1 oz.	0.11
	Cottage cheese, 1/2 cup	0.18
	Milk, skim, 1/2 cup	0.34
	Yogurt, nonfat, plain, 1 cup	0.57
Eggs	Whole egg, 1 large	0.25
Fruits	Banana, 1 medium	0.12
	Raspberries, fresh, 1 cup	0.11
	Strawberries, whole, 1 cup	0.10
Vegetables	Avocado, 1 whole	0.21
	Bok choy, shredded, cooked, 1 cup	0.11
	Broccoli, chopped, cooked, 1 cup	0.18
	Collard greens, chopped, cooked, 1 cup	0.20
	Kale, chopped, cooked, 1 cup	0.09
	Kelp, raw, 1 cup	1.60
	Mustard greens, chopped, cooked, 1 cup	0.09
	Peas, cooked, 1 cup	0.12
	Turnip greens, chopped, cooked, 1 cup	0.10
Breads and cereals	Bran flakes, 3/4 cup	0.44
	Oatmeal, cooked, 1 cup	0.05
	Millet, cooked, 1 cup	0.14
	Pita bread, whole-wheat, 1 large pocket	0.05
	Shredded wheat, 1 cup	0.08

continues

Riboflavin Content of Vegetarian Foods   (continued)

Food Group	Food	Riboflavin (mg)
	Wheat germ, $1/4$ cup	0.23
	Whole-wheat bread, 1 slice	0.06
Legumes	Garbanzo beans, cooked, 1 cup	0.10
	Kidney beans, cooked, 1 cup	0.10
	Lentils, cooked, 1 cup	0.15
	Navy beans, cooked, 1 cup	0.11
	Pinto beans, cooked, 1 cup	0.16
	Soybeans, cooked, 1 cup	0.49
	Soymilk, plain, $1/2$ cup	0.17
	Tempeh, 1 cup	0.18
	Tofu, firm, 4 oz.	0.13
Nuts and seeds	Almonds, 1 oz.	0.17
	Peanut butter, 2 Tbsp.	0.03
	Sesame tahini, 2 Tbsp.	0.14
Nutritional yeast	Red Star T-6635+, 1 Tbsp. flakes	2.40

Sources: USDA Nutrient Database for Standard Reference (www.nal.usda.gov/fnic/foodcomp/) or Manufacturer.

Vegetarians and Vitamin D

Where do we get the sunshine vitamin?

Silly question, right?

Well, yes and no. Most of us don't have to worry about getting enough vitamin D, but under certain circumstances, anyone—vegetarian or nonvegetarian—can be at risk of not having enough. In our society, though, nonvegetarians and vegetarians that use dairy products have some security measures built into their food supply to help protect them. Vegans—and anyone who doesn't use dairy products—should be aware of the issues surrounding vitamin D.

Making Vitamin D While the Sun Shines

Few foods are naturally good sources of vitamin D. Those that are aren't eaten by many vegetarians. Eggs are a source, and so is liver, which isn't recommended for anybody due to its high cholesterol content and because an animal's liver is a primary depository for environmental contaminants.

We humans are designed to manufacture our own vitamin D when our skin is exposed to sunlight. Theoretically, we don't have to get any from foods. Vitamin D is actually a hormone that regulates the body's calcium balance. It plays an important role in bone health.

Vitamin D is a fat-soluble vitamin, so we store what we make. During the summer months, we store enough of what we make to carry us through the winter months when we are exposed to less sunlight.

It takes about 20 to 30 minutes of summer sun on the hands and face two or three times a week for people with light skin to make enough vitamin D to carry them through the winter. The length of exposure that you need depends in part on how much pigment your skin contains. People with darker skin need more sun exposure, and people with light skin need less.

Heads Up!

Vitamin D is a fat-soluble vitamin and we store what we make or consume. Too much can be toxic, so this is another case of "more is not better." The Recommended Dietary Allowance is 5 micrograms or 200 International Units (IU) for adults. Be sure not to exceed this level if you are taking supplements. Better yet, consult a registered dietitian or your health care provider if you are unsure of whether or not you need a supplement.

The Risks of Rainy Days and Rest Homes

A hundred years ago, *Rickets* and *osteomalacia* were prevalent in cities throughout the world where people received inadequate exposure to sunlight. The cities were located at latitudes high enough to have short summers and long, gray winters, and the increasing urbanization of the cities created smoggy conditions that further blocked out the sunlight. Peoples' bodies didn't produce enough vitamin D as a result. They ended up with diseases of the bone, since without adequate vitamin D, the bones could not utilize calcium properly. In London, for instance, rickets plagued children whose bones were still developing, and osteomalacia, a disease in which the bones soften, was prevalent in adults.

In the United States, milk and other dairy products have been fortified with vitamin D for many years now as a public health measure to protect people that may have inadequate sunlight exposure. You get a vitamin D supplement, in effect, if you drink milk.

People at greatest risk live in large, smog-filled northern cities. Other people at risk include people who have very dark skin (especially those living at northern latitudes), people who are housebound

Veggie Talk

Rickets is a disease that causes deformity of the bones. It's prevalent in children who do not have access to adequate amounts of vitamin D. **Osteomalacia** is another condition of the bones in which a lack of vitamin D causes the bones to demineralize and soften. Weakened bones break more easily.

and rarely see the light of day, and people who don't have regular exposure to sunlight because of covering their entire bodies with clothing or covering their skin with sunscreen every time they go outdoors. As we age, our ability to produce vitamin D also diminishes, so older people may also be at greater risk of deficiency.

The Last Bite

Vitamin D is added to fluid milk, but the amount present has been determined to be unreliable. Some samples of milk have contained very little vitamin D, and other samples have contained many times the amount permitted by the government. The problem has to do with difficulties the milk industry has in dispersing the vitamin D evenly throughout large vats or tanks of milk.

Vegan Sources of Vitamin D

The best source of vitamin D is regular exposure to sunlight. This may seem to contradict advice given to avoid the sun, since too much sunlight exposure can cause skin cancer. The best approach may be to allow yourself limited exposure to sunlight. In other words, go outdoors for brief periods of time without sunscreen, then wear sunscreen the remainder of the time.

Vegans have other sources of vitamin D in addition to sunshine. Some milk substitutes are fortified with vitamin D, as well as some brands of margarine and breakfast cereals. Supplements are another option, but anyone taking a daily supplement should be sure not to exceed the RDA. Read labels to be sure that you are not taking too much, or consult a registered dietitian.

VegetarianVitamin D Sources

	Food	Vitamin D (mcg)
Vegetarian	Egg, 1 large	0.68
	Margarine, 1 tsp.	0.50
	Milk, skim, 1 cup	2.50
Vegan	Bran Flakes, Post, ²/₃ cup	1.23
	Corn flakes, Post Toasties, 1 cup	1.23
	Grape-Nuts, Post, ¹/₄ cup	1.23
	Potato milk, Vegelicious, 1 cup	1.0

	Food	Vitamin D (mcg)
Vegan	Raisin Bran, Post, ¹/₂ cup	1.23
	Rice milk, Rice Dream, 1 cup	2.5
	Soymilk, EdenSoy Extra, 1 cup	1.0
	Westsoy Plus, 1 cup	2.5

Source: Bowes and Church's Food Values of Portions Commonly Used, 17th Edition *(HarperPerennial, 1997), or Manufacturer.*

Get into the Zinc Zone

Whether or not you've made it into the "zinc zone" is debatable, because there is some disagreement among scientists as to what are appropriate recommended levels of intake. At the present time, the Recommended Dietary Allowance for zinc for women is 12 milligrams per day and 15 milligrams for men.

Both vegetarians and nonvegetarians alike have trouble meeting the RDA for zinc. Some scientists think that that's because the RDA has been set too high. Recommendations in other parts of the world are substantially lower, primarily due to differences of opinion about how well zinc is absorbed. Like the other nutrients we've discussed already, zinc too is found in relatively high concentrations in animal products, and setting recommendations for intake at levels that are high encourages people to continue eating animal products.

As with many other nutrients, the human body is able to adapt to varying levels of zinc content in the diet. If there's a lot of zinc present, your body absorbs less. If there's a shortage of zinc, your body becomes more efficient at absorbing what is present. This may in part account for the fact that vegetarians tend to have satisfactory zinc status. There may be other reasons, as well.

Heads Up!

Foods can be fortified with different forms of vitamin D, including vitamin D2 or vitamin D3. Vitamin D2, called ergocalciferol, is made by irradiating provitamin D (from plants or yeast) with ultraviolet light. Vitamin D3, called cholecalciferol, is made from fish liver oils or lanolin, which is sheep-wool fat. Vegans do not use products that have been fortified with vitamin D3, since it is derived from an animal source. Usually the food label will state the form of vitamin D used. If it does not, you may have to check with the manufacturer to determine the source.

Factors Affecting Zinc Absorption

As in the case of dietary iron, there are several factors that either inhibit or enhance the absorption of zinc.

Veggie Talk

Phytates are acids present in such plant products as wheat bran, whole-wheat breads and cereals, legumes, and nuts. Phytates bind with certain minerals, such as iron and zinc, and when present in excess can inhibit the body's absorption of these minerals.

Heads Up!

If you take a calcium supplement, take it between meals or before bedtime so that the calcium doesn't interfere with zinc absorption from your meals.

On the side of inhibiting absorption is phytic acid or *phytate*. The phytates in whole grains and several other plant products can bind with zinc and prevent the body from absorbing it. Wheat bran is rich in phytates, which is one reason that bran fiber supplements are generally not a good idea. Excessive amounts of phytates in the diet can upset your zinc balance.

Vegetarians have an edge when it comes to zinc due to their moderate protein intakes. In contrast, the high protein intakes of meat eaters cause a substantial increase in their zinc requirements. Various cooking and food preparation methods may also increase the availability of zinc. For example, sprouting seeds, cooking or serving foods in combination with acidic ingredients such as tomato sauce or lemon juice, and soaking and cooking legumes may all be ways of making zinc more available to the body.

Zinc Sources for Vegetarians

Vegetarians should be aware of the need for zinc and strive to eat foods that are rich in zinc frequently. I may sound like a broken record, but I can't emphasize enough the importance of limiting sweets and greasy, junky foods—"empty calorie foods"—that displace nutrient-dense foods that are good sources of zinc, iron, calcium, and other important nutrients and phytochemicals.

Food Sources of Zinc for Vegetarians

Food Group	Food	Zinc (ml)
Dairy	Cheddar cheese, 1 oz.	0.88
	Milk, skim, 1 cup	0.95
	Yogurt, nonfat, plain, 8 oz.	1.80
Breads and cereals	Bran flakes, 3/4 cup	3.75
	Oatmeal, cooked, 1 cup	1.15
	Shredded wheat, 1 cup	0.99
	Wheat germ, 1 Tbsp.	1.18
	Whole-wheat bread, 1 slice	0.54

Food Group	Food	Zinc (ml)
Legumes	Garbanzo beans, cooked, 1 cup	2.50
	Kidney beans, cooked, 1 cup	1.89
	Lentils, cooked, 1 cup	2.52
	Millet, cooked, 1 cup	1.58
	Navy beans, cooked, 1 cup	1.93
	Pinto beans, cooked, 1 cup	1.85
	Soybeans, cooked, 1 cup	1.98
	Soymilk, plain, 1 cup	0.56
	Tempeh, 1 cup	3.00
	Tofu, firm, 1/2 cup	1.23
Nuts and seeds	Almonds, 1 oz.	0.69
	Peanut butter, 2 Tbsp.	0.93
	Sesame tahini, 1 Tbsp.	0.07
Nutritional yeast	Red Star T-6635+, 1 Tbsp. flakes	1.00
Vegetables	Bok choy, cooked, shredded, 1 cup	0.29
	Collard greens, cooked, chopped, 1 cup	0.80
	Kale, cooked, chopped, 1 cup	1.17
	Kelp, cooked, chopped, 1/2 cup	0.48
	Mustard greens, cooked, chopped, 1 cup	0.15
	Peas, cooked, 1 cup	1.90
	Potatoes, baked, 1 potato	0.45
	Spinach, cooked, chopped, 1 cup	1.34
	Sweet potato, 1 medium	0.41
	Tomato, 1 medium raw	0.11

Sources: USDA Nutrient Database for Standard Reference (www.nal.usda.gov/fnic/foodcomp) or Manufacturer.

To Supplement or Not to Supplement?

That's a tough question.

With the exception of vitamin B12 for vegans, vegetarians can generally get the nutrition they need from foods and don't need supplements unless they have reason to believe that their intake is not sufficient. In the case of vitamin D or calcium, for instance, vegetarians who are in doubt should consult a registered dietitian who is knowledgeable about vegetarian diets for an assessment of their need for supplements.

Recently, however, the National Academy of Sciences has recommended for the first time that certain population groups take supplements, whether they are vegetarian or not. Specifically, the Academy recommends that vegetarian and nonvegetarian adults alike over the age of 50 take a vitamin B12 supplement to ensure that they have enough. The Academy also recommends that women who are in their childbearing years take a folic acid supplement, since it may be difficult for many to reach the recommended level of intake of 400 micrograms per day. Vegetarians do, however, have folic acid intakes that are much higher than nonvegetarians.

As for supplements of other nutrients, the experts are split on the issues of which ones, how much, and for whom. There are valid differences of opinion, since the science is so new and still evolving. If you happen to be a member of the Coke and French fries crowd, some nutrition scientists would recommend that you take a multiple vitamin and mineral supplement, just to be on the safe side. On the other hand, others would make a case for redoubling your efforts to clean up your diet and get what you need from whole foods rather than supplements. Admittedly, whole foods contain phytochemicals and other substances not contained in a tablet.

Helpful Hint

If you don't have access to your own registered dietitian, you might be interested in visiting the web site of Dr. Andrew Weil, author of *Spontaneous Healing* (Ballantine Books, 1996) and *Eight Weeks to Optimum Health* (Fawcett Books, 1998) at www.drweil.com for an assessment of your supplement needs. His approach is sensible, and at this site you can answer a questionnaire and receive a list of recommendations tailored to your lifestyle and risk factors.

In addition to vitamin B12 and folic acid for women in their childbearing years, many nutrition scientists feel that a good case can be made for taking supplements of anti-oxidant nutrients—vitamins A, C, and E, selenium, and mixed carotenes (as opposed to beta-carotene alone). That's for vegetarians and nonvegetarians alike, even though vegetarians tend to have more antioxidants in their diets than nonvegetarians. Since we are exposed to more environmental contaminants than ever before, especially in urban areas, it's possible that our need for antioxidants is greater than could be met on an ordinary, healthful diet. The additional antioxidants are ammunition against the production of harmful free radicals.

Or so it's thought at this time. Remember, the science of nutrition is in its infancy. At the time of this writing, a report had just been published by a group of British scientists who found that a supplement of 500 milligrams of vitamin C—much less than the amount taken by many people—could damage people's genes by promoting the release of free radicals. The scientists found that, while vitamin C is typically described as an antioxidant, it can also have oxidative properties and can convert iron to a form that can damage the heart and other organs. The vitamin C that is present in foods acts as an antioxidant and is health-supporting, but the form found in supplements acts as an oxidant and has a damaging effect.

So, the science is changing rapidly, and peoples' individual needs also vary. Your best bet is to check with a registered dietitian or your health care provider for more guidance in this issue.

The Least You Need to Know

➤ Vegetarians generally get plenty of riboflavin from plant products. Many nutrition scientists also think that the recommendations for riboflavin intake are set too high.

➤ Most people can get all the vitamin D they need through regular exposure to sunlight.

➤ Vegetarians tend to have satisfactory zinc status.

➤ Vegans need a reliable source of vitamin B12, but other supplements are not necessary for vegetarians unless there are special circumstances.

Part 3
You're Special

You're planning a vegan pregnancy? Congratulations. Or maybe baby is already here and you're having food fights over peas and carrots. Mom and Dad are eating a low-fat, vegetarian diet and want to know if the whole family can eat that way, including Grandma and Grandpa, who have their own needs because they're getting up there in age.

Maybe you have a vegetarian teenager who would like you to think that she's one of those "air plants" that can basically live on nothing, with an occasional Twizzler and Coke at the movie theater. Or you're an athlete chowing down on 4,000 calories a day, all of them vegetarian, and you just want to know if you're getting what you need.

The chapters that follow are for all of you who have or know someone who has special needs and wants to know how to meet those needs on a vegetarian diet.

Chapter 8

Vegetarian Mommy-to-Be

In This Chapter

➤ Getting into top nutritional form before you become pregnant

➤ Pregnancy strategies for getting enough calories, protein, calcium, iron, vitamin D, and vitamin B12

➤ Dealing with the queasies and the munchies and other hurdles

➤ Breast-feeding baby

Never mind all of the free advice from your mother-in-law and the inquiring minds asking if you plan to read to your baby in utero. Say you're pregnant and that you're a vegetarian and all sorts of alarms go off. Take all of the outside assistance that most pregnant people experience and multiply that by 100. You might even be tempted to make your reservations at the funny farm right now.

You probably know that it's perfectly safe and healthful to eat a vegetarian diet—and even a vegan diet—when you're pregnant. Then why is it that other people get so anxious when a vegetarian becomes pregnant? After all, vegetarians in other parts of the world have been having healthy babies with little fanfare or angst over their diets for centuries.

But that's just the point. It happens "over there." Not here. Remember: Vegetarian diets are still largely a lifestyle choice that is outside our culture. Many or most of your family and friends haven't had personal experience with a vegetarian diet, and most were not raised in a vegetarian tradition. So, they're anxious, and anxieties heighten when there's a baby involved.

In this chapter, we'll put some of those worries to rest.

Planning Your Pregnancy

Not every pregnancy is planned, but if there's a chance that you might have a baby in, oh, say the next nine months or so, then it's a great time to be proactive and get yourself into great nutritional shape. The longer you have to eat well before you become pregnant, the better for you and your baby.

The prepregnancy advice for vegetarians is pretty much the same as for nonvegetarians, with one or two exceptions for which vegetarians may need to take special care. On the other hand, vegetarians often go into pregnancy with an edge, because their weights are likely to be closer to ideal and they're more likely to have been consuming plenty of folic acid–rich foods which help to prevent *neural tube defects*.

Going in Eating Well

The longer you can eat well before you become pregnant, the better off you and your baby will be. People who are well-nourished have immune systems that are stronger, and they're less likely to succumb to many common illnesses such as colds and flus.

By limiting junk foods and stocking up on plenty of nutritious vegetables, whole grains, and fresh fruits, vegetarians are likely to have substantially higher intakes of folic acid as compared to nonvegetarians. This is important because folic acid has been identified as being instrumental in preventing neural tube defects in babies. What's more, having high folic acid intakes *before* pregnancy increases the chances that your baby will be protected, because the period of risk for neural tube defects occurs in the very earliest stage of pregnancy, before many women even realize that they're pregnant.

Another benefit to being well-nourished before you become pregnant is that your iron stores are likely to be higher. Many American women go into pregnancy with low iron stores and put themselves at risk for iron deficiency while they're pregnant. Maternal blood volume increases by about 50 percent during pregnancy, and women who go into pregnancy with low iron stores are more likely to become anemic.

Veggie Talk

Neural tube defects such as spina bifida are a type of birth defect that involves an incomplete closure of the spinal cord.

Start Out in Good Physical Condition

The beginning of pregnancy is not the time to start a new or vigorous exercise program, but if you establish an exercise routine prior to pregnancy, then it's likely you can continue that level of activity throughout your pregnancy. Staying physically active will help you maintain muscle tone and strength as well as help to promote normal laxation, or bowel movements, during a time when many women experience problems with constipation and hemorrhoids. Your health care provider will give you more information and advise you about exercise during pregnancy.

Fluids and Rest

Drinking plenty of fluids, especially water, and getting plenty of rest round out the picture of a healthful prepregnancy lifestyle. Vegetarian women are likely to have higher dietary fiber intakes than nonvegetarian women, and having plenty of fiber in the diet, along with fluids, helps to promote normal laxation and diminish problems with constipation and hemorrhoids.

Heads Up!

If you smoke tobacco or use illicit drugs, or if you are a habitual alcohol user, the time to stop is before you become pregnant, since there are substantial advantages for you and your baby to beginning pregnancy in top physical condition.

Nine Months and Counting!

Okay, the test strip turned blue, and you're on your way to becoming a mommy. The questions are beginning to trickle in:

"You're eating for two now. How are you going to get enough protein?"

"…and calcium, and iron, and vitamin B12…?"

The questions you have now that you're pregnant are probably the same ones that you had when you first went vegetarian. Understanding the ways that pregnancy changes your nutritional needs and how those needs can be met on a vegetarian diet will give you the confidence you need to enjoy your vegetarian pregnancy and minimize worries.

Nine Months and…Expanding

Vegetarians are more likely than nonvegetarians to go into pregnancy at weights that are closer to ideal. Women who go into pregnancy at close to their ideal weights can expect to gain from 25 to 35 pounds. If you are overweight when you begin your pregnancy, you may gain less—between 15 and 25 pounds—and if you are thin when you become pregnant, it's healthy to gain more weight—between 28 and 40 pounds.

Weight gain varies with individuals, however, so it's important to get prenatal guidance from a health care provider, whether that's your medical doctor, nurse practitioner, or midwife.

In the first three months of pregnancy it's commonplace to gain very little weight—a few pounds at most. Weight gain picks up in the second and third trimesters of your pregnancy, and a weight gain of about 1 pound a week is typical. Once you begin gaining weight after the third month of pregnancy, you'll need about 300 calories per day more than what you needed before you became pregnant. Women who need to gain more weight will need slightly more calories, and women who need to gain less weight will need fewer calories.

Most vegetarian women have weight gains that follow similar patterns to those of nonvegetarian women. Vegan women are more likely to be slender going into pregnancy. They may be more likely than other women to have low calorie intakes, since their diets tend to be bulky. If you are having trouble gaining weight, consult your health care provider for individualized advice. The following tips may also be helpful:

➤ *Eat snacks between meals.* Even something light and easy to fix, like a bowl of cereal with soymilk, half of a peanut butter sandwich or peanut butter on crackers, a bowl of hearty soup such as lentil or split pea soup, or a frozen, ready-to-heat bean burrito are a few suggestions.

➤ *Substitute starchy, more calorie-dense foods for bulkier, low-calorie foods.* For example, instead of filling up on a lettuce and tomato salad, try a thick soup made with vegetables and barley. Choose starchy vegetables such as potatoes, sweet potatoes, peas, and corn more often than low-calorie choices such as green beans and cucumbers. (Don't give up the folic acid-rich greens, though!)

➤ *It's easier to drink calories than it is to chew them.* When it's calories that you need, many people find that drinking shakes and smoothies is an easy way to get them in. If you use dairy products, you can make shakes or smoothies using ice milk or frozen yogurt mixed with fresh fruit. Vegans can use tofu, soymilk, or other milk substitutes and nondairy ice cream substitutes.

If you happen to have the opposite problem and are beginning your pregnancy overweight, now is not the time to actively reduce. At most, you'll want to control your weight gain by limiting sweets and fatty or greasy foods that are concentrated in calories and offer little in the way of nutrition in return. Plan to lose weight gradually with diet and exercise after the baby is born.

How Much Protein Do I Need?

It's the first thing people have questions about and the nutrient about which most vegetarians have the least need to be concerned. For pregnant vegetarians, including vegans, it's still the least of their concerns.

The recommended level of protein intake during pregnancy is 60 grams per day for most women. That's about 10 grams more protein than a woman needs when she's not pregnant. Most women, including vegans, are already exceeding that level of protein intake before they become pregnant. They typically get even more during pregnancy, since their calorie intakes increase by 300 calories a day, and protein makes up part of those 300 calories. So you can see that getting enough protein during pregnancy is nothing to worry about.

Any of these food choices adds an extra 10 grams of protein or more to your diet:

A Quick 10 Grams of Protein

A peanut butter sandwich on whole-wheat toast

A baked potato topped with 1 ounce of shredded cheese (regular or soy)

A ½ cup of flavored yogurt (regular or soy) with a bagel

A bowl of vegetarian chili and a couple of crackers

A bowl of bran cereal with soymilk

Two pieces of vegan French toast with maple syrup

A bowl of navy bean soup with a half of a tofu salad sandwich

---

Counting on Calcium

Counting the milligrams of calcium in your diet wouldn't be much fun, and fortunately it's not necessary.

Recommendations for calcium for pregnant women are higher than for women who are not pregnant. Current recommendations call for 1,200 milligrams of calcium per day during pregnancy and while a woman is breast-feeding her baby. Since vegans typically get less calcium than other vegetarians and nonvegetarians, it may be more challenging for them to meet this level of calcium intake. On the other hand, there is some evidence that the body becomes more efficient at absorbing and retaining calcium during pregnancy, and that may offset lower calcium intakes. Until that can be confirmed, however, vegans and other pregnant women should aim for the 1,200 milligram target.

The best way to do that is to try hard to get three or four servings of calcium-rich foods in your diet each day. Refer to Chapter 4, "Boning Up on Calcium," for a list of good calcium sources.

Helpful Hint

If you need help getting enough calcium in your diet when you're pregnant, try these ideas:

➤ Go for big-portion sizes of calcium-rich foods. Instead of a wimpy ½-cup serving of cooked kale, go for it and take a 1-cup helping.

➤ It may be easier to drink your calcium than to chew it. Have some calcium-fortified orange juice, or make smoothies with calcium-fortified soymilk, fresh or frozen fruit, and tofu that has been processed with calcium.

Vitamin D

Vitamin D goes hand-in-hand with calcium to ensure that your baby's bones and teeth develop normally. Pregnant women should be sure that their vitamin D intakes are adequate, whether from sunlight exposure or from fortified foods. Review Chapter 7, "The Other Suspects: Riboflavin, Vitamin D, and Zinc," for more information.

What About Iron?

With any luck, you stocked up on iron before you got pregnant, so that you began your pregnancy with adequate iron stores.

It's also common for women to be advised to take an iron supplement of 30 milligrams per day during the second and third trimesters of pregnancy. This is when maternal blood volume skyrockets and iron levels plummet.

You're also well advised to keep the junk foods to a minimum to ensure that there will be enough room in your diet for the good stuff, including foods that are high in iron. Is there an echo in here?

Musings on B12

We've already said that vegans need a reliable source of vitamin B12 in their diets. When you're vegan and you're pregnant, the importance of this cannot be stressed enough. Not only does the baby need vitamin B12 from its mother while he's developing, he also needs it when he's breast-feeding. So, vegan women need to have a reliable source of vitamin B12 before, during, and after pregnancy. See Chapter 6, "And Vitamin B12?" for the particulars.

Meal Planning Made Easier

What most pregnant women need is someone to make their meals for them. Now *that's* meal planning made easy!

Okay, so you don't see that happening within the next nine months. Here's what you do:

Make It Easy on Yourself

You can do that by permitting yourself to take some shortcuts for a while.

➤ *Use more convenience foods.* Frozen vegetarian entrees and snacks such as burritos and ready-to-heat sandwiches and veggie burger patties can reduce meal prep to minutes. Open a can of lentil soup and eat it with whole-wheat toast, or have a bowl of cereal with soymilk for dinner. Canned beans, canned soups, breakfast cereals, frozen waffles, burritos, and microwave popcorn are all nutritious and quick.

➤ *Order out for meals when you're too tired to cook.* Chinese vegetable stir-fries with steamed rice, a falafel sandwich and side of tabouli, or a vegetarian pizza may be just what you need.

➤ *Become a weekend cook.* Make a big batch of vegetarian chili or lasagna and freeze part of it. You can take it out and reheat it when you don't feel like cooking. Fix a big fresh fruit salad or mixed green salad one day and eat it over the next three days. (But don't put dressing on your salad until you're ready to eat it! It'll get soggy.) Muffins and quick breads freeze well too.

A Meal Planning Guide

When you're pregnant, you don't really have to eat different foods from the ones you eat when you're not pregnant—you just need about 300 calories per day *more*. And it becomes more important that you limit the junk.

So, if you'd like more guidance in choosing foods and planning meals, the information in Part 5, "Meal Planning Made Easy," is helpful. Eat according to your appetite, and pay attention to the overall quality of your food choices.

Troubleshooting the Queasies and the Munchies

Pregnancy is a time for some strange food aversions and even stranger cravings. They're usually harmless and pass by the end of the first three months of pregnancy. Not always, but usually. The same is true of that infamous bane of the pregnant set— nausea—better known as morning sickness and known by some as morning, noon, and nighttime sickness.

These aspects of pregnancy affect vegetarian and nonvegetarian women alike.

When Queasy Makes You Uneasy

Morning sickness may be the most uncomfortable symptom of pregnancy and, for many women, overcoming it is a matter of waiting it out. In the meantime, there are some things that you can do to minimize its effects.

➤ *Eat small, frequent meals or snacks.* Don't give yourself a chance to get hungry between meals, because hunger can sometimes accentuate feelings of nausea.

➤ *Eat foods that are easy to digest,* such as fruits, toast, cereal, bagels, and other starchy foods. Foods that are high in carbohydrate such as these take less time to digest. In contrast, fatty or greasy foods such as chips, pastries, cheese, heavy entrees, and rich desserts take longer to digest and may be likely to give you more trouble.

➤ *Check in with your health care provider for guidance* if nausea keeps you from eating or drinking for more than one day and night.

Pickles and Tofu Ice Cream

If you're having cravings for something outlandish like, say, tofu cheesecake with chocolate sauce or a hummus and green tomato sandwich, the best thing to do is...go for it! This phase isn't going to last forever, and, let's face it, pregnancy is a time when all sorts of hormonal changes are taking place and things can be topsy-turvy for a while. There's not much you can do about it, it's not necessary to control it, and it's probably not going to hurt you. As long as you aren't chewing on radial tires or the clay in your backyard, you should be just fine.

Heads Up!

Studies have demonstrated that problems in pregnancies result from drinking the equivalent of 5 cups of coffee or more per day. It's best to err on the side of caution and eliminate caffeine altogether during pregnancy until it's otherwise demonstrated to be benign. Or, if you must drink caffeine, limit your use to 1 or 2 cups of caffeine-containing beverages per day, including coffee, tea, colas, and other soft drinks that contain caffeine.

After the Baby— Breast-Feeding

You might be surprised to learn that you need even more calories when you're breast-feeding—about 200 more calories per day—than you did when you were pregnant. Most women need an additional 500 calories a day when they are breast-feeding as compared to their need before they were pregnant. No wonder many women find that its during the time that they're breast-feeding that they begin losing some of the extra weight they gained while they were pregnant.

Your nutrient needs are just a little higher when you are breast-feeding than when you were pregnant. For instance, you need about 5 grams more protein. You'll easily get the extra nutrients in the additional calories that you'll be eating. Remember: Vegans need to be sure to get a reliable source of vitamin B12. Be sure to include plenty of fluids too. Water is always the best choice.

The Least You Need to Know

➤ Vegetarians and vegans can get all the nutrients they need during pregnancy, although vegans need to be sure to continue to include a reliable source of vitamin B12 in their diets.

➤ It's a good idea to be well-nourished prior to becoming pregnant.

➤ Take stock of other lifestyle factors before you become pregnant. Get plenty of physical activity and rest, and stop smoking.

➤ Avoid alcohol when you are pregnant, and avoid or limit beverages containing caffeine.

➤ Eat according to your appetite when you are pregnant. Limit the junk, and concentrate on more nutrient-dense foods.

➤ Morning sickness and cravings come with the territory. They usually pass with the first trimester of pregnancy and usually aren't dangerous.

➤ Your nutritional needs while you're breast-feeding are similar to when you are pregnant. Keep up the good work.

Chapter 9

Vegetarian Baby and Toddler

> **In This Chapter**
>
> ➤ Baby's first food: breast or bottle and must-knows about each
>
> ➤ Stepping up to solids and how to proceed
>
> ➤ Advice about adapting vegetarian diets to small children's needs
>
> ➤ Meal planning guides for babies and young children

Enter a world in which the little people wear mashed potatoes in their hair and toss more of their food onto the floor than into their mouths. Hey, when was the last time you smeared smashed peas up and down your arms and hid cracker bits behind your ears?

You were probably two feet tall and had three chins. Me too.

The scenario hasn't changed much, and it doesn't make any difference if your child is a vegetarian.

Baby's First Vegetarian Food

We all start out as vegetarians when you get right down to it. There aren't many kids who start out life guzzling fluid fish or hamburger.

Milk is our first food. Humans make milk for human babies. The alternative is as close a replica as can be made in a laboratory.

Breast Is Best

Breast milk is the perfect first food for babies, because it's tailor-made for them. At no other time in our lives do most of us have a diet so well-suited to our needs.

From birth through at least the first six months and longer, if possible, breast-feeding your baby is the best choice, bar none. There are several reasons:

➤ Breast milk is ideally suited to a baby's nutritional needs. The composition of breast milk makes it the perfect food for human babies. Even baby formulas can't compare, because most nutrition scientists acknowledge that there are probably substances present in breast milk that are needed for good health but have not yet been identified and, therefore, are not available in synthetic formulas.

➤ Breast milk contains protective substances that give your baby added immunity or protection against certain illnesses. Breast-fed babies are also less likely to have problems with allergies later in life.

➤ Breast-fed babies are more likely to maintain an ideal weight.

➤ Breast milk is convenient and sterile.

➤ Breast-feeding is good for Mom, since it helps the uterus to return to its former size more quickly and aids in taking off excess "baby fat."

The babies of vegetarian women have an added benefit. Vegetarian women have substantially less environmental contaminants in their breast milk as compared to nonvegetarian women. The diets of vegetarian women contain only a fraction of the amount of pesticide residues and other contaminants that nonvegetarian women consume. These contaminants are concentrated in animal tissues and fat, and women who eat the animal products store the contaminants in their own tissues and fat. Consequently, when they produce breast milk, they pass the contaminants on to their babies through their milk.

The Last Bite

Some people are sticklers for details. Here's the question: Can babies who drink breast milk be considered vegans, or do they have to drink a synthetic soy formula to be considered vegans? The answer: Oh, come on! Vegans who breast-feed their babies consider their babies vegans too.

When Breast Milk Is a No-Go

Women who breast-feed their babies get lots of applause, but women who can't breast-feed shouldn't be chastised. There are many reasons why some women can't or don't want to breast-feed. Those who don't will need to feed their babies a synthetic baby formula instead. Just as with breast-fed babies, formula-fed babies need their formula and nothing but their formula for at least the first four to six months, if not longer.

There are several brands of baby formula on the market, and your health care provider will probably recommend a few to you. Most are based on cow's milk, altered to be more easily digested and more closely resemble human milk. Others contain animal fat or other animal by-products. Vegans don't use these formulas. There are other baby formulas that contain no animal products and are soy-based. These formulas, including such brands as Isomil, Prosobee, and Soyalac, are acceptable for use by vegans.

Heads Up!

Commercial soymilks are not the same thing as infant soy-based formulas, and they are not appropriate for infants. If you do not breast-feed your baby, be sure that you feed her a commercial infant formula, *not* the commercial soymilks that are meant for general use (such as EdenSoy, Westsoy, and others). When your child is older, these will be fine, but not in infancy and toddlerhood.

How Long Is Long Enough?

Babies should be breast-fed or bottle-fed exclusively for the first four to six months of their lives. They need no other food during this time. In fact, if you start solid foods sooner, your child is more likely to become overweight and develop allergies. Resist the temptation to start solids too early.

There are a few clues to look for that will tell you when it's time to begin introducing your baby to solid foods. This will happen sometime between four and six months of age.

➤ Your baby reaches about 13 pounds in weight or doubles its birth weight.

➤ Your baby wants to breast-feed eight times or more during a 24-hour period.

➤ Your baby takes a quart of formula or more in a 24-hour period and acts like she is still hungry and wants more.

Heads Up!

If your baby is bottle-fed, don't put anything in the bottle except breast milk, formula, or water for the first six months. Sugar water drinks, soft drinks, and iced tea are inappropriate for babies and small children, and fruit juices and diluted baby cereals should not be introduced until after the six-month point. Nothing is more nutritious or beneficial to your baby for the first six months than breast milk or infant formula.

Once your baby reaches one of these milestones, it's time to introduce solid foods—gradually.

A Few More Pointers

You should be aware of a few more issues concerning your baby's nutritional needs during the first 12 months:

➤ Remember: If you are a vegan mom, it's critical that you take a vitamin B12 supplement while you're breast-feeding to ensure that your baby has a source of vitamin B12 too.

➤ As regards vitamin D, if you aren't sure if your baby is getting enough, consult your health care provider. Babies over the age of three months who have limited exposure to sunlight need a vitamin D supplement of not more than 400 International Units (IU) per day.

➤ Beyond the first four to six months of age, breast-fed babies are usually started on iron supplements. Your individual health care provider will advise you on this issue.

A Solid Start

What's the nearly universal first solid food for babies, vegetarian or not? Baby cereal. Usually rice cereal, since almost every baby can tolerate it.

It's best to give your baby iron-fortified, baby rice cereal for at least the first 18 months.

Rather than abruptly discontinuing breast- or bottle-feedings, introduce small amounts of solid foods one at a time. Start gradually, and continue breast- or bottle-feedings as usual. Begin by mixing baby rice cereal with breast milk or infant formula and offering a few tablespoons. Work up to two feedings a day, totaling about ½ cup.

From there, you'll gradually add other foods, one at a time, a little at a time, and your baby will increase the amounts at her own pace.

Heads Up!

Cow's milk should not be given to infants under the age of one year. Cow's milk can cause bleeding in the gastrointestinal tract of human babies and lead to anemia. Studies have also linked cow's milk given to infants with an increased risk for insulin-dependent diabetes.

The Solid Starting Lineup

There aren't any hard and fast rules about how to introduce solid foods to babies—just some general guidelines. For instance, all babies—whether their families are vegetarians or not—start out eating the foods that are the easiest to digest and least likely to cause problems such as allergic reactions or choking. Those foods are cooked cereals and mashed or pureed fruits and vegetables and their juices. Protein-rich foods and foods that are high in fat are introduced later. Foods are usually introduced one at a time, so that if a baby does have a sensitivity to a food, it will be easier to pinpoint the culprit.

Once your baby becomes accustomed to cooked cereals and mashed and pureed fruits and vegetables, she can move on to table foods. You can refer to the following table to get an idea of how to proceed. Remember, these are merely suggestions and not carved in stone. Your health care provider will give you additional guidance.

Getting Started

The two feeding guides that follow are suggested schedules for feeding vegetarian babies from four through 12 months of age, as well as toddlers and preschoolers ages one through four years. A feeding guide for school-aged children is provided in Chapter 10, "Kids' Stuff or Adults Only? Vegetarian Diets for Children and Teens." You'll notice that the guides exclude all animal products. If you prefer to include dairy products and/or eggs, they can be substituted for soy products where indicated.

Heads Up!

Many health care providers are not familiar nor comfortable with the concept of vegetarian diets for children. Be assured that vegetarian diets are perfectly safe and ad–equate for children and that they have numerous advantages over nonvegetarian diets. They are outside our culture at this time, and that is the primary reason you will meet with resistance by health care providers. You may also find a lack of support for vegetarian diets in baby and child care books you read. Again, be assured that these opinions are not consistent with scientific knowledge.

Feeding Schedule for Vegan Babies Ages Four to 12 Months

	Four to Seven Months*	Six to Eight Months	Seven to 10 Months	10 to 12 Months
Milk	Breast milk or soy formula	Breast milk or soy formula	Breast milk or soy formula	Breast milk or soy formula (24 to 32 oz.)
Cereal and bread	Begin iron-fortified baby cereal mixed	Continue baby cereal; begin other breads with milk	Baby cereal; other breads and cereals	Baby cereal until until 18months; total of four servings (1 serving = ¼ slice bread or 2 to 4 Tbsp. cereal)

continues

Feeding Schedule for Vegan Babies Ages Four to 12 Months (continued)

	Four to Seven Months*	Six to Eight Months	Seven to 10 Months	10 to 12 Months
Fruits and vegetables	None	Begin juice from cup; 2 to 4 oz. vitamin C source; begin mashed vegetables and fruits	4 oz. juice; pieces of soft/cooked fruits and vegetables	Table-food diet; allow 4 servings per day (1 serving = 1 to 6 Tbsp. fruit and vegetable, 4 oz. juice)
Legumes and nut butters	None	None	Gradually introduce tofu; begin casseroles, pureed legumes, soy cheese, and soy yogurt	Two servings daily, each about ½ oz.; nut butters should not be started before one year

*Overlap of ages occurs because of varying rate of development.

Source: Simply Vegan, Third Edition, *by Debra Wasserman and Reed Mangels, Ph.D., R.D., 1998. Reprinted with permission from The Vegetarian Resource Group, PO Box 1463, Baltimore, MD 21203; (410) 366-8343; www.vrg.org.*

The following feeding guide is for toddlers and preschoolers ages one through four years. If you need assistance adapting the food guide for your individual child or need more help with menu planning, contact a registered dietitian familiar with vegetarian diets and working with families.

Meal–Planning Guide for Toddlers and Preschoolers Ages One to Four

Food Group	Number of Servings
Grains	6 or more (a serving is ½ to 1 slice of bread; or ½ to 1 cup cooked cereal; or grain, or pasta; or ½ to 1 cup ready-to-eat cereal)
Legumes, nuts, seeds	2 or more (a serving is ¼ to ½ cup cooked beans, tofu, tempeh, or TVP; or 1½ to 3 oz. meat analog; or 1 to 2 Tbsp. nuts, seeds, or nut or seed butter
Fortified soymilk, infant formula, or breast milk	3 (a serving is 1 cup)

Food Group	Number of Servings
Vegetables	2 or more (a serving is ¼ to ½ cup cooked or ½ to 1 cup raw vegetables)
Fruits	3 or more (a serving is ¼ to ½ cup canned fruit; or ½ cup juice; or 1 medium fruit)
Fats	3 (1 tsp. margarine or oil)

Adapted from: Simply Vegan, *Third Edition, by Debra Wasserman and Reed Mangels, Ph.D., R.D., 1998. Reprinted with permission from The Vegetarian Resource Group, PO Box 1463, Baltimore, MD 21203; (410) 366-8343; www.vrg.org.*

Smart Starts

Vegetarian diets are associatedwith numerous health advantages, so starting children out on the right foot helps to cement good eating habits that will follow them into adulthood. Even so, once young vegetarian children begin eating table foods, there are a few issues about which you should be aware.

The Bulk Factor

Vegetarian diets—particularly low-fat orvegan diets—can be bulky. Many plant foods are high in fiber and relatively low in calories. Since young children have small stomachs, they may become full before they've had a chance to take in enough calories to meet their energy needs. For this reason, it's important to be sure to include plenty of calorie-dense foods in the diets of young vegetarian children.

Kids Need More Fat

When diets are based on bulky plant products, one of the ways in which young children can be assured of getting enough calories is by not overly restricting dietary fat. Some adults may want to keep their fat intakes to a minimum, especially for weight control, and plant-based diets help them do that. But a plant-based diet can backfire for young children if their fat intake is too controlled.

For that reason, using plant sources of fat liberally can help provide young children with the extra calories they need during a period of their lives in which they are growing and developing rapidly. So, for instance, adding a slice of avocado (nearly all fat) to a sandwich is fine, or using nut and seed butters on sandwiches and vegetable sticks is also a good idea.

Heads Up!

Children under the age of one year should not be given honey or corn syrup. These foods, which can carry Clostridium spores that cause botulism, can cause food poisoning in young children.

Kids Need Snacks

Another way to ensure that vegetarian kids get enough calories is to include between-meal snacks in their diets. In the case of toddlers, you'll need to make sure that you don't give them things that they can choke on. For instance, grapes and whole tofu hotdogs are dangerous because they can easily get stuck in the esophagus. If you give them to a small child, they should be sliced in half or into quarters. Be careful with chips, nuts, and other small items that can lodge in a small child's throat. Young children should be supervised when they are eating.

A few nutritious snack ideas include:

➤ Soy yogurt

➤ Small pieces of fresh fruit

➤ Single-serving aseptic boxes of fruit juice or soymilk

➤ Graham crackers

➤ Tofu processed with calcium—cubes or made into smoothies or pudding

➤ Whole-grain cereal "Os"

➤ Bowl of cooked cereal or dry cereal with soymilk

➤ A dab of smooth peanut or almond butter on a cracker

The Least You Need to Know

➤ Babies should be fed breast milk or infant formula exclusively for the first four to six months, and, ideally, for at least the first year.

➤ Vegan moms should be taking a vitamin B12 supplement, especially if they're breast-feeding.

➤ Solid foods should not be started before four to six months of age.

➤ Vegetarian diets can be totally appropriate for young children and are associated with health advantages.

➤ Vegetarian children should not have their fat intakes overly restricted and should be given snacks between meals.

Chapter 10

Kids' Stuff or Adults Only? Vegetarian Diets for Children and Teens

In This Chapter

➤ What to expect for growth rates in vegetarian kids

➤ How to ensure that kids and teens get the nutrition they need

➤ A meal-planning guide for school-aged children

➤ Ways to motivate kids to eat their vegetables

➤ Healthful fast-food ideas for teens on the run

➤ Handling school meals, weight concerns, and other challenges

A 1995 Roper Poll conducted for the nonprofit Vegetarian Resource Group found that children from eight to 12 years of age are becoming vegetarians at twice the rate of adults. They're doing it because they have compassion for animals and an interest in saving the planet from environmental destruction caused by raising animals for food. Many of these kids are "going it alone" and are the only vegetarians in their households. You've got to admire that kind of courage. But when Mom and Dad aren't vegetarians themselves, there can be some hand wringing over questions and concerns about whether vegetarian diets are adequate for kids.

But even in homes where vegetarianism is the norm, people have questions about vegetarian nutrition for kids. It's understandable, considering that vegetarian diets are outside the mainstream, and most health care providers, school teachers, friends, and relatives don't have personal experience with a vegetarian lifestyle.

So, here's the first piece of insight: Feeding any child, vegetarian or not, takes time, patience, and care.

A diet that is haphazard, heavy on chips and soft drinks and light on fruits and vegetables, or otherwise carelessly planned, is not likely to meet the needs of growing children. On the other hand, a well-planned vegetarian diet offers health advantages over nonvegetarian diets for kids, and it helps to put into motion a lifestyle of healthful eating that, with any luck, will become a pattern for a lifetime.

In this chapter, we'll take a look at the most common questions and concerns that caregivers have about vegetarian diets for children and teenagers.

The Growth Factor

Some people worry about growth rates in children who don't eat meat. They have concerns that children raised on vegetarian diets will suffer from growth retardation.

There have been reports in the scientific literature over the years about poor growth in vegetarian children, but a closer look at the studies settles that concern for most of us.

The growth problems occurred in a couple of circumstances:

➤ The children lived in poverty in developing countries and didn't have enough to eat.

➤ The children did not live in poverty but were being fed bizarre, inadequate diets that were severely limited in variety and calories.

Of course, malnutrition, not vegetarianism, causes growth retardation. Any child, vegetarian or not, who doesn't have enough to eat will suffer from nutritional deficiencies and may have difficulties developing properly.

In this book, we're talking about vegetarian—including vegan—diets that contain adequate calories and a variety of foods to ensure that nutritional needs are met. As stated earlier in this book, not only do reasonable vegetarian diets meet nutritional needs, but they are associated with health advantages as well.

So, What's a Normal Rate of Growth, Anyway?

Questioning growth rates in vegetarian children begs the question "What's a normal rate of growth for a child, anyway?"

Your pediatrician has growth charts on which she plots your child's height and weight at regular intervals and compares them to population norms. You may even be doing this yourself at home. Growth rates are usually reported in percentiles. For instance, one child may be growing at the 50th percentile for height and weight, while another child of the same age may be growing at the 90th percentile. Still another same-aged child may be growing at the 25th percentile. Is one child healthier than the other?

Not necessarily. Within any group of people, we'd expect to see 50 percent growing at the 50th percentile, 25 percent growing at the 25th percentile, and so on. That's called *normal distribution*. In other words, variation is normal within population groups. A child growing at the 25th percentile isn't necessarily healthier or less healthy than a child growing at the 90th percentile.

What's important is for a child growing at a particular rate to continue growing at that same rate. If the growth rate declined, that would be a signal to investigate the reason for the decline. So a child growing at the 35th percentile who continues to grow at the 35th percentile is probably fine. But if that child's rate of growth should falter, then the parent or health care provider should look into possible causes.

What Are Your Expectations?

Kids fed on a Western-style, meat-and-potatoes diet are expected to go through growth spurts at certain ages. Most of us hope that our children grow up to be "big and strong." We aim for football-player-sized kids and worry that the playground bully is going to pick on our child if he's too small. As a culture, we value BIG and TALL.

The Last Bite

The percentage of American children who are overweight has risen to the point where public health nutritionists now consider childhood obesity to be a major public health problem. The problem is attributed to diets that are too rich in fat and too low in fiber, as well as to declining levels of physical activity among children, who now spend more time than ever in front of the television and computer. Vegetarian children are more likely to be at their ideal body weights. Their diets contain substantially more fiber and less total fat, saturated fat, and cholesterol.

Do Vegetarian Children Grow at a Different Rate?

The growth rates of lacto and lacto ovo vegetarian children are similar to the growth rates of nonvegetarian children. However, there is very little information about growth rates of vegan children in this country. A peek at the growth rates of children in China eating a near-vegan diet has given scientists some idea of what we might expect to see, however.

Helpful Hint

Ask your health care provider for a growth record form so that you can follow your child's rate of growth at home. He or she can show you how simple it is to plot your child's height and weight monthly or quarterly. That way, you can rest assured that your child is making satisfactory progress, and you'll be the first to know if there's a problem.

In the population study called the China Project, scientists found that the children eating a near-vegan diet grew more slowly than American children eating a standard, Western meat-and-milk-containing diet. The Chinese children attained full adult stature eventually, but they took longer to get there. They grew over a period of about 21 years, as compared to American children, who stop growing at about the age of 18 years. Chinese girls reach menarche, or have their first menstrual cycle, at an average age of 17 years as compared to 12 years in American girls. In the Chinese, this later age of menarche was associated with lower rates of breast cancer in Chinese women, theoretically because they were exposed to high levels of circulating estrogen hormones for a shorter period of time.

So, it's possible that American vegan children may grow more slowly than other children, but we don't know if that's good, bad, or indifferent. It's likely that if there is a difference, the difference may be associated with health benefits in children eating a healthful vegan diet.

The most important thing for parents of vegetarian children to know is that if they follow their child's rate of growth, their child's growth rate should be constant. If it takes a nose dive, that's the time to investigate and intervene. In the meantime, if a child is growing and is otherwise healthy, there's no need to worry.

How to Make Your Child Grow Like a Weed

Vegetarian diets have health advantages for everyone, but a few of the characteristics that make vegetarian diets so healthful can also be pitfalls for children if you aren't aware of them and take precautions. Primarily, we're talking about the bulkiness of the diet and the fact that some children can fill up before they have taken in enough calories.

In Chapter 9, "Vegetarian Baby and Toddler," I described three ways in which you can ensure that your young children get enough calories in their diets. It's important to continue to be aware of these issues for older children as well.

Small Stomachs, Bulky Foods

Be aware of the potential bulkiness of a vegetarian diet and be sure to include plenty of calorie-dense foods. That means emphasizing starchy, high-calorie foods such as breads, cereals, and starchy vegetables such as beans, peas, potatoes, and others, and minimizing low-calorie, bulky foods such as large lettuce salads and low-calorie raw vegetables. It's okay to include those foods in your child's diet, but don't let them displace too much of the higher-calorie foods.

Vegetable Fats Are Fine

Feel free to use some vegetable sources of fat in your child's diet, such as seed and nut butters, olive oil, and avocado slices. These fats are a concentrated source of calories and, while some adults may want to limit fatty foods themselves for weight control, kids need the extra calories for growth.

Count on Snacks

Give your kids nutritious snacks between meals. In Chapter 9, I listed some snacks that are good choices for younger children. For older children and teens, this list can be expanded to include:

➤ Muffins

➤ Whole-grain cookies

➤ Whole-grain crackers

➤ Dried fruit (brush teeth after eating)

➤ Popcorn

➤ Cereal and soymilk or skim cow's milk

➤ Fresh vegetable sticks with hummus or black bean dip

➤ Frozen fruit bars

➤ Bean burritos and tacos

➤ Bagels

➤ Sandwiches

➤ Fresh fruit

➤ Smoothies made with soymilk and fresh fruit, ice cream substitute, or nonfat dairy products

➤ Veggie burgers

➤ Individual frozen vegetarian pizzas

➤ Frozen waffles with maple syrup, jam, or jelly

➤ Whole-grain toast with jam or jelly

Helpful Hint

Like other types of vegetarian diets, vegan diets can be healthful for children. If you have recently switched to a vegan diet and your child loses weight or does not seem to be growing as quickly, add sources of concentrated calories, such as vegetable sources of fat, and substitute more starchy foods for lower-calorie, bulkier foods. Also refer to the meal planning guide later in the chapter.

A Nutrition Reminder

When it comes to designing a vegetarian diet for kids and teens, you need to pay special attention to a few key nutrients.

Protein

The most foolproof way of ensuring that your child gets enough protein is to make sure she gets enough calories to meet her energy needs. When a child's diet is too low in calories, the body will burn protein for energy. As I mentioned earlier in this book, protein and calorie malnutrition go hand in hand. When there are enough calories in the diet, protein can be used for building new tissues instead of being burned for energy.

So, the primary ways in which you'll ensure that your child has enough protein is to be sure that she has enough calories to meet her energy needs as well as a reasonable variety of foods, including fruits, vegetables, grains, legumes, nuts, and seeds.

Some of the foods that are especially good sources of protein and are also likely to be hits with children are:

➤ Bean burritos and tacos

➤ Veggie burgers

➤ Veggie hotdogs

➤ Hummus or other bean dip with vegetable sticks or tortilla chips

➤ Peanut butter on apple chunks or celery sticks

➤ Peanut butter sandwiches or crackers

➤ Tofu salad sandwiches

➤ Soymilk and fruit smoothies

➤ Tofu or nonfat ricotta cheese and vegetable lasagna

➤ Vegetarian pizza

➤ Nonfat or soy yogurt

➤ Nonfat or soy cheese on crackers

➤ Tempeh sloppy Joes

Calcium

Children and teens are in a period of rapid growth, and they need plenty of calcium in their diets to accommodate the development of their teeth and bones. As we've already discussed in Chapter 4, "Boning Up on Calcium," there are other factors (presence of vitamin D, absorption and retention of calcium) that are equally as important as having adequate amounts of calcium in the diet—or more so. Nevertheless, it's a good idea to encourage three servings of calcium-rich foods each day. Aim for big servings—1 cup at a time. Your kids won't eat their vegetables? We'll tackle that one a little further on in this chapter. Keep in mind, though, that calcium-fortified orange juice and fortified soymilk are easy ways to add calcium to the hit-or-miss diet of older kids and teens.

Iron

Many of the foods that are high in calcium also happen to be high in iron, so if you can fix these foods for your family or have quick-and-easy sources on hand for your kids to serve themselves, you'll get a double benefit. (Refer to Chapter 5, "What About Iron?" for a list of good iron sources.)

Remember too that it's important for vegetarians to have good food sources of vitamin C present at meals to increase the body's absorption of the iron present in that meal. Really, the practical translation of this is to make fruits and vegetables readily available to your kids. With plenty of fruits and vegetables on the menu, you'll help ensure that your kids get enough calcium, iron, and vitamin C. Strategies for increasing the likelihood that your child will eat these foods are coming right up.

Incidentally, if you're thinking that getting kids to eat fruits and vegetables is an insurmountable challenge and a reason to nix the idea of a vegetarian diet, think again. All kids need plenty of fruits and vegetables, regardless of whether or not they eat meat or drink cow's milk. Adding meat or milk to your child's diet would displace even more plant matter from your child's diet. The answer to getting kids to eat well goes beyond whether or not they are vegetarians. But we'll get to that in a minute.

> **Helpful Hint**
>
> Kids will eat foods that are presented appealingly and are convenient to eat. If you want them to eat fruits and vegetables, consider keeping a bowl of seasonal fresh fruit on the kitchen counter or table, fresh fruit salad in the refrigerator, and cut up, fresh vegetables in a container on the top shelf—in plain sight—in the refrigerator. Bags of baby carrots that are already peeled are a favorite. Keep hummus, salsa, and black bean dip on hand for dipping fresh vegetable sticks.

Vitamin B12

All vegans, including children and teens, need a reliable source of vitamin B12 in their diets. If your kids are eating a vegan or near-vegan diet, they should be eating vitamin B12–fortified foods regularly or taking a vitamin B12 supplement. If there's any doubt about whether fortified foods are providing enough vitamin B12, the safest bet is to have your kids take a supplement. (See Chapter 6, "And Vitamin B12?" for more information about vitamin B12.)

Vitamin D

The important thing to remember about vitamin D and children is that vitamin D, in concert with calcium, is critical for the normal growth and development of bones and teeth. (Vitamin D is covered in Chapter 7, "The Other Suspects: Riboflavin, Vitamin D, and Zinc.") If you have any doubts about whether or not your child is at risk of not getting enough vitamin D, ask a registered dietitian or your health care provider for an assessment and recommendation.

Others

Of course, we could keep right on going from there and list numerous other nutrients, their roles in the growth and development of children, and the importance of including good food sources in the diet. When it gets right down to it, however, the real issues are ensuring that your child gets:

➤ Adequate calories

➤ A reasonable variety of foods

➤ A reliable source of vitamin B12 for vegan and near-vegan children and adequate vitamin D

➤ A limited amount of junk foods, so that these foods don't displace more nutritious foods from the diet

A Meal–Planning Guide for School-Aged Children

The meal-planning guide that follows is suitable for school-aged children up to 12 years of age. The guide excludes all animal products. If you prefer to include dairy products and/or eggs, they can be substituted for soy products where indicated.

Daily Meal-Planning Guide for School-Aged Children

Food Group	Number of Daily Servings
Grains	6 or more for four- to six-year-olds; 7 or more for seven- to 12-year-olds (a serving is 1 slice of bread; ½ cup cooked cereal, grain, or pasta; or ¾ cup to 1 cup ready-to-eat cereal)
Legumes, nuts, seeds	1 to 3 for four- to six-year-olds; 3 or more for seven- to 12-year-olds (a serving is ½ cup cooked beans, tofu, tempeh, or TVP; 3 oz. of meat analogue; or 2 Tbsp. nuts, seeds, or nut or seed butter
Fortified soymilk	3 (a serving is 1 cup fortified soymilk)
Vegetables	1 to 1½ for four- to six-year-olds; 4 or more for seven- to 12-year-olds (a serving is ½ cup cooked or 1 cup raw vegetables)
Fruits	2 for four- to six-year-olds; 3 or more for seven- to 12-year-olds (a serving is ½ cup canned fruit or ¾ cup juice; or 1 medium fruit)
Fats	4 for four- to six-year-olds; 5 for seven- to 12-year-olds (a serving is 1 tsp. margarine or oil)

*Adapted from Simply Vegan, Third Edition, *by Debra Wasserman and Reed Mangels, Ph.D., R.D., 1998. Reprinted with permission from the Vegetarian Resource Group, PO Box 1463, Baltimore, MD, 21203; (410) 366-8343; www.vrg.org.*

Making Fruits and Vegetables Your Child's Best Friends

Now, the real challenge is how to get Johnny to eat his vegetables.

If you haven't learned by now, it's usually a losing battle to try to force people to do things they don't want to do. Kids are no exception.

There are some strategies, however, that may increase the likelihood that Johnny will eat his vegetables. More importantly, there are some things that you can do to increase the likelihood that your children will grow up enjoying healthful foods and will make them a part of their adult lifestyles one day.

The Last Bite

When some people say that their whole family is vegetarian, they mean their cat and dog too. Dogs are naturally omnivorous and can fare well on a diet that excludes meat. Cats, on the other hand, are carnivorous and need the nutrients found in meat. Specifically, cats must have a source of the amino acid taurine in their diets, and there is none in the plant world. If you don't feed your cat meat, you must provide a taurine supplement. Your veterinarian may or may not be receptive to the idea of a vegetarian diet for cats and dogs, just as many human health care providers are not familiar with vegetarian diets for people. For more information, see *Dr. Pitcairn's Complete Guide to Natural Health for Dogs and Cats*, by Richard Pitcairn, Susan Hubble Pitcairn, and Michael W. Fox (Rodale Press, 1995). Also see *The New Natural Cat: A Complete Guide for Finicky Owners*, by Anitra Frazier and Norma Eckroate (E. P. Dutton, 1990).

Set the Example

Model the behavior that you want your children to adopt. If you want your child to like broccoli and sweet potatoes, let them see you enjoying them yourself.

What if you don't like broccoli? There's no need to pretend to like something that you don't. Children can spot a fake. But you don't have to sneer at it, either. If you don't care for a food, fix it for the others in your household, and don't make a big show out of the fact that there isn't any on your plate.

Attitude Is Everything

Present foods with a positive attitude. It will make all the difference in the world. At the same time, don't push. You also don't have to be obvious—a wide grin and "Aren't these lovely Brussels sprouts?" isn't necessary, but present the food with an air that says that you have every reason to expect that your family is going to be pleased with this food.

No Need to Be the Hall Monitor

It's no use trying to be the diet police. You don't have to eat foods that you don't like, and you can let your child express food preferences too. We don't all like the same foods. If your child expresses dislike for a food that you'd like to see her eat, play it low-key. She may come around in time. If not, there's no need to fret. There are hundreds of different vegetables, fruits, and grains. If your child doesn't like one or another, there are plenty of others to take its place.

Helpful Hint

The Vegetarian Resource Group publishes the brochure, "Vegetarian Nutrition for Teenagers!" For a free copy, send a self-addressed, stamped, business-sized envelope to VRG, PO Box 1463, Baltimore, MD 21203 or call (410) 366-8343.

Allow Freedom of Choice

Children prefer a measure of freedom like everyone else. If your child turns up his nose at a particular food, offer one or two other choices. For instance, if your child says, "No!" to cooked carrots, offer a few raw carrots with dip or steamed, mixed vegetables instead. If your child refuses these, let it go. The next meal will bring new choices.

The Family That Plans Meals Together Eats Together

Get your children involved in meal planning. Ask about their ideas and preferences. Then take your child shopping for food. Children are more likely to eat what they've had a hand in choosing. If you are buying apples or pears from a bin, let your child pick out two or three and put them into the bag. Let older children have even more responsibility. Send your teen to the opposite side of the produce aisle to pick out a head of cauliflower. Who cares if it's the best one? It's more important that your kids become involved.

Foster the Spirit of Adventure

Have some fun experimenting with new fruits and vegetables. You and your child are on even ground when you pick up a food at the supermarket that's totally new to both of you. Try something challenging, such as a really strange-looking piece of exotic fruit or a spaghetti squash.

If you get it home and taste it and find that you don't like it, that's okay. It's part of the process of trying new things. Sometimes you hit on a new favorite, and sometimes you turn up with a dud. At least you tried, and finding those new favorites makes it all worthwhile.

Prepare Meals Together

Your kids will be more likely to eat food that they've had a hand in fixing. Supervise young children and let them help with simple tasks like retrieving canned goods from the pantry or dumping prepared ingredients into a pot. Older kids can help wash and peel fruits and vegetables for salads and assemble other ingredients for casseroles and stir-fries.

Grow Your Own Food

Let your kids learn how their foods grow and help them gain an interest and appreciation for fresh foods. Plant a windowsill herb garden, grow a pot of tomatoes on your back porch or apartment balcony, or plant a small kitchen garden or a full-sized backyard garden—whatever makes sense for your lifestyle, on a small scale or large.

The Last Bite

Antonia Demas, Ph.D., Director of the Food Studies Institute in Trumansburg, New York, has developed an innovative elementary school curriculum that teaches children about foods using a hands-on, experiential approach that combines nutrition, anthropology, and the arts. Using her method, children learn about and prepare foods from other cultures, drawing from the healthiest traditions of those cuisines. In her studies, Dr. Demas has found that children who have classroom exposure to new foods are five to 20 times more likely to choose those foods when they are subsequently served in the school cafeteria, as compared to children who had no previous exposure to the same foods.

Extra Special Challenges

Sooner or later, all vegetarians and those who love them will stumble upon the many challenges—some big, some small—that occur when meat-and-potatoes converge with veggie-burger-hold-the-cheese. From the relatively mundane dilemma of what to take along in the car on a road trip to the more sophisticated skill of planning meals for vegan house guests who happen to be observing Passover.

School Lunch

There's no getting around it—it's tough to find a healthy school lunch, and it's tougher to find a healthy, vegetarian school meal. Even the U.S. Department of Agriculture's surveys of its own program have found that most, if not all, school meals are too high in fat and too low in fiber and do not meet the Department's Dietary Guidelines for Americans.

Over the past several years, lots of time, energy, and money have been poured into revamping the school meals programs and bringing them into compliance with current dietary recommendations. The fact is, however, that they aren't anywhere close to being there. Steps have been taken in the right direction, though, and some of the regulation changes that have taken place over the past few years have made more vegetarian options feasible. *Feasible*, not necessarily *available*.

For instance, yogurt can be served and credited to schools as a meat replacement, and nondairy cheeses can be served in lieu of dairy cheeses if they are nutritionally similar. Schools also have the option of using a nutrient-based menu-planning system if they so choose. A nutrient-based menu-planning system allows the school to evaluate meals based on overall nutritional composition, rather than on whether or not a meal consists of a specified number of servings from various food groups. Theoretically, a nutrient-based system would make it easier to offer meatless menus, since servings from the "meat group" wouldn't be mandatory. In reality, a rare few schools in the nation are using this system, since changing to the new system from the old "food-groups" system would take more time and energy than most schools are willing to devote. Why bother, when the regulations permit them to continue using the old system?

To be fair to the schools, I should point out that the issue is complex. The system has limitations, and radical changes can't be expected to take place overnight. School food-service personnel certainly have the kids' best interests at heart. It's just that kids who want vegetarian options at school aren't going to find many, and kids who want vegan options are going to find even fewer.

What to do?

➤ Take a bag lunch. If it's not too uncool, your child might want to consider packing a lunch from home. Hummus or peanut butter doesn't need refrigeration for the few hours that it's in a locker before lunch. A bagel, a muffin, some carrot sticks with some hummus or salsa for dip, and some fresh fruit are also portable and practical. If a microwave oven is available at school, soup cups are convenient and add variety. Just add hot water, stir, and it's a meal. In addition to prepared soups "in a cup," you can buy vegetarian chili and rice or pasta dishes that require only hot water to become a hot lunch. Natural foods stores usually have the biggest selection.

➤ If your child wouldn't be caught dead with a bag lunch, then there are a couple of other options. Ask the school for a copy of the cafeteria menu. You and your child can sit down together and peruse the menu for the best choices each day. Think about whether or not an entree could be easily modified by the school to make it vegetarian. For instance, if macaroni and cheese with ham is on the menu, could the school set aside one serving without ham for your child? If spaghetti with meat sauce is scheduled, with a day or two's notice, could the school provide a meatless sauce for your child? If there's not going to be an appropriate vegetarian entree, could your child take one or two side dishes from the cafeteria line and supplement them with something brought from home, such as a sandwich?

The Last Bite

If it hasn't occurred to you that your child may not share your enthusiasm for eating a vegan or vegetarian diet at school, give it some thought. Though surveys show that kids are adopting vegetarian diets at twice the rate of adults, your child may or may not want to comply away from home. Most experienced vegetarians find that strong-arm tactics do little good in getting kids to eat what parents want them to eat. Set a good example at home, encourage your child to eat well while away, then let your child choose. More about issues such as these in Chapters 14, "Are We in This Together?" and 15, "Avoiding the Coke and French Fries Trap: Assorted Practical Pointers."

Finding satisfactory vegetarian meal options at school can be a frustrating experience, but it's not impossible. Since the circumstances are different for each student and each school, you might also want to consider sitting down with school food service personnel and discussing practical solutions that both your child and the school can live with.

The Last Bite

If your school's biology curriculum calls for the dissection of animals, there may be options for kids who have an ethical objection to learning about anatomy this way. Some cities and states have policies that give students alternatives, such as plastic models and computer simulations of a dissection. At least three states—California, Florida, and Pennsylvania—have laws giving students the right to use an alternative method. Students who want to learn more about alternatives to dissection can also call a toll-free hotline for more information—(800) 922-FROG.

When Weight's the Issue

Older children and teens are body-conscious. More likely than not, the girls want to lose weight and the boys want to gain it.

If diet is the cause of too much pudge, the culprits are probably chips, candy bars, fast foods, and other sweets and fatty foods. Clean up your diet. Replace the junk foods with more fresh fruits and bigger helpings of vegetables, whole grains, and legumes. Have a lentil soup cup instead of a large order of fries. Eat a big apple instead of a bag of nacho chips.

If the diet is already up to snuff, then the answer is probably exercise—lack thereof. Get moving. For teens, aerobics classes and weight-lifting are excellent ways of increasing cardiovascular fitness as well as overall strength, and burning more calories will help you lose weight. If you find that going to the gym becomes a chore and you're not enjoying yourself, find something that you do enjoy. Take up biking or hiking or canoeing. Switch activities depending upon the season. Snow ski in the winter and swim in the summer. Mix it up to avoid getting into a rut. Go in-line skating on cool, sunny days, and play racquetball at the gym when the weather is poor. Learn to play tennis. Take a class on kayaking. Make physical activity a permanent part of your family's lifestyle now so that you can keep your weight down as both you and your children age. Weight-lifting at the gym may not be appropriate for younger kids, but parents can get them involved in swimming lessons, tennis, figure skating, gymnastics, and other age-appropriate activities.

The Last Bite

Eating disorders are more common in teens—especially girls—than in adults. However, there's no cause-and-effect relationship between vegetarian diets and eating disorders, such as anorexia nervosa (self-starvation) and bulimia (binge and purge). Some anorexics do stop eating meat, but it's likely to be due to the effects of the anorexia that cause a loss of the taste for meat. Being vegetarian in itself does not induce an eating disorder. Eating disorders have psychological origins, and people with eating disorders need psychiatric or psychological intervention.

Teen boys are more likely than teen girls to feel that they are too skinny. Nature will probably take its course, and today's string bean will be tomorrow's 40 Regular. It's just that it's sooner for some beans than for others, and the waiting and comparing of physiques can get a little nerve-wracking.

So, if your teen wants to gain weight, the way to do it is simply to eat more of "the good stuff." Increase serving sizes at meals, and add healthful snacks between meals. Smoothies and juice blends add easy, quick calories. Increasing weight-bearing exercise will also help the body to add more muscle tissue, within limits, of course.

For individual assistance with weight control issues, see a registered dietitian.

Teen Athletes

If your teen is active in sports, you may wonder if he or she is getting enough protein, other nutrients, and calories on a vegetarian diet. This topic is explored more thoroughly in Chapter 12, "Vegetarian Athletes and Sportsmeisters," but the quick answer is this: Teens have higher needs for some nutrients to begin with, since they are in a period of rapid growth and development, and being vigorously physically active increases those needs slightly. However, teens who are physically active also take in more calories to accommodate their higher activity level. Assuming those extra calories are coming from wholesome foods and not junk, they'll get the additional nutrients they need in the extra calories they'll be consuming.

The increase in nutritional needs resulting from physical activity is really very small for most "nonelite" athletes and is essentially inconsequential. Nutrient recommendations have a generous margin of safety worked in. Professional and Olympic-level athletes are the people who may truly have substantially increased needs for certain nutrients and may have to be more careful in planning their diets (see Chapter 12).

The Least You Need to Know

➤ Children who follow healthful vegetarian diets should be expected to have satisfactory rates of growth.

➤ Since some vegetarian diets can be bulky and low in calories, make sure younger children, who have small stomach capacities, meet their energy needs with snacks that include vegetable fats such as nut and seed butters or avocado.

➤ The best way to ensure that vegetarian children get enough protein is to ensure that they have enough calories in their diets as well as a reasonable variety of foods.

➤ Vegan and near-vegan kids need a reliable source of vitamin B12 and adequate vitamin D.

➤ Be careful that junk foods don't displace too many nutritious foods from the diet.

➤ Increase the likelihood that your kids will eat fruits and vegetables by setting a good example yourself, taking a positive attitude, getting your kids involved in meal planning and preparation, and resisting the temptation to push too much.

Chapter 11

Vegetarian Diets for Older Adults (New Tricks for Old Dogs!)

> ## In This Chapter
>
> ➤ How nutritional needs change with age
>
> ➤ Dietary recommendations for older adults
>
> ➤ Ways in which vegetarian diets reduce common age-related problems
>
> ➤ How vegetarian diets mesh with therapeutic diets for various illnesses
>
> ➤ Tips for making meal prep easier

Have you hit the age of 40 yet? If so, have you noticed how much younger you seem (in your own eyes) as compared to your parents at the same age? True, your perspective is different now. But your parents at 70 years of age seem so much younger than your grandparents did at the same age. It's not just a matter of fashion. People are staying healthy longer these days. It's not completely uncommon to meet someone who is 100 years old.

More people are enjoying a generally healthy and vital old age, but age-related health problems *do* increase as we age. We consider conditions such as constipation, hemorrhoids, and weight gain to be normal parts of the aging process. We figure that diabetes and high blood pressure are bound to crop up eventually. After all, other elderly family members had the same ailments.

The science of *gerontology* is still young, but scientists are gaining insights into some of the aspects of aging that most of us take for granted as being part of growing old. There is a similar pattern of changes that takes place among all humans as we age, but these changes can occur sooner or later for different individuals. Some people never develop certain conditions. These differences among people can be due to genetics as well as lifestyle factors.

Diet is one of the lifestyle factors that makes an undeniable difference in the way that people age. We've already discussed the fact that vegetarians have lower rates of coronary artery disease, high blood pressure, diabetes, some forms of cancer, obesity, gallstones, and kidney stones. Vegetarians generally also live longer than nonvegetarians. Granted, some of the health and longevity differences may be due to lifestyle factors such as a higher level of physical activity and not smoking, which are more typical of vegetarians. But a vegetarian diet confers nutritional advantages too, and these translate into improved quality of life for many older adults.

In this chapter, we'll look at some of the ways in which a vegetarian diet affects older adults.

Veggie Talk

Gerontology is the study of normal aging.

Nutritional Needs Change with Age

Older folks have been at the back of the line when it comes to research on the body's nutritional needs throughout the lifecycle. Nutrition scientists are getting there, but we still know very little about how the aging process affects the body's ability to digest, absorb, and retain nutrients. Until we know more, recommended intakes for most nutrients for older adults are simply extrapolated from the recommendations for younger people.

Blame It on Metabolism

Yes, what you've always heard is true: Your metabolism declines as you age. Unfair! Unfair! But the sad, hard fact is that you need fewer calories the older you get, assuming that your physical activity level stays the same. In fact, if your activity level decreases, then your calorie needs decline even further. Oh, woe!

It gets worse. If you consume fewer calories, your intakes of protein, vitamins, minerals, and other nutrients also decrease. Unfortunately, as far as anyone knows right now, your nutritional needs do not. Your needs for certain nutrients may actually rise. So that means you have to be extra careful to eat well. You have to get the same amount of nutrition that you got when you were younger (and eating more calories), but you have to get it with less food. If you haven't caught my drift, that means that you have to eat fewer *empty calorie foods*. Less junk. Fewer sweets, snack chips, cakes, cookies, candy, soft drinks, and alcohol. Empty calorie foods are nutritional freeloaders—they displace more nutrient-dense foods and provide little nutrition in exchange for the calories.

Your Needs for Certain Nutrients May Increase

A great deal of research is still needed on how nutritional needs change for older people, but scientists are reasonably sure that needs do change. That may be due, in part, to the fact that absorption of certain nutrients declines with age. For example, older people are thought to produce less stomach acid, which is vital in helping the body absorb vitamin B12. That's why the recently revised federal recommendations for vitamin B12 intake for older adults were raised to 3 micrograms per day, as compared to 2 micrograms for younger people. This is especially noteworthy for older vegans, who need to be careful to have a reliable source of the vitamin in their diets.

More food for thought: If you are an elderly couch potato, your calorie needs may be very low. In that case, your intake of many nutrients may be marginal or inadequate, since you may not be eating very much. If you're a vegetarian and your calorie intake is low, your protein intake may actually be an issue. Some scientists think that protein needs are somewhat higher for older people. Since vegetarians already get less protein than nonvegetarians—usually an advantage—intakes for elderly people who have low calorie intakes may dip *too* low.

Veggie Talk

Empty calorie foods are foods that provide little in the way of nutrition in exchange for the calories they contribute to the diet.

Current research also indicates that older people don't manufacture as much vitamin D, and some scientists think that vitamin D needs for older people may be as much as twice current recommendations. On the other hand, if vitamin D production naturally decreases with age, maybe that's the way nature intended it to be. In either case, older adults need to have a source of vitamin D in their diets or have enough sunlight exposure to allow them to produce it. Older vegetarians who don't drink milk or eat other dairy products should be aware of this, since they can't count on getting their vitamin D from fortified dairy products as other people do. If their exposure to sunlight is limited, they should use vitamin D–fortified foods such as some brands of soymilk or get their vitamin D from a supplement.

As I've explained earlier, vitamin D and calcium work hand-in-hand to keep your bones strong. Bone loss accelerates with age, so recommendations for calcium intake are high for older people as compared with people in middle age. All the more reason for older folks to be frugal with their calories and save them for nutritious foods, rather than filling up on sweets and junk.

Getting What You Need (and Avoiding What You Don't Need)

The general dietary recommendations for older adults are actually not dissimilar to those for younger people. Get enough calories to meet your energy needs and maintain an ideal weight, eat a variety of wholesome foods, including fruits, vegetables, whole grains, legumes, and a limited number of seeds and nuts. Drink plenty of fluids, and limit the sweets, junk, and other empty calorie foods.

Move It or Lose It

Regular exercise is an important component of a healthy lifestyle, and it's just as important for older adults as it is for the younger crowd. When you're regularly and vigorously physically active, you burn more calories. Therefore, you can eat more. The more food you consume, the more likely it is that you'll get the nutrients you need. You're also likely to preserve more bone and muscle tissues when you exercise regularly, especially when the activity is weight-bearing, such as walking or using weight sets. If you stay physically active, you'll also be more likely to keep your weight at an ideal level.

The Last Bite

To assess your own diet, start with keeping a food diary that you can compare against the food guide in Chapter 18, "A Daily Vegetarian Food Guide." To do that, record everything that you eat or drink for a few days to a couple of weeks. It doesn't matter what you write on—a notepad, index cards, or legal pad will do. Just be sure to note what you ate or drank (be specific—was it whole-wheat bread or white? Regular salad dressing or fat-free?), the portion size (estimate it), the date, and even the time and where you were. These details can be very helpful if you take your diary to a nutritionist for evaluation. Just keeping the diary may also make you more aware of your eating habits and areas that need attention.

Who's Old? Me??

You knew you were getting old when your eyebrows started turning gray. Or when that stray hair sprouted on your chin. Yeah, things were changing.

Besides the obvious outward signs of aging—wrinkles, lines, and gray hair—there are other common complaints of people when they get older. Most have to do in some way with the digestive tract. They start getting constipated, or they have more trouble with heartburn and indigestion. Some of these problems are the effect of a decrease in the production of the stomach secretions that aid digestion, or they're in some other way a result of a body that's not functioning as efficiently as it once did.

On the other hand, many of these problems are the result of lifelong assaults on the body via a poor diet, or lack of regular exercise, or any of a host of destructive habits, such as smoking or abusing alcohol. For instance, if you've been exercising, eating plenty of fiber, and drinking enough water for the last 20 years, you're much less likely to have hemorrhoids or varicose veins.

Eating a vegetarian diet can help prevent or delay many of the common problems associated with getting older, and a vegetarian diet can also help alleviate some of the problems once they've developed.

Constipated and Cranky?

Constipation is nearly always due to dietary factors. Regardless of your age, you need plenty of fiber in your diet from fruits, whole grains, vegetables, and legumes, plus plenty of fluids (see Chapter 2, "Why Go Vegetarian?"). Regular exercise also helps to promote normal laxation.

Older adults develop problems with constipation when their calorie intakes dip too low. They're eating less, so they take in less fiber. If they're eating too many desserts and junk foods, they may be getting even less fiber. Older people are also notorious for being physically inactive. Both of these factors—low fiber intake and low activity level—can cause you to become constipated.

You can take steps to get yourself "moving" again. Keep the following points in mind:

➤ You can't have too much fiber in your diet. Be sure to eat plenty of fresh fruit, vegetables, whole-grain breads and cereal products, and legumes. Review Chapter 2 for more information about dietary fiber.

➤ Make it a habit to drink fluids frequently. Water is best. You don't necessarily have to count eight glasses per day, but keep a pitcher of water on your desk and a bottle of water in your car, and drink them regularly. Stopping for a sip every time you pass a water fountain is a good idea.

➤ Prunes and prune juice have a laxative effect for many people.

Heads Up!

Constipation can be made worse if you are taking certain medications, including antacids made with aluminum hydroxide or calcium carbonate, or if you are a habitual laxative user.

Helpful Hint

In addition to cutting the fat in your diet, you can help prevent heartburn by avoiding reclining immediately after a meal. If you do lie down for a nap after lunch, put a couple of pillows under your back so that you're elevated at least 30 degrees and aren't lying flat. Avoid overeating. It may help to eat smaller, more frequent meals.

➤ Keeping fatty foods and junk foods to a minimum is a smart move because these foods are usually low in fiber and will displace other foods that might contribute fiber to your diet.

➤ You won't be as likely to need antacids if you keep your fat intake low. Fat takes longer to digest than other nutrients, so it stays in the stomach longer and can promote indigestion and heartburn.

➤ Regular physical activity keeps your muscles (including those in your abdomen) toned and helps to prevent constipation.

Since vegetarian diets tend to be lower in fat and higher in fiber than nonvegetarian diets, older vegetarians are less likely to have problems with constipation.

Heartburn Heartache

Vegetarians have less heartburn because they tend to have less fat in their diets. If you are a vegetarian and do have trouble with heartburn, examine your diet. You may be eating too many high-fat dairy products or greasy junk foods such as chips, donuts, and French fries.

The Goods on Gas

You may prefer to call it flatulence. It's intestinal gas, which can be caused by a number of things, including the higher fiber content of a vegetarian diet. More than just a social problem, gas can cause discomfort in your abdomen, and it can cause you to belch or feel bloated. Before you incriminate your beans and cabbage, though, be aware of a few other causes of gas that might be exacerbating your problem, including:

➤ Carbonated beverages

➤ Swallowing too much air when you're eating

➤ Certain medications (ask your pharmacist if any of the medications you take may be culprits)

If you do think it's your diet, though, you've got a few options. Consider these gas busters:

➤ Single out the foods that are the culprits. Beans? Cabbage? Onions? Eliminate one at a time until you reduce your gas production to a level you can live with. The foods that cause gas in one individual don't necessarily cause gas in everyone else and, unfortunately, the foods that do cause gas are among the most nutritious.

➤ Try using a product such as Beano, which uses enzymes to break down some of the carbohydrate that causes gas. Products such as these come in liquid form—you squeeze a few drops on the food before you eat it. Its effectiveness varies from person to person.

➤ Get active. People who exercise regularly have fewer problems with gas.

➤ Give it time. If you're new to a vegetarian diet, your body will adjust to the increased fiber load over several weeks, and your problem with gas should subside.

➤ Avoid carbonated beverages.

➤ Eat slowly and chew your food thoroughly to minimize the amount of air that you take in with each bite.

Excuses, Excuses...

You're diabetic and you follow a special diet? Maybe you're on a special diet for high blood pressure or heart disease. It doesn't matter. A vegetarian diet is compatible with restrictions for any diet and, in many cases, a vegetarian diet is the ideal for your condition.

For instance, people with diabetes may be able to reduce the amount of medication or insulin they presently take if they switch to a vegetarian diet. The fiber content of vegetarian diets helps to control blood sugar levels. If your health care provider told you to switch to chicken and fish instead of red meat to protect your heart, a vegetarian diet that limits high-fat dairy products and eggs is even better.

Vegetarian diets are usually low in fat and high in fiber, so they help people control their weight. Weight control is an important component of the dietary management of diabetes, heart disease, high blood pressure, arthritis, and many other conditions.

There's no reason that you can't eat a vegetarian diet, whatever the ailment. If you need help adapting a vegetarian diet to your special needs, contact a registered dietitian with expertise in vegetarian nutrition. The American Dietetic Association's referral service can find a dietitian in your area. Call (800) 366-1655.

Make It Easy on Yourself

Do you have little time for shopping and preparing meals from scratch? Does arthritis make it difficult to open bottles and packages, or does poor eyesight make it difficult for you to read package instructions or drive to the grocery store? Do you live alone and find it difficult to cook for one?

You don't have to be old to want to make meal planning easier on yourself. There are lots of reasons for wanting your meals to be quick and convenient to prepare. There are also lots of ways to save yourself time and energy planning meals.

If You Cook

If you do cook meals from scratch—even occasionally—it's a great idea to make enough of a recipe so that you can freeze part of it for later when you don't feel like cooking. Foods that freeze especially well include vegetarian chili, lasagna, casseroles, cookies, muffins, quick breads, and soups. If you freeze them in small batches or single servings, they're even more convenient. Muffins and cookies can be taken out of the freezer one or two at a time. Other foods can be heated as needed.

Helpful Hint

When you make rice, make more than you'll need for one meal. Leftover rice will keep in the refrigerator in an airtight container or covered dish for a week or more. Reheat it and top it with vegetarian chili, black beans, or sautéed vegetables. You can even use leftover rice to make rice pudding.

Veggie Talk

There's no legal definition for the term **natural foods**, but within the food industry it's generally understood to mean foods that have been minimally processed and are as close to their natural state as possible.

If You Don't

Just because you don't cook doesn't mean you can't eat well. There's nothing wrong with a bowl of whole-grain cereal with soymilk for lunch or dinner occasionally. Some commercial vegetarian frozen entrees are also good choices. Natural food brands that you find in natural foods supermarkets (and increasingly in the regular neighborhood supermarkets too) can be particularly good choices. They tend to be lower in sodium and higher in fiber than mainstream brands.

But first a word about *natural foods*. These are foods that have been processed, but still remain close to their natural state. Natural foods may have been altered by grinding, chopping, drying, freezing, heating, fermenting, or separating, but they have not been altered through a chemical process (such as the hydrogenation of oils). They are free of artificial flavorings and colorings, preservatives, and any other additives that do not occur naturally in the food. The term "natural" doesn't necessarily apply to hormone use, organic feed for animals, nor to environmental practices used to grow the food.

Try frozen bean burritos, ethnic dishes such as Indian curried vegetables, Chinese stir-fries, and others. Vegetarian burger patties are also quick and convenient. Some other goodchoices for quick meals or snacks include:

➤ Flavored soy yogurt

➤ Soup cups (just add hot water)

➤ Packets of instant hot cereal

➤ Individual servings of canned fruit or soy pudding

➤ Boil-and-serve bags of frozen vegetable combinations

➤ Instant rice

➤ Bagels

➤ Vegetarian baked beans

➤ Fresh fruit

➤ Baking potatoes and sweet potatoes (microwave them or bake in the oven)

➤ Canned fruits packed in their own juice

➤ Whole-grain crackers

➤ Nut butters such as peanut butter and almond butter

➤ Fresh vegetables, cut and packaged, such as celery and carrot sticks and broccoli and cauliflower florets

➤ Canned refried beans or canned whole beans

➤ Flour tortillas

Helpful Hint

If you are not familiar with the many convenient natural food products that are on the market today, you might be interested in perusing my book, *The Natural Kitchen* (Berkley Books, 1999), which takes you aisle by aisle through the natural foods store and points out some great starter foods for people who have never before set foot in a natural foods store.

Getting Motivated

Many older people live alone. Some have lost a spouse or companion, some feel depressed due to medications they're taking, physical disabilities, or complications with preparing meals for themselves. All of these factors can make a person lose interest in taking care of him- or herself and eating well.

There are some ways of coping. Sometimes it's easier to eat smaller, more frequent meals or snacks, rather than trying to keep up with a three-meals-a-day schedule. Relying on some of the quickie foods listed earlier can also be helpful. It may also help some people to eat in a group with others. Just being with other people is a good way to lift your spirits. Local vegetarian organizations usually hold regular potluck dinner meetings, and some organize regular restaurant gatherings and special holiday meals. Getting active with a local vegetarian society can be a good way to meet others like yourself and to enjoy a meal in the company of others.

The Last Bite

The National Meals on Wheels Foundation and the Vegetarian Resource Group (VRG) have created a four-week vegetarian menu for use in Meals on Wheels programs nationwide. The menus can also be used in other congregate meal settings or senior centers. The menus are lacto ovo vegetarian, but instructions are provided for adapting the menus for vegans as well. The menu set is available, free of charge, by calling the VRG at (410) 366-8343 or writing to PO Box 1463, Baltimore, MD, 21203. You can also request the menu set via e-mail at vrg@vrg.org or on the World Wide Web at www.vrg.org.

The Least You Need to Know

➤ A vegetarian diet can help prevent, delay, or lessen the severity of many of the diseases and conditions that are often thought to be a normal part of the aging process.

➤ Scientists presently have little information about how the nutritional needs of older adults differ from those of younger people.

➤ Most older adults need fewer calories as they age, but their nutrient needs probably stay the same or increase.

➤ It's important for older adults to balance their calorie intake with their energy needs, eat a variety of wholesome foods, limit the junk, get plenty of fluids, and get regular physical activity.

Chapter 12

Vegetarian Athletes and Sportsmeisters

In This Chapter

➤ Getting the right mix of protein, carbohydrate, and fat

➤ What athletes need to know about vitamin and mineral requirements

➤ How to replace fluids

➤ Meal planning before, during, and after events and workouts

➤ Tips for handling pregame jitters and other challenges

Everyone has their reasons for going vegetarian. When I was 16 years old and a competitive swimmer, a book by Murray Rose caught my eye and inspired me to change my lifestyle forever. Murray Rose was an Australian swimmer who attributed his athletic endurance to his vegetarian diet. Rose was a three-time Olympic gold medallist and world record holder in swimming in Melbourne in 1956. He won a gold medal, a silver medal, and another world record at the 1960 Olympic Games in Rome. I'm not sure that the switch to a vegetarian diet improved my own athletic performance, but it didn't hurt, and the diet stuck.

In this chapter, we'll look at the special nutritional needs of vegetarian athletes.

Gaining the Competitive Edge

Today, we know that vegetarian diets can be advantageous for *athletes*. Some, but not all, studies have shown that vegetarian athletes have greater endurance than those who are not vegetarian. What seems to make the most difference in athletic performance is the overall make-up of the diet. Of critical importance is eating a diet consisting primarily of carbohydrate, with adequate amounts of protein and fat. That describes most vegetarian diets to a tee. Athletes who eat a typical American-style diet that emphasizes meat as the main course have a much harder time getting the optimal mix of nutrients in their diets.

Can athletes do well on a vegetarian diet? You bet. A vegetarian diet is tailor-made for helping athletes achieve optimal performance.

The following table lists some successful vegetarian athletes.

Famous Vegetarian Athletes

Surya Bonaly (France), Olympic figure skater

Andreas Cahling (Sweden), champion body builder and Olympic gold medallist in the ski jump

Chris Campbell (USA), Olympic wrestler

Desmond Howard (USA), professional football player and Heisman trophy winner

Peter Hussing (Germany), European super heavy-weight amateur boxing champion

Billie Jean King (USA), champion tennis player

Carl Lewis (USA), Olympic runner and gold medallist

Ingra Manecke (Germany), champion discus thrower

Bill Manetti (USA), power-lifting champion

Edwin Moses (USA), Olympic gold medallist and world record holder in track

Martina Navratilova (USA), champion tennis player

Paavo Nurmi (Finland), long-distance runner, Olympic gold medallist and holder of 20 world records

Bill Pearl (USA), weight lifter and four-time Mr. Universe

Dave Scott (USA), six-time winner of the Ironman triathlon

Protein Pointers

The experts differ in their opinions about how much protein athletes need. Some question whether physical activity level affects the body's need for protein at all, and others feel that needs are higher, depending upon the kind of activity.

Both the American Dietetic Association and the Canadian Dietetic Association recommend that athletes aim for $1^{1}/_{2}$ grams of protein per kilogram of body weight, or almost double the amount recommended for nonathletes. Some scientists differentiate and say that endurance athletes need a little less than that, and strength athletes need a little more. The extra protein isn't needed primarily for muscle development, though, as you might think. Instead, it's needed to compensate for the protein that athletes burn up as fuel. Some athletes need a tremendous number of calories to meet their energy needs, and if they don't have enough fuel from carbohydrates and fats, their bodies turn to protein for energy. When that happens, they need extra protein in their diets so that enough will be available for building and repairing tissues. (For more information about protein, see Chapter 3, "Protein Power.")

Veggie Talk

For the purposes of this chapter, the term **athlete** applies to a person who is vigorously physically active most days of the week for extended periods of time. Swimmers, runners, or triathletes who are training hard are considered athletes. Going to the gym three times a week to work out on the stair climber and lift weights is great, but it's not enough activity to make any appreciable difference in your nutritional needs. Ditto for golfers and weekend warriors.

The Last Bite

Studies on the protein requirements of athletes have focused on young male subjects. Female athletes and older adult athletes may have different needs. It's likely that the protein needs of female athletes are lower than those of male athletes, and the needs of older adult athletes may be higher. Remember, the relevance here is for elite, Olympic, and professional-level athletes—those who are in serious training rather than the rest of us who are just trying to stay in reasonably good shape.

Getting Enough Protein

Since athletes need more calories than people who are less active, they tend to consume more protein via the extra food they eat. Usually, just getting enough calories to meet your energy needs and eating a reasonable variety of foods is enough to ensure that you'll get the protein you need. That's especially true for endurance athletes, such as swimmers, cyclists, runners, and triathletes. Athletes who strength train (weight-lifters, wrestlers, and football players, for example) may need to be more aware of getting enough protein-rich foods in their diets, especially if their calorie intakes are low. Any athlete who is restricting calories to lose weight while training should also be more careful to get enough protein.

Protein Boosters

It's easy for athletes to add protein to a vegetarian diet. Each of the following foods would add at least 10 grams of protein (as well as other nutrients) to your diet:

➤ Large bowl of whole-grain cereal with soymilk

➤ Bagel with peanut butter

➤ A 12-ounce soymilk smoothie with wheat germ and strawberries

➤ Cup of vegetarian chili over a cup of rice

➤ Tempeh sloppy Joe

➤ Cup of soy yogurt with ¹/₂ cup Grape-Nuts

➤ Pita pocket with hummus and grated carrots

➤ Large baked potato topped with a cup of lentil soup

➤ Two bean burritos

➤ A bean taco and a bean burrito

➤ Large plate of pasta tossed with olive oil and vegetables

Heads Up!

A little protein is a good thing, but too much isn't. High-protein, high-fat meals actually make athletes sluggish and are generally bad for your health. Instead of eating a steak before competing, athletes are better off eating a big plate of spaghetti with tomato sauce, a heaping helping of stir-fry with vegetables and tofu, or bean burritos with rice and vegetables.

Remember: Plant Proteins Are Winners

Don't forget that there are advantages to getting your protein from plant sources. Plant sources of protein are associated with better kidney function and lower rates of some types of cancer and heart disease.

Loading Up on Carbs

For athletes, it's all about carbohydrate.

It's well known that a diet that consists primarily of carbohydrates—vegetables, pasta, rice and other grains and grain products, fruits, and legumes—improves an athlete's stamina and results in a better performance. Athletes that restrict their carbohydrate intake show poorer performance levels. It isn't surprising, then, that vegetarian diets have advantages for athletes, since vegetarian diets tend to consist primarily of carbohydrate-rich foods.

The Last Bite

Athletes used to "carbohydrate load" before an event. They would restrict their carbohydrate intake and load up on fat and protein for a few days, then they would gorge on carbohydrate-rich foods for a couple of days just before their event. The idea was that this method would maximize their muscles' storage of fuel and result in better performance. Now we know that it's more effective just to eat a high-carbohydrate diet all the time. Most vegetarians are, in effect, in a constant state of carbohydrate load.

Fueling Up Your Muscles

When you eat a diet that is high in carbohydrate, your body stores some of the carbohydrate in the form of *glycogen* in your muscles and liver. Whether you engage in endurance events such as swimming, cycling, or running, or in shorter, high-intensity activities, such as a ski jump or running a sprint or the high hurdles, your muscle and liver glycogen stores are a vital energy supply and a critical determinant of your ability to perform your best.

Veggie Talk

Glycogen is the form of sugar that is stored in your muscles and liver. Your body calls upon its stockpile of glycogen for energy during athletic events.

The Right Carbs

Getting enough calories and carbohydrate in your diet helps to ensure that the protein in your diet is available for the growth and repair of tissues and doesn't have to be sacrificed and burned for fuel.

But not just any carbohydrate will do.

Soft drinks, candy, snack cakes, and other junk foods consist mainly of carbohydrate, but we've already said that they're empty calorie foods. Anyone who depends on his (or her) diet to help him feel and perform his best needs to take pains not to let the junk displace the more nutrient-dense foods from his diet. Junk-food forms of carbohydrate do provide calories, so they can help keep your body from needing to burn protein for fuel. But you need the nutrients in the more wholesome foods too. You've got to look at the big picture, not just a little piece of it.

Helpful Hint

Some elite-level athletes have tremendously high calorie needs, and many carbohydrate-rich foods are bulky. They can be so filling that some athletes can get full at meals before taking in enough calories. For that reason, it can be fine for athletes to include some refined foods in their diets, despite the fact that most other people need more fiber. For instance, some athletes may choose to eat refined breakfast cereals or white bread instead of whole-grain products.

Good choices for carbohydrate include pasta, beans, rice, potatoes, lentils, breads, cold and hot cereals, soymilk, all vegetables, all fruits, and combinations of all of these.

Some Fat Can Be Okay

Everyone—athletes included—should limit their intake of saturated fat, and people who are overweight should limit their total intake of fat. But there are some situations in which a little extra fat added to the diet can be just the right move, particularly when the fat that's being eaten is from a plant source.

In Chapter 10, "Kids' Stuff or Adults Only? Vegetarian Diets for Children and Teens," we discussed the fact that some added fats can be okay for young vegetarian children, since they have relatively high energy needs, and vegetarian foods can be bulky and filling and low in calories. Likewise, some vegetarian athletes may have trouble getting enough calories if their diets are too bulky.

If you are having trouble getting enough calories on a vegetarian diet, it's fine to use a little extra peanut butter, almond butter, or olive oil on your toast, bread, or crackers. Avocado slices on a sandwich, guacamole dip, tahini, olives, seeds, and nuts are also nutritious and versatile. Just a little bit of any of these can boost your calorie intake by hundreds of calories—a scary thought for anyone who wants to lose weight, but useful information for the skinnies looking for a convenient source of extra calories. (See also "Tips of the Trade" later in the chapter.)

The Last Bite

Calorie needs of athletes vary widely, from female swimmers consuming 2,600 calories per day to male cyclists in the Tour de France burning 8,500 calories per day.

Meeting Your Vitamin and Mineral Needs

Generally speaking, a well-planned vegetarian diet that emphasizes adequate calories and variety and limits the junk should provide athletes with all of the nutrients they need. Under certain circumstances, though, a few nutrients may deserve some special attention.

Calcium

Athletes have the same needs for calcium as nonathletes, but some female athletes who train intensely may be at risk if their level of training causes them to become *amenorrheic*. Like post-menopausal women, women who have stopped having their periods have lower levels of estrogen, and that can lead to accelerated loss of calcium from the bones. Of course, you already know that there are several factors affecting bone health, and that the amount of calcium you absorb and retain from your diet is more significant than how much calcium your diet contains in the first place. Nevertheless, if you are a female athlete who has stopped having periods or skips periods, the recommendations for calcium intake are higher for you. That means you need to push the calcium-rich foods and have less room in your diet for junk. (See Chapter 4, "Boning Up on Calcium," for more information about calcium.)

Veggie Talk

Amenorrhea is the cessation of regular menstrual cycles. Amenorrhea isn't caused by vegetarian diets—any female athlete may stop having periods when training too intensely.

Iron

All athletes—vegetarian or not—are at greater risk of iron deficiency due to iron losses in the body that occur with prolonged, vigorous activity. Female endurance athletes are at the greatest risk, as well as athletes who have low iron stores. (Go back to Chapter 5, "What About Iron?" for a refresher on iron.) There's no need to take a supplement unless blood tests show that you need one. Men, in particular, should avoid taking unnecessary iron supplements due to the connection between high intakes of iron and coronary artery disease.

Other Vitamins and Minerals

Vegans need to remember to have a reliable source of vitamin B12 in their diets. Some studies also show that exercise raises the need for riboflavin and zinc. Other research is pointing to advantages for athletes who get plenty of antioxidant nutrients (vitamins C, E, and the carotenoids) in their diets. But now we're speculating. Don't pull out your hair. At this point, the most practical advice for anyone is simply to do your best to eat well.

The Last Bite

Many vegetarian athletes have questions about creatine supplements, which come in the form of creatine monohydrate. Some studies have shown that creatine supplements improve the performance of athletes engaged in high-intensity (as opposed to endurance) activities. Vegetarians get virtually no creatine in their diets, since it's found in animal muscles. Companies that produce creatine supplements assure vegetarians that the supplements are not made from animal sources. Nevertheless, more research is needed before nutritionists can recommend creatine supplements to athletes, and the prudent choice is to avoid them for now. Rarely can any supplement beat the benefits of simply eating a healthful diet.

Meal Planning Before, During, and After Events

Whether you are in training or getting ready for an athletic event, what you eat and when you eat it can make a difference in your level of performance.

Before the Event

If you generally eat a high-carbohydrate, vegetarian diet, you're ahead of the game already. When it gets closer to the time of the event in which you'll be competing, it's time to pull a few more tricks out of your sleeve.

In the hours before the event, you should eat foods that are easy to digest and will keep your energy level up. High-carbohydrate foods are good choices, but now's the time to minimize your fat and protein intakes. Fat, in particular, takes longer to digest than other nutrients. You want your stomach to empty quickly to give your food time to get to the intestines where it can be absorbed before you burst into action. That's the reason to keep your fat intake low at this point. Avoiding foods that are concentrated in protein is also a good idea immediately before an event, since protein also takes a bit longer to digest than carbohydrate. That leaves fruits, vegetables, and grains as the best choices in the hours before an event.

It's also a good idea to avoid foods that are excessively high in sodium or salt, since these foods can make you retain fluids, which may impair your performance or make you feel less than your best. Foods that are especially high in fiber are probably best saved for after the event too, since you'll probably want your large intestine to be as empty as possible during the event. High-fiber foods can cause some people to have diarrhea and others to become constipated before athletic events, especially when they're anxious.

Some good pre-event light meal and snack ideas include:

➤ Bowl of cereal with soymilk

➤ Soymilk and fruit smoothie

➤ Bagel with jam

➤ A banana and several graham crackers

➤ Pancakes or waffles with syrup

➤ Toast or English muffins and a cup of soy yogurt

➤ Tomato sandwich and a glass of fruit juice

➤ Cooked vegetables over steamed rice

➤ Pasta tossed with cooked vegetables or topped with marinara sauce

Helpful Hint

The rule of thumb is to give yourself one hour before the event for every 200 calories of food you eat, up to about 800 calories. In other words, if you eat a meal that contains 400 calories, it's best to eat it two hours before the event.

During the Event

Have you ever played a set of tennis in the blazing sun on a hot summer day or paddled a canoe or kayak for several hours on a river in the middle of August?

If so, you might have needed as much as 2 cups of water every 15 minutes in order to replace the fluids your body lost during heavy exercise in the extreme heat. Many athletes don't pay enough attention to fluid replacement, and it's critical to your health and optimal performance that you do.

Water is the best choice for exercise sessions or athletic events that last up to 90 minutes. After that, there's a benefit to getting some carbohydrate in addition to the water to help boost your blood sugar and prolong the period of time before your muscles tire out. There may also be some benefit to eating or drinking carbohydrate sooner than 90 minutes when the activity is of very high-intensity, such as racquetball or weight-training.

How much carbohydrate should you get?

Aim for about 30 to 80 grams of carbohydrate per hour. Sports drinks are fine for this purpose and may be more convenient than eating a solid food.

Heads Up!

It's important to drink $1/2$ cup to 1 cup of water every 10 to 20 minutes while you are exercising and, when possible, when you are competing. If you are working out in a gym, make it a point to take frequent breaks to visit the water fountain. One good gulp or several sips can equal $1/2$ cup to 1 cup of water. In other settings, keep a water bottle with you on a nearby bench, in your boat, or strapped to your bike.

An added advantage is that they provide fluid as well as carbohydrate. For most brands of commercial sports drinks, that means aiming for $1/2$ cup to 1 cup every 15 minutes, or twice as much every half hour. In lieu of a commercial sports drink, some people might prefer to drink fruit juice diluted 1:1 with water. For example, mix 2 cups of apple juice or cranberry juice with 2 cups of water, and drink it over a one hour period.

Fruit is also a good choice for a carbohydrate boost. A large banana contains at least 30 grams of carbohydrate, and so do two small oranges.

After the Event

After the event or exercise session, protein can come back to the table. Protein is needed for the repair of any damaged muscles. Your body also needs to replenish its stores of muscle and liver glycogen, amino acids, and fluids. So calories, protein, carbohydrate, and fluids are all very important immediately after an athletic event. The sooner you begin to replace these nutrients, the better. In fact, studies have shown that your body is more efficient at socking away glycogen in the minutes and hours immediately following the event than it is if you wait several hours before eating.

Tips of the Trade

A few last pointers for vegetarian athletes or any athlete who wants to maximize his or her athletic performance:

➤ If your calorie needs are high, add snacks between meals. Dried fruit mixtures, bagels, fresh fruit, soup and crackers, hot or cold cereal with soymilk, a half sandwich, soy yogurt or a smoothie, a bean burrito, or baked beans with toast are all excellent choices.

➤ If you have trouble getting enough calories with meals and snacks, reduce your intake of the bulkiest foods, such as salad greens and low-calorie vegetables, and eat more starchy vegetables such as potatoes, sweet potatoes, peas, beans, and lentils. Liquids can be an especially efficient way to add extra calories—try fruit or soy yogurt shakes and smoothies. Make your own blends using wheat germ, soy yogurt and soymilk, and frozen or fresh fruit. Remember too that some added vegetable fats can be fine for athletes who need a compact source of extra calories.

➤ Take a portable snack in your gym bag, backpack, or bike pack for immediately after your workout to replace carbohydrate and protein and provide calories. Fresh fruit, a sports bar, a bagel, or a package of crackers and bottle of fruit juice are good choices.

➤ Keep fluids with you when you work out—fruit juice, sports drinks, or bottled water.

➤ Don't work out when you're hungry. Your session will suffer. Take a break and have a light snack first.

➤ If you get the pre-event jitters, limit foods to those that are easy to digest and are low in fiber. Some athletes who get too nervous to eat any solid food before an event may find that it's possible to drink a smoothie or eat yogurt.

The Least You Need to Know

➤ Weekend athletes and most of us who exercise a few times a week for muscle tone and cardiovascular health have nutritional needs that are essentially the same as those who don't exercise.

➤ Elite athletes have higher protein needs than other people. Most can easily get the extra protein in the extra calories they consume.

➤ An athlete's diet should be primarily carbohydrate, with moderate amounts of protein and a small to moderate amount of fat from plant sources.

➤ Eat a high-carbohydrate, low-fat, low-protein meal up to four hours before an athletic event. Give yourself one hour before the event for every 200 calories you consume.

➤ During exercise, drink about $1/2$ to 1 cup of water every 10 to 20 minutes.

➤ Plan to eat soon after an event to replace carbohydrate, protein, and fluids.

Part 4
Making the Switch

You've got the nuts and bolts behind you: the who, what, and why, along with the nutrition basics. Now it's time for action.

The next few chapters will get you poised to start living the vegetarian way with good-sense advice and strategies for making the transition.

Chapter 13

Choosing the Approach: Gradual or Cold-Tofu?

In This Chapter

➤ Deciding on the approach: gradual versus overnight

➤ Weighing the pros and cons of each approach

➤ Steps to take for a smooth transition

➤ A sample schedule for changing over

➤ Tips to ease the way

"Where are you going?" the cat asked.
"I don't know."
"Well, either road will get you there."

[The Cheshire cat to Alice, who had lost her way.]
—From *Alice in Wonderland* by Lewis Carroll.

Don't be like Alice, who didn't know which route to take to get where she wanted to go. Without a plan, you're less likely to achieve your goal. When it comes to changing your eating style, *how* you do it isn't as important as having a plan in mind for getting there.

We all have different personalities and styles of doing things. What's important is that you find a method that works for you. There's no right or wrong way of making a lifestyle change, as long as you are successful. So do what's comfortable for you. This chapter covers some of the things you might want to think about in formulating your own plan of action.

Heads Up!

If you are a diabetic and switch to a vegetarian diet, you should pay your health care provider a visit. Diabetics who adopt a vegetarian diet frequently need less insulin or oral medication and need to have their dosages adjusted.

The Overnight Approach

One day he's chewing on a 10-ounce rib-eye at a local steakhouse, and the next day he's ordering the tempeh burger at his neighborhood natural foods cafe.

Not a likely scenario, but some people do make the decision to go vegetarian overnight. They see a video or hear a lecture that inspires them, or they read a book or article about the horrors of the slaughterhouse. Worse, they visit a slaughterhouse in person. Instant vegetarian.

The transition typically isn't flawless, but these people are motivated to make the change as soon as possible. Some people just prefer to make big changes quickly as opposed to dragging them out over months or years. That's fine.

The Pros of Instant Vegetarianism

There are some benefits to making the switch to a vegetarian diet in one fell swoop:

➤ *You get to enjoy the benefits sooner.* People who make big changes right away tend to notice the benefits sooner, especially if they have health concerns. For example, they may begin losing weight right away if they're overweight, or their blood sugar level may drop if they're diabetic. In some cases, blood sugar levels decrease enough to allow the medication to be discontinued altogether. However, don't attempt to change your medications without checking with your doctor or other health care provider first.

➤ *Immediate gratification.* Your personality may be such that you need the satisfaction that comes with taking immediate action and reaching your goal as soon as possible.

➤ *You know you'll get there in this lifetime.* In comparison to people who take the gradual approach, people who make the change all at once jump one big hurdle and arrive at their goal. They don't run the same risk that the others run of getting stuck in a rut along the way and never moving on to the goal.

The Cons

If you take the instant route to gratification, you'll soon find out you've got no time to develop the necessary new skills and to put supports in place. It takes time to soak up the background information about nutrition and meal planning, as well as learn how to deal with all sorts of practical issues such as eating out, handling questions from friends and family, and so on. These are some of the things that are necessary for a successful transition, and if they're not taken care of before you dive in, your entry can a bit sloppy, or you can do a big belly flop.

If you opt for the overnight approach, use your wits to do the best you can at the outset, but make it a point to come up with a plan for smoothing the transition as soon as possible. Get yourself educated, get a plan, and get some support as soon as possible (we'll discuss this more in Part 7, "Veggie Survival Strategies").

Helpful Hint

"Cold-tofus" are the folks I'm most likely to meet three years later who tell me, "I used to be a vegetarian, but now I eat some chicken and fish..." They're also the ones most likely to be living on iceberg lettuce salads, chewing their knuckles because they are hungry or have no energy.

Overnight Works Best When...

Some people don't have a choice. They may have witnessed a scene that won't let them ever again look at a package of hamburger the same way. They're going vegetarian, and there's no looking back. No time for planning, no time for reading up on the subject. Move over and make room at the salad bar.

If you make the decision to switch that quickly, then you'll need to do the best you can until you can get your hands on some resources to help you continue successfully on that path.

The overnight approach works best for people who:

➤ *Have done some homework.* Even a little bit of reading or talking with another vegetarian about basic nutrition questions and ideas for quick and easy meals can help immensely.

➤ *Are surrounded by support.* The overnight approach is easier for people who live or work with other vegetarians and have someone they can emulate or question about basic nutrition and meal-planning issues.

➤ *Are relatively free of other distractions.* It's easier to make a big change overnight if you don't have a new baby, a new job, or an 80-hour work week.

Heads Up!

If you have switched to a vegetarian diet but find yourself tired and hungry or irritable, you may not be eating enough. Some people who switch overnight haven't had time to figure out what they can eat. They end up eating only a few different types of foods, and they often don't get enough calories.

The Gradual Approach

Most people fare best taking the gradual approach to adopting a vegetarian diet, letting their diets evolve at their own pace as they master new skills and educate themselves about this new eating style. Eventually they become secure and comfortable with meal planning and handling a variety of food-related situations.

The Pros of Gradual

Other advantages to taking the gradual approach:

➤ *Your new eating habits are more likely to stick.* By making changes gradually as you collect the information and support you need to make it work, you build a strong foundation.

➤ *The gradual approach may be less disruptive to your routine,* since you have more time to adapt to each change every small step of the way.

The Cons

There are two disadvantages to taking the gradual approach as opposed to making the switch overnight. Keep these in mind and try to avoid them:

➤ *Getting stuck in a rut along the way.* You can get stuck anywhere along the line and never make the transition to a full-fledged vegetarian diet. Some people cut out red meat as one step toward a vegetarian diet, but never make it any further. They're forever stuck in the chicken and fish rut, and before long they're considering jumping off the Empire State Building. Or they get as far as substituting cheese and eggs for meat, but they don't get beyond it. Their blood-cholesterol levels are soaring because they're living on cheese omelets, macaroni and cheese, and grilled-cheese sandwiches. Don't let this happen to you. Have a plan to keep moving.

➤ *Procrastinating and dragging the change out too long.* Some people will grab any opportunity to take it easy. If you take too long to make the change, it may never happen. Don't delude yourself. If you want to adopt a vegetarian diet but it's been a year since you started, it's time to put pen to paper and develop a more structured plan with dated goals for getting there.

Steps for Making the Change

When you adopt a vegetarian eating style, you'll need to master skills in a variety of areas, including:

➤ Basic vegetarian nutrition

➤ Grocery shopping and stocking your kitchen with staples

➤ Meal planning and fixing new recipes

➤ Dealing with social situations surrounding family, friends, and business associates

➤ Eating away from home at the office, restaurants, school, friends' homes, or while traveling

➤ Establishing new food traditions for holidays and special occasions

Whether you choose to make the switch to a vegetarian diet overnight or gradually, there are a variety of ways in which you can tackle these areas of change. It's just a matter of personal preference. You may be especially interested in nutrition and devour books on the subject, or you may love to cook and find yourself experimenting with recipes long before you get around to thinking about vegetarian meals while traveling. You may like to read, or you may prefer talking to other vegetarians or attending lectures instead.

Whichever way you choose to proceed is up to you. The following guide is only one suggestion for planning a reasonably paced transition to a vegetarian eating style.

Break It Up

Have you ever had to write a term paper or thesis? Cringe! Any large project can seem overwhelming when you look at it in its entirety.

Instead, break the project up into smaller pieces, and focus on only one piece at a time. Psychologically, this may make it easier for you. It can also get you moving if dwelling on the immense size of the task causes you to become immobilized. Write down your steps if you'd like to, and check them off as you master each one. This can give you a sense of accomplishment and help keep you motivated along the way.

Heads Up!

It helps to set time goals in your plan for transitioning to a vegetarian diet. If you can keep these "deadlines" in your head, fine. If not, or if you find yourself dragging your feet getting to the next step, you may need more structure. Write your plan down on paper, and break it down week by week. Give yourself a reasonable amount of time to complete each task, and stick to your plan.

Draw up a weekly or monthly plan of action outlining the things upon which you want to focus each step of the way. For instance, you might want to concentrate on reading several books and other written materials for the first two months. From there, you might pick up a few vegetarian cookbooks and experiment with recipes, adding a few meatless meals per week to your schedule for the next month. You may step it up to five meatless days per week for the next few months, and begin attending your local vegetarian society's meetings.

Your plan should reflect your lifestyle, your personality and preferences for making these changes, and any constraints that may have to be factored in, such as cooking for a family, traveling frequently, and so on.

Read, Read, Read

If you're not a reader, skip to the next step. If you do like to read, however, there are many, many excellent resources. It's a great idea to spend several weeks to a few months reading everything you can get your hands on that pertains to vegetarian diets. There's a lot of material out there to help you. Reliable resources are listed in Chapter 26, "Getting Educated About Everything Vegetarian."

Some books and magazines may seem to cover the same subjects, but it's worth reading them all, because each author presents the information in his or her own style, and the repetition of the subject matter in different words can help you learn. You'll find materials on all aspects of vegetarianism. Read them, and you'll build a solid foundation for your transition.

Seek Out Other Resources

Once you begin to tap into books and magazines and other resources on vegetarianism, you'll become aware of videos, lectures, television programs, audiotapes, vegetarian groups, and other sources of information about a vegetarian lifestyle. Take advantage of them and soak up the information like a sponge. Right now you're in the information-gathering stage.

Begin Cutting Out Meat

While you're doing the background work, reading and soaking up other forms of information about vegetarian diets, you can start reducing your meat intake in some easy ways:

➤ Add two or three meatless main meals to your diet each week. Begin with some easy and familiar entrees, such as spaghetti with tomato sauce, vegetarian pizza, bean burritos, vegetable lasagna, and pasta primavera.

➤ Try some vegetarian convenience foods, such as veggie burger patties, veggie breakfast meats, frozen vegetarian dinners, veggie hotdogs, and others. They're quick and convenient. Many supermarkets now carry most or all of these, but you can find a large selection at natural foods stores. Substitute these foods for their meat counterparts.

➤ When you do eat meat, make it a minor part of the meal rather than the focal point of the plate. Use meat as more of a condiment or side dish. Keep portions small, and use it only in dishes in which the meat is extended by mixing it with rice, vegetables, pasta, or other plant products. For instance, rather than eating a chicken breast as the entree, cut it up and mix it into a big vegetable stir-fry that feeds four to six people.

Keep Going

From there, just keep going. Add a few more meatless meals to your weekly schedule and live with it for a month or so. Set a date beyond which you'll be eating only vegetarian meals. Mark that date with a big star on your calendar, then cross off each day that you're meat-free after that.

Practice, Practice, and Practice Some More

From this point on, it's all about practicing and continuing to expand your base of knowledge and experience. Expect some bumps in the road, but keep on going. Experiment with recipes, new foods, and vegetarian entrees at restaurants, invite friends and family over to your place for meals, read some more about nutrition and meal planning, and allow yourself more time to get comfortable with your new lifestyle.

The following table gives a reasonable timeline for someone making the switch to a vegetarian diet. Use it as a flexible guide to help you plan your own transition.

Twelve-Month Transition to a Vegetarian Eating Style

Time Frame	What to Do
First two months	*Read about basic nutrition, meal planning, dealing with social situations, and other aspects of vegetarian diets.* Check books out at the library, buy a few good resources at the bookstore, send away to vegetarian organizations for materials, and subscribe to vegetarian magazines. Attend lectures, listen to audiotapes, or view videos on the subject. Absorb information.
Month three	*Begin to reduce your meat intake.* Add two or three meatless meals to your repertoire each week, experiment with new products, make a list of all of the vegetarian foods that you already enjoy, and when you do eat meat, make it a minor part of the meal, rather than the focal point of the plate.
Months four through six	*Cut back even more on your meat intake.* Plan five meatless days each week. Limit meat use as a condiment or side dish or minor ingredient in a dish. Plan a cutoff date after which you'll move on to all vegetarian meals. Mark that date on your calendar. A week or two before that date, stop buying meat and products containing meat, such as soup with ham or bacon and baked beans with pork.

continues

Twelve-Month Transition to a Vegetarian Eating Style   (continued)

Time Frame	What to Do
	Keep a diary or log of everything you eat for several days. You'll refer to it later to gauge your progress. Be specific about the ingredients. For example, if you eat a sandwich, make note of the kind of bread and filling you chose.
Months six through eight	*Look into joining a local vegetarian society or attending a national vegetarian conference.* Continue reading and absorbing information. Continue experimenting with new recipes. Go out to eat and order vegetarian entrees at restaurants.
Months eight through 12	*Practice.* Continue to seek new information. Socialize and invite friends and family to your home for vegetarian meals. Look back over the past year and evaluate how you have handled holidays and special occasions, vacations, and breaks in your routine. Are there situations that need attention, such as eating away from home or finding quick and easy meal ideas? Keep a food diary for several days and compare it to your first one.

More Tips for Getting from Here to There

You're on your way! Now, here are some more tips to make the journey a little easier.

Make a List of Foods You Like

For those who are just starting out, make a list of the vegetarian foods that you already enjoy, and fix them often.

You probably already eat a number of vegetarian foods, but you haven't thought of them as being vegetarian until now. Here are some examples:

➤ Vegetable stir-fry over rice

➤ Macaroni and cheese

➤ Vegetarian lasagna

➤ Tomato sandwiches

➤ Pancakes

➤ Bean burritos and tacos

➤ Grilled-cheese sandwiches

➤ Spaghetti with tomato sauce

➤ Pasta with pesto

➤ Pasta primavera

➤ Spinach pie

➤ Lentil soup

➤ Minestrone soup

➤ Baked potato topped with broccoli and cheese

Some of your other favorite foods can probably be easily modified to make them vegetarian. Some examples:

➤ *Chili.* Make it with beans instead of meat.

➤ *Bean soups.* Leave out the ham or bacon.

➤ *Sandwiches.* Load up on lettuce, tomatoes, mustard, chopped or shredded vegetables, add a little cheese if you like, and leave out the meat. Use pita pockets, hard rolls, and whole-grain breads to give sandwiches more personality.

➤ *Burgers.* Buy veggie burger patties instead.

➤ *Breakfast meats.* Use veggie versions of link sausage or patties and veggie bacon. They taste great and can replace meat at breakfast or in a BLT.

➤ *Hotdogs and luncheon meats.* Buy veggie versions. All natural foods stores carry them, and so do some supermarkets. They look and taste like the real thing but are far better for you.

➤ *Meatloaf.* Even that all-American food can be made with lentils, chopped nuts, grated vegetables, and other ingredients. Vegetarian cookbooks include several variations. They're delicious.

➤ *Pasta sauces.* Why add meat or meat flavorings when you have basil, oregano, mushrooms, red peppers, sun-dried tomatoes, pimentos, black olives, and scores of other delicious ingredients to give sauces flavor? Great on cannelloni, stuffed shells, manicotti, ravioli, and fettuccine.

➤ *Stuffed cabbage.* Instead of pork, fill cabbage leaves with a mixture of rice, garbanzo beans, and seasonings. It's worth perusing vegetarian cookbooks for gems like this one.

Be Kind to Yourself

Many people are their own worst critics. While you don't want to delude yourself into thinking that you're making progress when you're not, you also don't want to be too harsh with yourself if you have a setback now and then. Change takes time and patience.

Occasional slips are normal. If you have to eat cereal for dinner for an entire week, or if you have to pick the pepperoni off the pizza rather than refusing it altogether at a friend's house on Super Bowl Sunday, don't let it get you down. If you have a lapse from your plan, pick up where you left off and start again. No one is keeping score but you.

The Last Bite

Be aware that interruptions in your routine, such as a vacation, holiday, or sickness, can trigger a lapse in your eating plan. In times of stress or a break in the usual routine, it's common for people to fall back into old familiar patterns, including old ways of eating. Give yourself a break, then start fresh again. With time, you'll learn how to handle these breaks in routine and won't be derailed.

Browse Through Vegetarian Cookbooks

Go to the library and check out all of the vegetarian cookbooks that you can find. If you have a friend who's a vegetarian, borrow his or her cookbooks. Then begin to page through each one. Read the names of the recipes. If you see one that grabs you, look at the ingredient list. If it inspires you, fix it. When you find a cookbook with lots of recipes that appeal to you, go to a bookstore and buy it, or order it by mail from a vegetarian organization or catalog. Natural foods stores also carry a good selection of popular vegetarian cookbooks.

Do this to orient yourself to the options on a vegetarian diet. You'll be surprised at the variety. You may also notice lots of ethnic foods borrowed from cultures that have vegetarian traditions. There's more variety on a vegetarian diet than on a meat-centered diet, and reviewing cookbooks will help you see that.

Tour a Natural Foods Store

Head to your neighborhood natural foods store. Walk up and down all of the aisles, including the frozen foods case. You'll find dozens of vegetarian foods. Buy a few on this trip, then try a few more next time.

When you sample new products, expect to find a few duds. That comes with the territory. Try another brand of the same type of product, since there can be a lot of variation from one brand to the next. Once you start experimenting with new foods, you'll discover a long list of great products that will become regulars in your repertoire.

Accentuate the Positive

Some people hit the floor happy each morning, and others have to work at it. Likewise, some people see the fun in a challenge, and others just see the challenge.

Many people think of the restrictions when they visualize a vegetarian diet. They focus on the "don'ts"—don't eat hamburger, steak, fish, shrimp, chicken, turkey, sausage, hotdogs, gelatin, beef broth, chicken fat, and so on. They see a big hole in the middle of their plates where the meat used to be.

It's a mindset and an attitude. It doesn't have to be that way.

Any experienced vegetarian will tell you that there is more variety on a vegetarian diet than on a nonvegetarian diet: more choices, more interesting foods, and no bare spots on their plates.

That's another mindset, and a positive attitude. Try to keep all of the good choices in mind when you think about meal planning, and don't bother to waste energy thinking about what you used to eat. In time, you won't even have to try. Eventually, you'll reach the point where meat and meat products don't even cross your mind.

Helpful Hint

Keeping a food diary can help you chart your progress as you adopt a vegetarian eating style. It can be fun to compare "before" and "after." Keep a log of what you eat each day for several days at the outset of your transition, then file it away. Six months later, keep another log for several more days. Compare this one to the first one and note the changes. You can do this every so often to help you evaluate your progress. A food diary can also help you recognize if you are stuck in a rut.

The Least You Need to Know

➤ There's no right or wrong way to make the transition to a vegetarian diet. Choose an approach that is comfortable for you.

➤ If you go vegetarian overnight, begin to educate yourself about nutrition and meal planning, and find sources of support as soon as possible to help you successfully maintain your new eating style.

➤ If you choose the gradual approach, be sure not to get stuck in a rut. Set clear goals and evaluate your progress from time to time.

➤ Lapses are normal. If you fall back into your old pattern of eating for a day or two, just pick up where you left off and go back to vegetarian meals as soon as possible.

➤ Keep a positive attitude and focus on the many vegetarian foods from which you have to choose, rather than on the meat that you don't want to eat anymore.

Chapter 14

Are We in This Together?

In This Chapter

➤ Issues to consider when you're in a mixed relationship

➤ How to handle family meals when you're the only vegetarian

➤ Improving the odds that your family will be receptive

➤ Rules of the house and how to negotiate them

➤ Relating to others beyond your own four walls

Some food fights are easy to settle. He likes chunky and she likes creamy? Keep two jars of peanut butter in the cupboard. Big deal. Butter versus margarine, mayo against Miracle Whip. If only all differences in food preferences were so easy to handle.

If you're a vegetarian, chances are good that you're the only one in your household. Like May–December romances, partnerships between a steak-and-potatoes type and a Buddha's delight can present extraordinary challenges. An awareness of the issues and the manner in which you approach those challenges can spell success or disaster for your relationships.

Of course, many people will find that going vegetarian poses no particular problems and that their families, partners, and roommates will fall easily into line with their new lifestyle. This chapter, however, is for those whose choice is being met with resistance from family and friends.

WASH ME

Helpful Hint

If you get into a relationship with someone who isn't a vegetarian, don't bank on him or her changing. If he or she does, great. If not, be prepared to negotiate your lifestyle together. Being realistic about such matters can potentially avert traumatic realizations and disappointments down the road when the person you thought would eventually see it your way doesn't. Used-to-be-vegetarians are often people who were once pushed into it by a partner or friend.

This chapter will help you sort out the issues and help you plan your strategy for dealing with mixed marriages (and other food-related relationships) and preserving the harmony at family meals. We'll also cover some public-relations tips for maximizing the potential for success in relationships outside your immediate circles.

Odds Are You're Going It Alone

Vegetarian and natural-living magazines feature classifieds for vegetarian singles seeking other vegetarian singles. But most of these folks will be members of the lonely hearts club for a long time unless they relent and let a nonvegetarian into their lives. After all, true vegetarians are only about 1 percent of the population. Sad but true.

The vast majority of vegetarians are unique in their households. If you're going it alone at home, there are numerous issues that will have to be addressed by you and your partner and immediate family. Some will be unique to your living situation, but some challenges are common to many others in your predicament.

One Meal or Two?

Should you fix a standard meat-two-vegetables-a-starch-and-a-salad meal, and just let the vegetarian dodge the meat and fill up on the rest? Or do you fix a separate entree for the vegetarian?

Some families feel burdened by this problem. Nobody wants to get stuck cooking two meals for the same table. Should the meals be vegetarian, so that everyone can eat them? After all, there are lots of meatless dishes that most nonvegetarians enjoy.

No answers here. Like the other questions that follow, this is a situation that requires discussion and negotiation among all parties concerned. Unless you face it head on, it will bite you from behind.

Should the Vegetarian Be Expected to Cook Meat?

Let's say that you're the head cook in your household, and you're a vegetarian. Should you be expected to fix meat for nonvegetarian members of the household?

This one would probably be easier to tackle if you were already a vegetarian coming into the relationship, and the expectation that you would not handle or touch meat was set up front. If you've had a change of heart and become a vegetarian after the fact, it may be a touchier issue. After all, now you're upsetting the apple cart.

Is there a sous-chef in your home? Maybe it's time for a nonvegetarian member of your household to learn how to cook meat. You can prepare meals together, and you can be in charge of everything but the meat. On the other hand, you might not want to be subjected to the smell of cooking meat, and you might not want meat to touch your kitchen counter or pots and pans. I don't blame you. But you'll have to hash this one out with your family. It may help to know that you're not alone. There are lots of people like you out there.

What About the Kids?

If you are a vegetarian parent partnered with a nonvegetarian, what will you feed your children? Of all the situations that mixed relationships face, this one has the potential to raise the roof the highest.

Nothing seems to charge the emotions like issues surrounding kids. If you have an opportunity to discuss this one before you have children, you may be able to diminish the problems. (You'll still have to deal with your extended family, but that's another chapter.) If not, then you will have to negotiate what your kids will eat, where, and when.

Some families make the decision that meals at home will be vegetarian, but away from home, it's every man, woman, and child for themselves. Others serve meat at home and let each individual decide for themselves what they will eat, with no pushing or prodding one way or another.

Helpful Hint

If you are having difficulty negotiating issues surrounding meals with your significant other or your family, it might help to talk to other vegetarians who have dealt with the same issues. Consider getting online and joining in on some of the vegetarian chats on the Internet. You can locate vegetarian chat groups through some of the resources listed in Part 7, "Veggie Survival Strategies."

Helpful Hint

Vegetarian diets can be healthful for children of all ages and can help establish a pattern of good eating habits that will be carried into adulthood.

If your child's diet is nonnegotiable for you and you want it to be vegetarian, then you'll have to work that out with your partner and define the terms. A marriage counselor may be able to help if you find your discussions getting contentious.

Be sure to check out Chapters 9, "Vegetarian Baby and Toddler," and 10, "Kids' Stuff or Adults Only? Vegetarian Diets for Children and Teens," for information about vegetarian diets for children, from babies to teens.

When the Boss Comes to Dinner

You're the family chef, and you're a vegetarian, but you're expecting guests for dinner, and it's not likely that they share your preference. Neither does the rest of your family. What do you serve?

There's more than one option, but it's another example of the kinds of situations that you are likely to encounter and have to negotiate in your relationships at home. In this case, if you don't want to fix meat yourself, you could have that part of the meal catered. You might opt to avoid the whole problem by taking your guests to a restaurant where they can order what they like. If you want to eat in but prefer that there be no meat in your home whatsoever, that's okay too. You'll need your family's support, though. Gotta talk about it.

Many other similar issues are likely to arise in mixed households. It's a good idea to try to anticipate them and discuss them with your partner and family before they cause too much conflict.

Keeping the Peace at the Family Table

It can be easier to find solutions to problems when you have some ideas about how other people have solved similar problems. When it comes to handling family meals, there are several options that might work for you as they've worked for others. Since every family is different, though, you might have to adapt these ideas to fit your own circumstances. At the least, they may spur you to think of a workable solution.

Separate Styles, Separate Entrees

This works best when the vegetarian is also the family chef. It's the most obvious solution, but it's also the most work.

The idea is simple: Fix a full-fledged, standard meat-containing meal for those who eat meat, and fix a separate, vegetarian entree for those who don't. The vegetarian can eat the vegetarian entree as well as the nonmeat components of the rest of the meal.

There's a hidden strategy here for the vegetarians. As any experienced vegetarian knows, the vegetarian option tends to look really tasty. Try setting a vegetarian pizza on the table with other pizzas at a party or any gathering. If you're vegetarian, you'd better grab fast, because all the nonvegetarians are going to want the vegetarian choice. Likewise, put a bowl of pasta topped with a marinara sauce on the table side by side with pasta and meat sauce. Conduct a bit of research, and see which bowl empties fastest. I'll put my money on the marinara—I've seen it happen too many times.

So, the strategy is that if you set out vegetarian entrees, everyone else is going to want them too. Eventually, you may be making nothing but vegetarian meals. The others may not even notice the transition. And all that arguing and teeth gnashing was for nothing.

Eat What You Can

Another option, of course, is for the vegetarian to simply eat large servings of whatever meatless foods are on the table. Mashed potatoes, steamed broccoli, salad, and a dinner roll make a great meal. There doesn't have to be a hole on your plate where the meat should be. You can cover that bare spot up with extra servings of the foods you like.

This is the same approach that many vegetarians use when they eat out at the homes of friends or others who don't serve vegetarian meals. They eat what they can of the meatless foods available. They don't draw attention to themselves (some vegetarians prefer it that way), and they don't give others the impression that it's hard to be a vegetarian in a nonvegetarian culture by whining about not having an entree.

This approach is passive and fairly nonconfrontational. Problems are most likely to arise if another family member becomes threatened by the fact that you are behaving outside the norm of the family. For some, it may appear that you are rejecting family values and traditions. You're not, of course. You're just changing them.

Heads Up!

Rarely does arguing and cajoling convince others to adopt your vegetarian eating style. In fact, taking the pushy route usually has the opposite result: People will resent the pressure and push right back the opposite way. Instead, play it cool and let them drool over your vegetarian foods instead. If they're good, let them have one bite. Eventually, they'll probably come around. At least part of the time.

The Last Bite

Food plays an important role in family traditions around the world. When you make a switch to a vegetarian eating style, you'll find new traditions to replace the old. For instance, instead of a Thanksgiving turkey, your family may serve a stuffed squash, a vegetable-walnut loaf, or a tofu "turkey." Whatever foods you substitute for meat will become the new favorites. Over time, they'll be just as much a source of enjoyment and tradition as the old foods.

The Vegetarian Least Common Denominator

Another sensible approach is to consider vegetarian foods to be the least common denominator. In other words, everyone—vegetarians and nonvegetarians alike—can eat vegetarian foods, so when you plan meals for the family or just the two of you, start with vegetarian choices. Choose foods that are vegetarian as prepared but to which a nonvegetarian can add meat if he or she so chooses.

For example, make a stir-fry using assorted vegetables, and serve it on steamed rice. A nonvegetarian can cook chicken (or shrimp, or beef) separately and cut it up into cubes and add it to his own dish. Rather than actually making two different entrees, you're modifying an entree for a meat eater. That should be considerably easier than fixing two distinct dishes.

All of the following foods are vegetarian as prepared or can easily be made without meat. Meat eaters can add small bits of meat (such as chicken or fish) if they so desire.

Vegetarian Dishes Easily Adapted for Meat Eaters

Bean burritos, nachos, or tacos

Italian stuffed shells, manicotti, cannelloni, or spaghetti with marinara sauce

Mixed green salad (large dinner-style)

Pasta primavera

Pesto pasta

Vegetable jambalaya

Vegetable lasagna with marinara sauce

Vegetable stir-fry

Vegetable soups or stews

Vegetarian chili

Vegetarian pizza

Vegetarian Consensus

If your family is congenial enough, you may be able to get away with making all vegetarian meals, providing the group likes the choices. Whether you go vegetarian all of the time or part of the time, it's a good idea to go out of your way to make foods that everyone likes.

So, begin by making a list of all of the family's favorite foods that just happen to be vegetarian. For instance, your list might include:

➤ Macaroni and cheese

➤ Grilled-cheese sandwiches

➤ Bean soup

➤ Minestrone soup

➤ Stuffed baked potatoes (with grated cheese and chopped broccoli)

➤ Most of the foods found earlier in the list of easily adapted vegetarian dishes

To that list, you can add some *transition foods* that appeal to most people. Transition foods are foods that look and taste like familiar meat-based foods. Examples include:

➤ Vegetarian burger patties and hotdogs

➤ Vegetarian cold cuts for sandwiches

➤ Vegetarian bacon and sausage links and patties

➤ Frozen, crumbled textured vegetable protein (for recipes that call for ground beef)

Finally, experiment with ethnic foods and other new vegetarian recipes. Let family members have input into planning, and incorporate their preferences into the menu. Before long, you'll have a list of family favorites a mile long.

Veggie Talk

Transition foods help meat eaters cross over to a vegetarian diet. These foods taste good and can be used in the same ways as their meat counterparts. Examples include veggie burgers and veggie hotdogs. Transition foods act like crutches or training wheels until the person becomes more comfortable planning meals without meat.

Get Them in the Mood

You can take some simple steps to make the other members of your household more receptive to vegetarian meals.

Give Them Something Good

First, remember that you're asking them to trade in some of their favorite foods. What would it take for you to give up something that you liked, or at least were familiar and comfortable with?

You'd probably want a substitute that tastes as good as or better than the food you gave up. You wouldn't want to be inconvenienced. You wouldn't want the change to leave you feeling less than satisfied with your meals.

Keep that in mind when you ask for your family's support. Make their favorite vegetarian foods often.

Give Them a Voice

People who are involved in any aspect of meal planning are more likely to be interested in eating the food. Get the family or your partner involved in meal planning to the extent that they want to be:

➤ Grow some of your own vegetables and herbs

➤ Ask for input about daily meal ideas and preferences

➤ Shop together

➤ Prepare meals together

➤ Plan menus together for special occasions and when guests visit

Don't Push

It's that simple. When you preach and push people to do something that they aren't ready to do, you'll probably get the opposite result.

Instead, teach by your own example. If your family or partner isn't ready to make a switch to a vegetarian diet, then quietly go about your life. Your actions will speak volumes, and the chances are good that, given time, the others will notice, get interested, and make some dietary changes of their own.

Here's a real life example:

My mother has been a vegetarian since I was a child. I remember the day that she went vegetarian.

I grew up in a typical, traditional, Midwestern meat-and-potatoes household. One day, my mother called the family to the table for dinner. We were all seated except my mother. She came to the table, but before sitting down, she briefly announced to us that from that day forward she would be a vegetarian. She didn't say another word about it. No explanation except, "This is what I've decided is right for me." She sat down, and we ate our dinner.

My mother didn't discuss her vegetarianism with anyone. With the exception of her family and close friends, most people didn't even realize that she didn't eat meat. At family meals, she continued to prepare meat for my father and my siblings, and then she would make a cheese omelet or toasted cheese sandwich for herself (a Wisconsonite stuck in the cheese-and-eggs rut) and eat the salad and vegetables along with it.

Time went by. Then, one by one, my sisters and brother and I went vegetarian ourselves. Nobody offered more of an explanation than to say to our mother, "You don't have to fix meat for me anymore." Eventually, the only person my mother was fixing meat for was my father. Many years later, meat also faded out of my father's diet.

Decades later, we're all still vegetarians.

There's no reasonable alternative if you want others to change. Ultimately, we all have to concern ourselves with our own food choices and let others choose for themselves too.

Put Your Best Food Forward

When people say that all they care about is how the food tastes, don't believe them. Appearances count. Food that is presented attractively *looks* like it tastes better. It sets the expectation that this food is going to be good.

Set an attractive table. Use a tablecloth or place mats. Place a vase with a sprig of foliage or flowers from the yard on the table. Show that you care.

Arrange foods in serving bowls or on plates with a little flair. It doesn't take much to toss a snip of parsley on top or to add a slice of fruit as a garnish on the side. Let's say that you've made French toast using soymilk and bananas instead of eggs and milk. You'd like your family to love this new breakfast concept. Instead of bringing the French toast to the table in a big stack on a utilitarian plate, slice each piece diagonally, fan the pieces out across a platter, and sprinkle them lightly with confectioner's sugar. Serve warm maple syrup in a small pitcher.

It's All About Attitude, After All

Attitude really is everything. If you present new foods with an upbeat, positive attitude, they're much more likely to be accepted. Show that you're interested in what others think of the food and that you'd like them to like it. Tell them about the dish you've made. Is it a staple in India? Can you eat it with your fingers?

Don't try to fake it, though, unless you're a professional actor. Overzealousness is usually not appreciated, either. Just be yourself, and others will be more likely to share your enthusiasm.

Rules of the House

In addition to working out a plan for family meals that promotes harmony among all members, you may also have to discuss how you'll handle such regular events as guests coming to stay at your house and friends dropping over and remaining for dinner.

For some people, these situations are nothing to get too excited over. It's business as usual. Whichever way the family has worked things out, it stays that way while the visitors are present.

After all, "When in Rome..." right?

It's not that easy for some people. Especially between partners, this kind of situation can cause friction, particularly when the lifestyle of the vegetarian in the household is still seen as an intrusion or unwelcome deviation from the norm. Having outsiders come in can cause built-up tensions to flare.

The meat eater's point of view may be that, if eating meat is the norm of the guests, the preferences of the majority should rule. Even attention drawn to the "vegetarian thing" may be unwelcome. In some homes, the nonvegetarian may feel uncomfortable with discussions about vegetarianism in the presence of guests. It's bad enough in the privacy of the home, but exposing such "eccentricities" to people outside the family can be embarrassing for people who think there's something "too different" about it.

In some circles, vegetarianism may be no big deal. In fact, there may well be other vegetarians among your guests. In that case, many people are comfortable having some vegetarian dishes and some meat dishes available, with everyone free to choose what they please. But if you are living with someone who doesn't support your choice of diet, it's a good idea to get the issue on the table and resolved before your guests arrive. You may decide to eat out, or you may opt to bring take-out food home. However you solve the dilemma, the important thing is to anticipate the problem and try to find a solution ahead of time. Then enjoy the visit.

Vegetarian PR, or How Not to Be a Nut Among the Berries

You may be a card-carrying vegetarian, but the manner in which you present your lifestyle to the world will make the difference between you being pegged a proselytizer or a model citizen. Hint: People really dislike self-righteous evangelists. You'll find it much easier to get along in the nonvegetarian world if people don't cringe when they see you coming.

There's a greater potential for you to "do good" and make a positive difference in the world if you present yourself in a way that leaves other people open to you and your message rather than making them feel shut out and defensive. Your vegetarian lifestyle choice will affect other people, whether they know it or not. It's probably going to make them stop and think about their own choices. This is your golden opportunity to teach others about the advantages of vegetarianism by being a role model.

The Making of a Diplomat

You may be quite content to live your vegetarian lifestyle without explaining your choice to anyone or attempting to convert them. If so, then you are probably the type that won't rub other people the wrong way. You're an undercover vegetarian rather than a walking and talking advocate. That's fine. Even in your relative silence, you're making a statement.

On the other hand, if you frequently find yourself engaged in debates or earnest discussions with other people about the merits of a vegetarian diet—whether you initiate the conversations or not—then it's a good idea to give some thought to your approach in handling these interactions.

Whether you just want people to leave you alone and let you live the life you choose or you hope to inspire others to consider adopting a vegetarian lifestyle, *diplomacy* is key. You're going to need to develop skills in dealing with social situations in which your vegetarian lifestyle converges with the nonvegetarian world. Those skills will come with time and experience. In the meantime, the material presented here provides some reality-based suggestions for you to consider in deciding what your own style will be in dealing with others.

The Big Turnoff: In-Your-Face Ethics

Maybe you've seen the fashion "dos" and "don'ts" features in women's magazines—photos of people who have their looks perfectly and tastefully coordinated versus the ones with visible panty lines, long skirts with short coats, and other fashion gaffes. Your physical appearance can give people the impression that you have it all together or that you're a frazzled wreck.

Similarly, the manner in which you conduct yourself in the presence of others also affects the way in which you are perceived. People who are belligerent, bossy, or brash come off as being uncouth. Even if their point of view is valid, others are likely to discount the message at best or be totally repulsed and reject it outright at worst.

Veggie Talk

Diplomacy as defined by *Webster's* is "skill in handling affairs without arousing hostility." Diplomacy is a key to getting along with non-vegetarians.

The Last Bite

Some people feel that the in-your-face approach has a place. Opinions are neither right nor wrong, of course. The bra burners of the 1960s drew attention to women's rights issues with their very visible demonstrations of activism, while most women advocated for change in subtler ways. Likewise, a peace activist may wage a hunger strike to draw attention to the cause while others promote peace behind the scenes. Ultimately, it's up to you how—and if—you advocate for vegetarianism. Attacking others, however, is a negative approach that is likely to alienate others and make them less receptive to your message.

Speak When Spoken to

"Why did you become a vegetarian?"

Most vegetarians have heard that question at least 25 times.

"If you don't eat meat, how do you get enough protein?"

They've heard that one just as many times.

"What do you eat for dinner?"

"Don't you miss meat?" (Alternate version: "Don't you just want a good steak once in a while?")

"If you're a vegetarian, why do you wear leather shoes?"

When someone inquires about your vegetarianism, the best response is a simple, straightforward answer. You don't have to expound on the basics. Just the facts will do. This is generally also not the time for the hard sell, nor is it the time to push someone else's buttons by criticizing that person's lifestyle.

You'll need to use your own judgement, but most of the time when people ask questions such as these, they're just exploring. They may not know much about vegetarianism, but you've piqued their interest. They may also be testing to determine what you're all about. Answer their questions concisely, but leave 'em wanting more. They'll ask when they want to know—and they may start asking you how they can become vegetarians themselves.

The Last Bite

Bumper stickers, buttons, and T-shirts with vegetarian slogans express your politics loud and clear. One makes a statement. Two emphasize the point. But when your car and body are blanketed with these items, you are shouting. Some people may perceive you to be hysterical, depending upon the degree of coverage of your car and clothing. Consider that there may be a point of diminishing returns in terms of the extent to which people will listen to you when you express your views this way.

Give Vegetarians a Good Name

The world would be a better place if more people were vegetarians. Those of us who have already made the switch know how nice it can be to live a vegetarian lifestyle. A vegetarian lifestyle is good for you, good for the animals, and good for our environment and planet.

The truth is, it's not particularly difficult to be a vegetarian, and there are many benefits. Why not advertise that fact? Some vegetarians present themselves in a way that makes it appear to be difficult and problematic to live a vegetarian lifestyle. Instead, aim for showing people how easy and pleasurable a vegetarian lifestyle can be. Take the positive tack if you'd like other people to give vegetarianism serious consideration.

Be Flexible

All vegetarians get stuck at a truck stop or a KFC once in a while, where there's virtually nothing on the menu that they'd eat. Those are the times when you kick into survival mode and take a can of juice or a soft drink and a bag of chips and just hang on until the next opportunity to eat some real food.

Most of the time, though, vegetarians have plenty of food choices, or they can make do with what there is. Whether you're a guest at someone's home, eating out on business, traveling, or out with friends, try to be flexible when it comes to your meals. By being flexible, you show others that you can be a vegetarian in this nonvegetarian society without your lifestyle creating too much conflict. It's a positive message, though it's very easy to project just the opposite message.

This is especially true for vegans. Vegans do find it more difficult than other types of vegetarians to eat away from home, especially when they're in the company of nonvegetarians or nonvegans and don't have total control over where the group goes to eat.

I remember an occasion when I was with a group of people, including two vegans, at a conference in Kansas City. When it came time to find a place to have dinner the first night, we literally roamed the streets for over an hour, wearily walking into one restaurant after another, reading the menus, finding few vegan options, and walking out again. Eventually, after everyone was frustrated and overly hungry, we settled on a Chinese restaurant and ate there every night thereafter for the rest of that week.

The Last Bite

Some vegetarians eat a vegan diet at home but occasionally make exceptions and eat foods containing dairy and/or eggs when they're away and have limited choices. The reason: They'd prefer not to isolate themselves socially from nonvegans to the extent that they might have to if they were to adhere strictly to a vegan lifestyle. They feel that by being "90 percent of the way there" they are achieving most of the benefits of a vegan lifestyle without sending others a negative message. It's the old argument of "diminishing returns." In setting an example for others, it may be more important to inspire lots of people to drastically reduce their intake of animal products than it is to inspire one or two to go vegan.

The impression I was left with was that it was no fun at all to be a vegan, and that it was tiresome and difficult to find something to eat away from home. In a mixed group of vegetarians and nonvegetarians, or vegans and nonvegans, it's better to avoid this kind of experience. Instead, anticipate the limitations and try to preempt them. Steer your party to a restaurant at which you'll be most likely to have choices right from the start. If you can't do that, then do your best to make do wherever you land.

Fill Your Plate

Show people that eating a vegetarian diet doesn't mean that you have to go hungry when you eat meals away from home. Fill up your plate with food. Let people see how colorful and appealing a meal without meat can be. Don't leave a hole on your plate or allow it to look empty as if you're deprived.

Be Positive in Your Outlook

Sometimes it's a matter of personality—some people are just naturally more cheerful than others. As much as possible, though, try to be positive in the way you interact with others where food is concerned. Your attitude will reflect on how people feel about you, and they will associate that feeling with how they feel about the concept of vegetarianism.

Reconciling Your Approach

Just as your decision to live a vegetarian lifestyle is a personal one, the manner in which you interact with other people is also your call. You can be tolerant or intolerant, kind and compassionate or confrontational.

Your approach may be different than another's. A concession on the part of one near-vegan to eat a food containing dairy or egg when they're away from home may be completely unacceptable to another vegan, just as someone's decision to eat a piece of turkey at Thanksgiving might be an abhorrent choice to other vegetarians.

In understanding others' choices, it can help to remember how complicated and deeply personal the subject of vegetarianism can be for everyone. Reconcile your approach as you see fit. Then work at projecting a positive image. Show others that you are confident, content, and at ease with your lifestyle.

The Least You Need to Know

➤ Most people are the only vegetarians in their households.

➤ Talk through meal planning with all family members concerned and negotiate a solution.

➤ Don't push others to adopt a vegetarian eating style. Instead, quietly pursue your diet choices and set the example without pressure on others to follow you.

➤ Many vegetarian foods are familiar favorites for everyone. Serve those often.

➤ Present vegetarian foods attractively and project a positive attitude about them.

➤ Discuss the rules of the house pertaining to entertaining guests in your home. Do it well before your company arrives.

Chapter 15

Avoiding the Coke and French Fries Trap: Assorted Practical Pointers

In This Chapter

➤ Don't lose sleep over the nutrition

➤ March to your own drummer

➤ Who's weird?

➤ How to go veg all the way: food, clothes, cosmetics, the works

➤ How not to be a casualty of the vegan ideal

At this point, you may be distracted by such errant thoughts as, "I need a degree in nutrition to get this right," or "I wonder if I'll be vegetarian enough?" Your mind may be leaping ahead to such concerns as, "Is my aberrant lifestyle going to ruin my chances of making partner in the firm?"

This chapter will help you put some of these issues into perspective.

You Can Be Your Own Nutritionist

In the opening of his book, *Baby and Child Care* (Pocket Books, 1998), Dr. Benjamin Spock wrote these famous words: "Trust yourself. You know more than you think you do." Likewise, while you may not have studied the metabolic sequence of the Krebs Cycle or be able to calculate an individual's caloric needs, if you're reading this book, you probably have enough gumption to get your diet mostly right.

The science of nutrition is complicated, but being well-nourished is a fairly simple matter. While it may sound strange coming from a nutritionist, there really is no need to become overly anxious about nutrition on a vegetarian diet. Remember: The primary reasons that people get up in arms over vegetarian diets is that they are a) uninformed and b) unfamiliar with the many vegetarian societies outside our culture.

When nutrition is an issue, it's not because vegetarian diets are lacking in necessary nutrients. It's because many people in our society don't eat well, whether they're vegetarian or not. Poor nutrition is a function of lifestyle in general. The greatest threats? Time and junk.

Helpful Hint

It may cost more if someone peels your carrots and washes your lettuce for you, but buying washed and cut fresh fruits and vegetables can be worth the extra cost if you end up eating more of them more frequently.

Do You Have the Time?

A friend once said, "Time is the only truly nonrenewable resource." He was so right.

How you spend your time is just as important as how you spend your money, or more so.

Since time is such a valuable commodity these days, we prioritize how we spend it. After all, there are only so many hours in a day. With all of the obligations that most of us juggle each day—work, family, keeping in shape, mowing the lawn, grocery shopping—it's no wonder peeling potatoes and assembling a casserole have been relegated to the back of the line. Many of us just don't take the time to fix meals from scratch any more. If it can't be on the table in 10 minutes or less (or eaten out of a bag), we don't eat.

When you depend on others to make your meals for you—food companies, fast-food joints, and the restaurant down the street—you lose a great deal of control over what goes into those meals, including how much salt and sugar they contain, what kind of fat is used, and how much. You're also more likely to choose impulsively, and choices made when you are overly hungry or stressed are less likely to be healthful.

The challenge, then, is finding ways to prepare good-tasting, health-supporting meals in a minimum of time at home. (Chapter 19, "When There's No Time to Cook: Quick and Easy Meals and Snacks," will get you started with some tips and ideas.)

The Last Bite

Some people think that vegetarian meals take longer to prepare because they contain vegetables that have to be peeled and chopped. Actually, any healthful diet contains plenty of fresh fruits and vegetables that may need some degree of preparation. One way to cut down on the time it takes to prepare a meal is to do some prep ahead of time. For instance, when you bring groceries home, take 10 or 15 minutes right away to wash, peel, and chop such items as carrots, broccoli and cauliflower florets, onions, and green peppers. Store them in an airtight container in the refrigerator. Later, when you're ready to make a stir-fry, salad, or vegetable lasagna, they'll be ready to use. Prep work is the last thing most people feel like doing when they're hungry and want to fix dinner in a hurry with a minimum of fuss.

Jettison the Junk

Junk foods are a threat because they're quick, they're convenient, we've acquired a taste for them, and they're everywhere you look. They're empty calorie foods, and they displace more nutrient-dense foods from your diet.

Whether you're a vegetarian or not, the junk is there to tempt you. As I've noted before, Coke and French fries are vegetarian, but the food of champions they are not. Not if someone makes a steady diet of them, anyway.

Vegetarians are a more health-conscious bunch than nonvegetarians, generally speaking. But not all vegetarians are immune to the call of junk. The usual suspects? Chips, cookies, cakes, processed snack foods, candy, soft drinks, and so on.

Vegetarians who shop at natural foods stores do somewhat better, since many of the treats made by natural product companies contain less salt, more whole grains and fiber, less sugar, and no hydrogenated fats. But even natural foods companies have some products in their lineups that qualify as nutritional losers.

Sometimes it's hard to be objective about our own diets. Do the best you can to judge the extent to which junk foods displace nutrient-dense foods from your diet. If you have any doubts about the accuracy of your self-assessment, keep a food diary for a week or two. Food diaries aren't perfect, but they're a pretty good mirror of your eating habits.

Do Your Own Thing

In life, when you play the comparison game, you usually lose. That's because there's almost always someone wealthier, better looking, smarter, and more accomplished than you. If you're vegetarian, there is usually someone who is more vegetarian than you too.

More Vegetarian?

Some of you know what I mean. Among some vegetarians, there seems to be a hierarchy of vegetarianism. The lacto ovo vegetarians are very pedestrian. They're beginners. They haven't quite evolved to the more ethically pure vegan ideal. They consume animal products—dairy and eggs—which subsidize the meat industry or otherwise exploit animals. They haven't yet shed the leather shoes and the wool coats.

The lacto ovo veggies think the fish eaters haven't gone far enough, and the vegans think the lacto ovo vegetarians are falling short. Not everyone is judgmental, but many are. In addition to being involved with their own diets, they're also policing everyone else's plates.

My advice: Listen and read and absorb all of the information you care to about vegetarian lifestyles. Then decide what's right for you and do it. Do your best to ignore negative messages from those who feel the need to preach. They too have needs to satisfy, but you don't have to be a part of it. The choice of a vegetarian diet—and which kind of vegetarian diet—is highly personal. It's nobody's business but your own.

Helpful Hint

To assess your own junk-food quotient, keep a food diary for a week or two. Review the results. For most people, one treat a day is a reasonable limit. A couple of cookies, a small dish of sherbet or nonfat frozen yogurt, a large handful of chips, or an ounce or two of chocolate shouldn't wreak too much havoc with your diet. Much more and you may start suffering some nutritional casualties.

Am I Weird, or What?

When you adopt a vegetarian lifestyle, you may have a sense of being isolated at times. That's especially true when you're surrounded by family and friends and the differences in your eating styles stand out. It's likely that you'll be the only vegetarian in your household. If feeling different is uncomfortable at first, keep the following points in mind.

You're One in a Hundred

More or less. Remember that only about 1 percent of the population is vegetarian. Lots of people call themselves vegetarians, but only a select few actually follow a true vegetarian lifestyle consistently. If you feel a little different, that's because you are.

You Alone Decide What You Put into Your Body

You may be different than 99 percent of the population, but you should feel confident in your decision to follow a vegetarian lifestyle. It's healthier, it's better for the environment, and it's the nonviolent choice. A vegetarian diet is the thinking man and woman's diet. People who opt for a vegetarian lifestyle tend to be more sensitive and socially responsible. They're deeper thinkers. Let's face it, we're brighter! (Of course, meat eaters reading this don't have to buy into my judgmental statement.)

You owe no one an explanation. You have every right to do your own thing.

Stand tall and take comfort in knowing that you're on the cutting edge of the nutritional curve.

Helpful Hint

When people adopt a vegetarian diet, the diet tends to evolve over time as they acquire new skills in meal planning and handling other situations relating to food. Don't let others cajole you into moving at a pace that doesn't feel comfortable for you, and don't let them make you feel bad about whatever level of animal products you include in your diet at any given time. Everyone does the best they can, and we all have different reasons and capacities for making lifestyle changes.

Vegetarian Diets Are Outside Our Culture

It bears repeating. Vegetarian diets are not a tradition in our culture. No wonder you feel a little strange. You'd fit right in if you lived in India or any other culture in which vegetarianism has been a tradition for thousands of years.

Going All the Way

How far you go in eliminating animal products in your lifestyle is up to you. Like your diet, your use of other animal products, such as wool, leather, silk, and others, may evolve over time as you figure out which alternatives will work for you.

The First Step—The Basic Vegetarian

A true vegetarian never eats meat, fish, or poultry, including foods made with by-products of these animal products. The operative word here is "eat," since some vegetarians do use some products that contain meat by-products. For example, some vegetarians use soap made with tallow, or they may use shampoo that contains animal proteins.

But a vegetarian doesn't eat these products. A vegetarian doesn't eat soup made with beef stock or rice flavored with chicken broth. A vegetarian also doesn't eat marshmallows or jelly beans made with gelatin.

Technically, a vegetarian wouldn't eat pie crust or refried beans made with lard or cheese made with animal rennet. It can be hard to avoid these ingredients, though, since it's not always possible to know if a food contains them. That's especially true if you are eating in a restaurant or in any situation in which you don't have a food label to read. In those cases, most vegetarians do their best to ascertain whether or not the food contains an objectionable ingredient. You can ask the wait staff in a restaurant, for instance, whether or not the beans contain lard, and you can ask the server in a cafeteria line if the pie crust contains lard.

The Last Bite

White table sugar can be made from sugar beets or sugar cane. About half of the sugar produced in the United States is made from sugar cane. Cane sugar is whitened by passing it through activated charcoal, which can be of animal, plant, or mineral origin. About half of the refineries use charcoal made from animal bones. Since you usually can't determine the type of sugar used in a product (it's just listed on the label as sugar), many vegans just avoid any product made with white table sugar (regular vegetarians usually don't boycott table sugar). Brown sugar, confectioner's sugar, and commercial granulated sugar may all be made from cane sugar. Many vegans prefer to use rice syrup, maple syrup, date sugar, or turbinado (raw) sugar when they want a sweetener. Some also use powdered sweeteners made from brown rice, unbleached granulated sugar cane, or fruit juice derivatives that can be found in natural foods stores.

Vegan versus Vegetarian

Vegetarians eat and use some animal products, such as milk, eggs, butter, wool, and leather. Vegans, on the other hand, avoid eating or using any and all animal products—as much as is humanly possible, that is.

So, whereas a vegetarian would eat a pancake that contains eggs and milk or would use a margarine that contains casein (a milk protein and thus an animal product), a vegan would not. A vegan would avoid a pie crust containing skim milk solids, pasta made with eggs, and sherbet that contains egg whites.

The Last Bite

Vegetarians do not eat animal products that require the death of an animal to obtain. For example, a vegetarian would not eat a chicken leg or drink beef broth. But some vegetarians would drink milk or eat an egg, since the use of these foods does not require the animal to die. Most vegetarians do, however, use animal by-products such as leather, wool, and silk. Vegans, on the other hand, use no animal products whatsoever, regardless of how those foods or products were obtained.

There are many hidden animal products in foods. Many are present in very small amounts. Some, such as casein and whey—both derived from dairy products—are acceptable for vegetarians to eat but are not acceptable to vegans. Others, such as rennet (which comes from the stomach lining of calves and other baby animals), are unacceptable to all vegetarians. The following table provides a list of many of these hidden animal ingredients.

Some ingredients can originate from an animal or a plant source, but you can't determine which by reading the label. In those cases, you'll need to call the manufacturer to inquire. You can also refer to materials made available by some vegetarian organizations listed in Chapter 26, "Getting Educated About Everything Vegetarian." *The Vegetarian Food Guide and Nutrition Counter* (Suzanne Havala, Berkley Books, 1997) also contains a list and definitions of hidden animal ingredients.

Hidden Animal Ingredients

Ingredient	What It Is	Its Use
Albumin	The protein component of egg whites	To thicken or add texture to processed foods
Anchovies	Small, silvery fish	Worcestershire sauce, Caesar salad dressing, pizza topping, Greek salads
Animal shortening	Butter, suet, lard	Packaged cookies and crackers, refried beans, flour tortillas, ready-made pie crusts

continues

Hidden Animal Ingredients   (continued)

Ingredient	What It Is	Its Use
Carmine (carmine cochineal or carminic acid)	Red coloring made from a ground-up insect	Bottled juices, colored pasta, some candies, frozen pops, "natural" cosmetics
Casein (caseinate)	A milk protein	An additive in dairy products such as cheese, cream cheese, cottage cheese, and sour cream
Gelatin	Protein from bones, cartilage, tendons, and skin of animals	Marshmallows, yogurt, frosted cereals, gelatin-containing desserts
Glucose (dextrose)	Fruits or animal tissues and fluids	Baked goods, soft drinks, candies, frosting
Glycerides (mono-, di-, and tri-glycerides)	Glycerol from animal fats or plants	Processed foods, cosmetics, perfumes, lotions, inks, glues, automobile antifreeze
Isinglass	Gelatin from air bladder of sturgeon and other freshwater fish	Clarify alcoholic beverages and in some jellied desserts
Lactic acid	Acid formed by bacteria acting on the milk sugar lactose	Cheese, yogurt, pickles, olives, sauerkraut, candy, frozen desserts, chewing gum, fruit preserves, dyeing and textile printing
Lactose (saccharum lactin, D-lactose)	Milk sugar	Culture medium for souring milk and in processed foods such as baby formulas and sweets, medicinal diuretics, and laxatives
Lactylic stearate	Salt of stearic acid (see stearic acid)	Dough conditioner
Lanolin	Waxy fat from sheep's wool	Chewing gum, ointments, cosmetics, waterproof coatings
Lard	Fat from the abdomens of pigs	Baked goods

178

Ingredient	What It Is	Its Use
Lecithin	Phospholipids from animal tissues, plants, and egg yolks	Cereal, candy, chocolate, baked goods, margarine, vegetable oil sprays, cosmetics, and ink
Lutein	Deep yellow coloring from marigolds or egg yolks	Commercial food coloring
Natural flavorings	Unspecified, could be from meat or other animal products	Processed and packaged foods
Oleic acid (oleinic acid)	Animal tallow (see tallow)	Synthetic butter, cheese, vegetable fats and oils; spice flavoring for baked goods, candy ice cream, beverages, condiments; soaps, cosmetics
Pepsin	Enzyme from pigs' stomachs	With rennet to make cheese
Propolis	Resinous cement collected by bees	Food supplement and ingredient in "natural" toothpastes
Stearic acid (octadecenoic acid)	Tallow, other animal fats and oils	Vanilla flavoring, chewing gum, baked goods, beverages, candy, soaps, ointments, candles, cosmetics, suppositories and pill coatings
Suet	Hard white fat around kidneys and loins of animals	Margarine, mincemeat, pastries, bird feed, tallow
Tallow	Solid fat of sheep and cattle separated from the membranous tissues	Waxed paper, margarine, soaps, crayons, candles, rubber, cosmetics
Vitamin A (A1, retinol)	Vitamin obtained from vegetables, egg yolks, or fish liver oil	Vitamin supplements, fortification of foods, "natural" cosmetics
Vitamin B12	Vitamin produced by microorganisms and found in all animal products; synthetic form (cyanocobalamin or cobalamin on labels) is vegan	Supplements or fortified foods

continues

Hidden Animal Ingredients   (continued)

Ingredient	What It Is	Its Use
Vitamin D (D1, D2, D3)	D1 is produced by humans upon exposure to sunlight; D2 (ergocalciferol) is made from plants or yeast; D3 (cholecalciferol) comes from fish liver oils or lanolin	Supplements or fortified foods
Whey	Watery liquid that separates from the solids	Crackers, breads, cakes, processed foods in cheese-making

What Do Your Clothes Say About You?

Vegans avoid clothing and fashion accessories made with fur, leather, wool, and silk. Vegetarian organizations can refer you to catalogs and stores that carry a wide range of vegan belts, shoes, purses, wallets, and other clothing items.

Some belts, shoes, and purses are now being made of such high-quality synthetic materials that it's difficult to detect that they aren't made with leather. Other vegan clothing options are always in style, such as straw or raffia purses, nylon wallets and purses, and canvas shoes.

Personal Care Items

For anyone who's never given it much thought, it can come as a surprise that so many personal care products, such as lotions, soaps, cosmetics, hair care products—you name it—are made with animal product ingredients. Again, check with some of the vegetarian and animal rights organizations listed in Part 7, "Veggie Survival Strategies," for a complete listing of items made with animal ingredients.

The Vegan Ideal

Some vegetarians hold the vegan lifestyle to be the ultimate goal. It's the pinnacle of ethical righteousness. The less dependent you are on foods of animal origin and animal by-products, the less you will contribute to the support of industries that exploit and harm animals and the environment.

Sooner or later, many vegetarians face a decision about how far they want to take their vegetarianism and whether or not to shoot for the vegan ideal.

To Go or Not to Go

Like the decision to go vegetarian in the first place, the decision to go vegan is highly personal. Given that basic vegetarianism is outside our culture, veganism is even further outside the norms of our society's traditions. Most vegetarians would acknowledge that it's far more challenging to aspire to a vegan lifestyle than it is to go for a vegetarian lifestyle.

That's because of the extent to which animal by-products permeate consumer goods. You can begin to understand this when you review the list of hidden animal ingredients in the table earlier in this chapter. From photographic film to medicines to personal care products, animal by-products show up everywhere. In many cases, the ingredients are unfamiliar to most people and are listed on labels by their chemical-sounding names, so it's tough to recognize them as having originated from an animal.

The Perfect Vegan

Realistically, it's nearly impossible to be consistently vegan in this culture. Most, if not all, vegans do eat or use animal products at some time or even regularly, even if they aren't doing it knowingly. It's just that it's too difficult to function in this society without taking some chances that an item contains an animal product.

For example, most vegans eat at restaurants at least occasionally. At some point, they may have to take the chance that the bread they are eating contains skim milk solids or another animal product or derivative. There may be honey in the breakfast cereal or an undetectable dash of Parmesan cheese on the croutons or in the salad dressing.

You may go to a salon for a haircut and find that the hairdresser uses a shampoo or conditioner that contains animal proteins, or you may wash your hands at a friend's house or in a public restroom and use soap that contains tallow. You may be served a meal on bone china.

It would be very difficult to avoid all animal products in every situation and still participate as a member of this society. Most vegans simply do the best they can and do not knowingly use animal products. They strive for the vegan ideal and may come close, but they don't necessarily achieve it.

The Last Bite

Most vegans do not use honey, since the harvesting of honey usually entails the disruption and death of some of the bees in the hive.

181

Which Is Better—Vegan or Vegetarian?

Whether or not you go vegan depends upon several factors, including your ability to make the extra effort required to sidestep animal products as well as to handle the additional social and practical complications. On top of that, people have valid differences of opinion about the effectiveness of adopting a vegan lifestyle.

For example, some people feel that a vegan lifestyle is the most ethical choice, since it minimizes or nearly eliminates dependence on animal products and therefore minimizes the exploitation and suffering of animals. They feel compromise is a cop-out, and they simply can't live with themselves unless they always do the best they can to be vegan in their lifestyle.

Another point of view is that when people try to follow a vegan lifestyle and are rigid about it and won't ever compromise, outsiders see the lifestyle as overly oppressive or restrictive and are turned off vegetarianism altogether. Some people feel that it sends the wrong message to others, and that a less-restrictive stance might increase the likelihood that others will see vegetarianism as a viable option for themselves.

Many people take a middle-of-the-road point of view and generally strive to minimize their use of animal products while sometimes giving in. By being "90 percent vegan," they feel that they contribute most of the benefits without crossing the line and sending a negative message to others.

Ultimately, you should do what feels right for you. Hopefully, understanding the difficulty of the decision and the many factors that people have to weigh will help you understand and tolerate other people's decisions about the choice of vegan or vegetarian and will help them to tolerate yours.

Heads Up!

A common term used in vegetarian circles is "vegan Nazi," as in, "The vegan Nazis won't permit any animal products to be served at the conference site." That unfortunate term is used to refer to vegans who are intolerant of anyone who isn't striving for the vegan ideal.

The Least You Need to Know

➤ There's no need to feel overwhelmed by the nutrition aspects of a vegetarian diet. Even though the science of nutrition is complicated, being well-nourished is a relatively simple matter.

➤ Limited time for planning and preparing wholesome meals and too much junk food are the two primary enemies of a healthful diet.

➤ Don't let anyone bully you into being "more vegetarian" than you are ready to be. The choice of a vegetarian diet and which kind of vegetarian diet are nobody's business but your own.

➤ It's normal to feel like the odd man out when you adopt a vegetarian diet, since vegetarian lifestyles are outside our culture.

➤ There are many hidden animal products in foods as well as in nonfood products such as cosmetics, medicines, personal care products, and others.

➤ Realistically, it's nearly impossible to be completely vegan in our culture due to the extent to which animal products permeate every aspect of our lifestyle. However, vegans strive for the vegan ideal.

Chapter 16

Assembling Your Vegetarian Kitchen

In This Chapter

➤ Tips for establishing a veg-friendly kitchen

➤ How to clean and organize cabinets, drawers, and counter tops

➤ Collecting the right equipment without creating an appliance graveyard

➤ Staples to keep on hand

➤ Top 10 must-have specialty products

You need a clean, well-organized, well-stocked kitchen, even if you don't have a lot of time to cook. When your kitchen is in shape, you'll eat better and you'll feel better too, because having things in order will give you peace of mind. You might even be more motivated to prepare meals.

Getting Started

For some people, the kitchen is their favorite room in the house. If you're one of those people, you've probably got one of every kind of kitchen gadget there is, and things are in order or you know where to find them. You probably enjoy cooking when you have the time.

For other people, the kitchen is strictly a matter of function—it's where you store your food and dishes, but you spend as little time in there as possible. Fixing meals is a necessity of life but not a hobby.

No matter what your attitude is about kitchens and cooking meals, there are some things that you can do to make the space more pleasurable and user friendly.

Clean Equals Carefree

Some individuals and companies adopt a segment of the highway and vow to keep it clean and neat. Why not start in your own home and adopt your kitchen?

The first thing I recommend doing is getting rid of anything that you don't use, including appliances, party favors, napkins, any other paper goods that have been collecting dust for a year or two, and any items that don't belong in the kitchen but may have made their way into your cupboards. Throw these things away, add them to your garage sale pile, or donate them to charity. This will help you free up space in your closets and cupboards so that the things you do use are accessible.

Empty your cabinets and drawers a few at a time and wash them out with soap and hot water. Wash your large appliances and microwave oven inside and out. Throw away any foods that have been sitting around unused in your freezer and any foods that are spoiling or otherwise won't ever be eaten in your refrigerator. Check your cupboards too, and pitch anything that is taking up space and that you know you won't ever use.

Get Organized

Over time, you've probably begun shelving items out of place and piling baking sheets, cake pans, and pots and pans on top of each other in unwieldy piles in your kitchen cabinets. Take them out, reorganize them, and store them in such a way that they are easy to see and reach. If you find that you don't have enough room to store items conveniently, consider creative ways of making more space.

For example, you might buy an overhead rack for pots and pans that can hang from your ceiling or a kitchen wall. That would free up some cabinet space. If there's room in your kitchen, you could add a baker's rack or a moveable island on wheels with extra drawers and shelves for storage. You'll be so much happier and your kitchen will be more user friendly if all of your appliances, dishes, pots, pans, and utensils are easy to access.

Label jars and canisters of baking supplies. Keep spices in a cool, dry place away from the heat of the stove. Unless you use huge quantities, buy oils and spices in small containers so that you can replace them more often and know that they're fresh.

Be Well-Equipped

Be equipped with the utensils and appliances you need to work efficiently, but don't get bogged down with too many gadgets that you don't use. Nobody likes a counter top that's so jammed with small appliances that there's no counter space to work on. For example, I gave away my electric can opener when I realized that I preferred to use an old-fashioned crank can opener and was able to get one more appliance off my kitchen counter. The little hand-held opener that I use is stored in a drawer.

Not everyone likes to own a large counter top mixer. Some people prefer a hand-held mixer. Some people don't use a mixer at all and only need a whisk. Think about your lifestyle and equipment needs, and pare it down wherever possible so that you don't waste money and cupboard and counter space.

Some kitchen equipment to consider:

1. Spatulas, wooden spoons, and whisks
2. Measuring cups (dry and liquid) and spoons
3. Mixing bowls in various sizes
4. A good set of kitchen knives, including a paring knife, a serrated knife, a French chef's knife for chopping vegetables, and a bread knife
5. Counter top mixer or hand-held mixer
6. Slow cooker (such as a Crock Pot)
7. Pressure cooker
8. Heavy duty blender/juicer
9. Baking pans and sheets
10. Food processor
11. Pots and pans in assorted sizes, some with nonstick surfaces

Helpful Hint

Consider dating groceries, especially canned and packaged goods, when you bring them into the house after shopping. Mark packages with the date they were purchased, using a grease pencil or permanent marker (stick-on labels can fall off cold or frozen packages). This will help you rotate your stock and use older foods first, helping to ensure that nothing stays in your cupboard or refrigerator too long and that what you have on hand is fresh.

Keep a Variety of Foods

Keep foods in a variety of forms on hand. There's no question that fresh is best, but it's not always the most convenient option. So plan to keep a range of fresh, frozen, canned, and packaged foods in your kitchen. The lists that follow will give you an idea of the types of foods you'll want to have on hand. The grocery lists in Chapter 17, "Shopping for a Vegetarian Kitchen," and the descriptions of food choices in Chapter 18, "A Daily Vegetarian Food Guide," will give you even more detail about the types of staples you'll want to have at home.

Breads, Cereals, and Other Grain Products

Grain products are versatile. They can be an accompaniment to a meal, such as a slice of bread or a couscous salad, or they can form the backbone of an entree, such as rice pilaf, a casserole made with buckwheat and vegetables, or a plate of spaghetti.

Among the many grains that are now available in natural food stores (and many supermarkets) are ones that may be unfamiliar to you if you're just beginning your research into vegetarianism. *Amaranth* and *quinoa* are from Central and South America, and both can be cooked and used similarly to rice, alone or in casseroles, or as hot cereal. Amaranth flour is also good for baking. *Spelt* and *kamut* are types of wheat from Europe. And *teff* is a grain from Africa where it is used to make the spongy, round, flat bread known as injera.

When you stock your kitchen, consider buying these types of grain products:

➤ Whole-grain mixes such as pancake mixes, pilafs, and baking mixes

➤ Bulk grains such as rice, rye, oats, buckwheat, barley, amaranth, quinoa, spelt, kamut, teff, millet, and others

➤ Whole-grain breakfast cereals, hot or cold

➤ Pasta in a variety of shapes and flavors

➤ Rice in several varieties such as brown, white, jasmine, arborio, and basmati

➤ Breads, rolls, bagels, English muffins, flour tortillas

➤ Frozen waffles and low-fat muffins

Helpful Hint

When you make a pot of rice (or any of a number of grains) make more than you need at one meal. The leftovers can be stored in an airtight container in the refrigerator for up to two weeks. Leftover rice can be reheated and served with steamed vegetables, bean burritos and tacos, topped with vegetarian chili, added to a filling for cabbage rolls, or used to make rice pudding.

Legumes: Beans, Peas, Lentils

Buy them dry in bags or bulk, or buy them canned. If you buy them canned, you can rinse them in a colander with water to remove most of the salt.

Beans, peas, and lentils are highly nutritious and endlessly versatile. You can combine several types of beans to make many-bean chili (garbanzos, pintos, red kidney beans, and white kidney beans are great). You can mash them for dips, soups, and spreads. You can combine them with rice, pasta, or other grains to make a variety of interesting vegetarian entrees. Other ideas:

➤ Bean or lentil soup

➤ Black bean burritos, nachos, or tacos

➤ Hummus

➤ Black bean dip

➤ Black beans with saffron rice

➤ Black-eyed peas with rice (known as Hoppin' John in the South)

➤ Baked beans with vegetarian franks

➤ Boston baked beans with brown bread

➤ Pasta with beans (known to Italians as pasta fagioli)

➤ Vegetarian chili (add a handful of corn kernels for a splash of color)

➤ Black bean cakes with salsa

➤ Variety of bean and vegetable combination dishes such as many ethnic entrees and casseroles

➤ Many types of beans: black, pinto, kidney, navy, black-eyed peas, garbanzo, cannelloni (white kidney beans), and others

➤ Lentils and split peas

➤ Dry, canned, and even frozen beans and peas

Veggie Talk

Amaranth is an ancient grain that was a staple food of the Aztecs of Central America. **Quinoa** (pronounced *KEEN-wah*) is a high-protein grain that was used by the Incas in Peru. **Spelt** and **kamut** (pronounced *kah-MOOT*) are types of wheat that have been popular in Europe for generations. **Teff**, one of the oldest cultivated grains, is commonly used in Ethiopia.

Helpful Hint

Small pressure cookers are now available that are safe and easy to use. They can cook dried beans in a fraction of the time that soaking and boiling takes. While canned beans are fine to use—especially when you rinse off the salt—many people like the flavor of beans made "from scratch" and find a pressure cooker a convenient way to substantially cut down prep time.

Fruits and Vegetables

The very best fruits and vegetables are those that are locally grown, in season, and fresh. Most of them are packed with vitamins, minerals, and phytochemicals. Frozen foods run a close second in terms of nutrition, and they're a perfectly acceptable alternative to fresh.

Helpful Hint

When you use canned vegetables, you'll save some of the vitamins and minerals that might have leached out if you can use the packing liquid in whatever dish you are making. For example, if you are making soup or a sautéed vegetable medley to serve over some kind of grain or pasta, dump the entire contents of the can into the pot. There may be some salt in the packing liquid, but you can leave out any additional salt that is called for in the recipe.

However, there are times when canned fruits and vegetables are more convenient or less expensive than fresh or frozen. Since heat destroys some vitamins, and time on the shelf can allow some nutrients to leach out into the water used in packing, canned vegetables tend to be less nutritious than fresh or frozen. However, that doesn't mean they're worthless! On the contrary, canned fruits and vegetables can make a sizable nutritional contribution, so there's no need to avoid them.

Meat Substitutes

More discussion about meat substitutes appears in Chapter 18, but you may want to try some of the following:

➤ Veggie burger patties

➤ Veggie hotdogs, cold cuts, bacon, and breakfast patties and links

➤ Tofu and tempeh

➤ Textured vegetable protein (TVP)

Dairy Products and Dairy Substitutes

If you do include dairy products such as cheese, milk, and ice cream in your diet, buy the nonfat varieties. Even the so-called low-fat items are too high in fat. The problem with dairy fat is that two-thirds of it is saturated, so the fat in dairy products is a real artery clogger.

You'll find some dairy product substitutes in the supermarket, but you'll find even more in the natural foods store. Experiment with:

➤ Soy, rice, potato, and oat milks and blends packaged in aseptic (shelf-stable) packages

➤ Soy cheeses

➤ Soy yogurt with active cultures

➤ Soy and rice frozen desserts

Convenience Foods

More about quick and easy meal ideas in Chapter 19, "When There's No Time to Cook: Quick and Easy Meals and Snacks," but you'll want to keep some shortcuts on hand for times when cooking is out of the question. For instance:

➤ Frozen vegetarian pizzas

➤ Frozen vegetarian entrees and ethnic dishes

➤ Frozen bean burritos

➤ Frozen vegetable and fruit mixtures

➤ Bean flakes for making nachos, burrito and taco fillings, bean soup, and bean dip

➤ Quick-cooking hot cereals and grains such as oatmeal and rice

➤ Veggie burgers and hotdogs

➤ Frozen waffles and low-fat muffins

➤ Soup cups (just add hot water) and mixes

➤ Washed and trimmed fresh fruits and vegetables

Top 10 List of Convenient Vegetarian Specialty Products

When you're setting up a vegetarian kitchen and in the mood to try some new products, there are several that come to mind that are especially helpful. These products have nutritional advantages and/or are especially convenient. You can find some of them in your neighborhood supermarket, and all of them can be found in natural foods markets.

Not all of these may appeal to you, and that's fine. None of them are strictly necessary, but many of the products make following a vegetarian or vegan diet much simpler.

Soymilk

Soymilk is a good choice for anyone who is lactose intolerant or just prefers to avoid dairy products. It comes in different flavors, including plain, which has a slight "beanie" aftertaste. It's usually packaged in shelf-stable aseptic boxes that need to be refrigerated after opening. Buy fortified soymilk, because it contains added vitamins A, B12, D, and calcium. You can substitute soymilk cup for cup in recipes that call for milk, you can pour it on your breakfast cereal, and you can enjoy it when you have a hankering for milk and cookies.

Powdered Vegetarian Egg Replacer

This is an egg substitute that is made from a mixture of vegetable starches. You just mix 1¹/₂ teaspoons of the powder with 2 tablespoons of water to replace one egg in virtually any recipe. The advantages: It stays fresh on a shelf in your cupboard almost indefinitely and is always on hand when you need it, there's no salmonella risk, and it's saturated fat– and cholesterol-free.

Vegetarian Burger Patties and Hotdogs

The burger patties can be made from soy or they can be grain- or vegetable-based. There's a wide variety and they all taste different, so you'll need to experiment to find your favorites. Some are meant to look and taste meat-like, and others don't look or taste anything like meat.

The hotdogs are typically made of soy, and they taste and look like the real thing. They even wiggle appropriately when you take them out of a pan of water with a fork. That's one of the advantages of these products: Kids can take them on picnics and to cook-outs and not feel too different for being vegetarians. You can cook these foods on a grill and serve them the same way their meat counterparts are served.

Of course, the nutritional advantage to these foods is that they're low in saturated fat, cholesterol-free, and many even contain a good dose of dietary fiber. They're quick, convenient, good tasting, and they work well as transition foods for people making the switch to a vegetarian diet. They can be the solution to a momentary "What should we make for dinner?" crisis.

Whole-Grain Breakfast Cereals

Hot or cold cereals are simply a good way to start the day. They're nutritious and satisfying. Plus, they make a perfectly good supper food from time to time. Once again, if you get stuck with "What can I have for dinner tonight?" you could do far worse than eating a bowl of cereal.

If you're getting a little weary of the cereal choices at your supermarket, check out a natural foods store. You'll be surprised at the variety, and I guarantee you'll hit on some new favorites.

Helpful Hint

Unlike cheese, tofu is never co-agulated with rennet. It's always safe for consumption by vegetarians and vegans alike.

Tofu and Tempeh

There are many new soy cookbooks on the market now, and some of them are listed in Chapter 26, "Getting Educated About Everything Vegetarian." You can use *tempeh* in many of the same ways that you might have used meat—to make sloppy Joe filling, barbecue, mock chicken salad, and a variety of other dishes.

Tofu is soybean curd. It's made much the same way that cheese is made by using a coagulant to curdle soymilk, separating the solids from the liquid, and pressing the solids into a block. Tofu packaged in aseptic containers is actually coagulated inside the package itself.

Tofu comes in different degrees of firmness, depending upon how much water has been pressed out. Different styles of tofu can be used in different recipes. For instance, soft tofu works well for making dips and sauces since it's easy to blend. Firm tofu works well in baked goods and as an egg replacer in many recipes (more about that in Chapter 20, "Recipe Magic!"). Extra-firm tofu is the style of choice for making stir-fries, since the cubes can hold up when they're jostled around in the pan.

Tofu and tempeh are nutritious and versatile. They're high in protein, low in saturated fat, cholesterol-free, and full of beneficial phytochemicals.

Organic Canned Beans

We've already talked about some of the virtues of beans. In natural foods stores, you can find *organic* canned beans, which, in addition to being convenient, have the added benefit of being grown without the use of synthetic pesticides and herbicides.

The term "organic" as it refers to foods is being hotly debated as this is written due to proposed government guidelines that will regulate the definition and use of the term on food packages. Up until now, the natural foods industry has used voluntary standards, and state rules for certifying foods as organic have varied from state to state. To be certified as organic, foods must also be grown in soil that has been free of prohibited substances for at least three years.

Veggie Talk

Tempeh is a traditional Indonesian food that is made from whole soybeans and is sometimes mixed with a grain such as rice. It's fermented and pressed into a flat, rectangular block. You could call it a cultured bean cake. In stores, it's usually sold refrigerated or frozen, vacuum-packed in plastic.

Veggie Talk

Tofu is a traditional Asian soyfood. It's white, nearly odorless, and bland, and it picks up the flavor of the foods with which it is cooked. Tofu makes a good substitute for eggs in many recipes.

Veggie Talk

Organic canned beans are convenient and have the added benefit of being grown without the use of synthetic pesticides and herbicides.

Dried Bean Flakes

These can be found in box mixes and in cardboard milk carton–like containers. The flakes can be made from black beans or pinto beans. They're especially handy for making burrito and taco fillings as well as bean dip. Just add boiling water to the flakes, and in five minutes you have a smooth bean puree.

Veggie Talk

The process of **hydrogenation** changes the chemical configuration of a vegetable oil in such a way that the oil is hardened, becoming a **hydrogenated fat**. An oil such as corn oil can be hydrogenated enough to make it hold the shape of a stick (margarine). Hydrogenated fats are often used in commercial baked goods, and they are added to many brands of peanut butter to keep the peanut oil in suspension and prevent it from settling out at the top of the jar. Like animal fats, hydrogenated fats stimulate your body to produce more cholesterol and are associated with increased rates of coronary artery disease.

Whole-Grain Mixes

You can find the biggest variety of these in natural foods stores. They're generally good products because they are free of *hydrogenated fats*, unnecessary additives, and refined flours, and they are often made with organically grown grains. There are mixes for a wide range of baked products such as gingerbread, cakes, brownies, cookies, quick breads, pancakes, and waffles.

Instant Soups

These are the products sold in single-serving cardboard cups. You add boiling water, stir, and enjoy. They're a good product to keep on hand for a quick snack, to pack in a bag lunch, and to take on a road trip (stop at a filling station/market for some hot water). The lentil soup variety makes a good, quick gravy. Just add hot water, stir, and let the soup rest for a few moments until it thickens. Then pour it over a baked potato, mashed potatoes, or toast. Compare labels and buy the varieties with the least amount of sodium.

Organic Canned Tomatoes

Like the organic canned beans, organic canned tomatoes have many practical applications and have the added benefit of being made with organically grown produce. This is especially nice in the case of tomatoes, on which mainstream growers tend to use a relatively large amount of pesticides. Use organic canned tomatoes to make pasta sauces, mix with cooked vegetables to make a variety of toppings for cooked grains, and to use in a wide range of other recipes for soups, stews, casseroles, and other dishes.

The Least You Need to Know

➤ It's a good idea to start with a clean, well-organized kitchen. Get rid of cupboard, counter, and drawer items that you never use and that take up space.

➤ Now's the time to assess your need for kitchen equipment such as knives, baking supplies, pots and pans, and small appliances.

➤ Keep a good variety of fresh, frozen, canned, and packaged foods on hand.

➤ You can find a big selection of excellent convenience foods in natural foods stores, and many can be found at your regular supermarket.

Chapter 17

Shopping for a Vegetarian Kitchen

In This Chapter

➤ Natural foods stores versus your neighborhood grocery store

➤ The merits of ethnic markets

➤ Ordering foods from co-ops and catalogs

➤ Your shopping style and what it means

➤ Tips for successful shopping

➤ Sample weekly and monthly grocery lists

"Do I have to shop at a health food store?"

"Is there a reason to buy alfalfa sprouts?"

In this chapter, we'll go beyond your neighborhood supermarket and explore places that you may never before have set foot in search of good foods. This chapter will cover shopping tips and strategies, some interesting new foods that you can try if you are so inclined, and sample shopping lists to guide you and help you to remember what you need.

What Are Natural Foods?

There's actually no legal definition for the term *natural foods*. Within the natural food industry, though, the term "natural" is generally understood to mean that a food has been minimally processed, is free of artificial flavors, colors, preservatives, and any other additives that do not occur naturally in the food.

Naturally Nutritious

Natural foods are frequently better choices than their mainstream counterparts, in part because they lack the undesirable ingredients of many commercially processed foods, and in part because they contain more nutritious ingredients.

Veggie Talk

The term **natural foods** is generally understood to describe foods that are as close to their natural state as possible, without synthetic flavorings, colorings, preservatives, and additives that do not occur naturally in the food.

For instance, natural breakfast cereals, baking mixes, and bread products contain no hydrogenated fats. They are usually made with whole grains, so they contain more dietary fiber, vitamins, and minerals than products made with refined grains. They're usually minimally sweetened, and when they are sweetened, there's often less sweetener used. Fruit juice is frequently used as a sweetener rather than refined sugar. There is typically less sodium in natural foods, and no monosodium glutamate or nitrites are used. The ingredients used in natural foods products are often organically grown too.

More Good Choices

Even within a particular category of food products, there are usually more healthful choices in a natural foods store. For instance, in a regular supermarket you may find one or two types of whole-grain pasta. In a natural foods store, you're likely to find an entire shelf of them.

Natural foods stores carry not only natural-style peanut butter but almond butter and cashew butter, as well. They carry numerous brands of whole-grain hot cereals and cold cereals, and an entire wall of natural fruit juice blends and alternatives to conventional soft drinks. They carry numerous brands of soymilk, as well as rice milk, oat milk, and potato milk too.

Conventional supermarkets are beginning to carry more natural foods, and they are even beginning to integrate those products with their regular lines, rather than shelving natural products in a separate "health foods" area. However, conventional supermarkets don't yet come close to carrying either the range of products or the number of products within a particular category that are carried by natural foods stores.

Competitive Prices

Natural foods stores used to be known as health foods stores. Twenty-five years ago, they were holes in the wall that smelled of incense and vitamins and were frequented by the long-hair-and-sandals set. The story is totally different today.

The general public is becoming much more familiar with natural foods stores, and natural foods superstores are springing up everywhere. These are large-scale stores that rival the selection and service of even the largest conventional supermarkets. Since natural foods products are being sold in greater quantities now, prices have come down as well. Large natural foods stores can often offer better prices than the small stores can offer on the same products, but conventional supermarkets may or may not offer more competitive prices. It depends upon the size of the supermarket and the volume of the item that the store can sell, among other factors. It pays to compare prices, and you may occasionally be surprised.

Helpful Hint

If there's a favorite product that you can buy at the natural foods store but which your regular supermarket doesn't carry, mention it to the manager of your store. The store may be willing to stock it at a competitive price.

The Regular Supermarket

Maybe you can remember when rice cakes and tofu were found only in health foods stores. Now there's an entire wall devoted to rice cakes in different sizes and flavors, and you can probably find several types of tofu in the produce section of your neighborhood grocery store. Well, things continue to evolve.

As I said earlier, supermarkets are bringing in more and more natural products. Why? Because they're selling. Retailers are being advised by industry specialists to sell the natural products side by side with their conventional counterparts. Put the Muir Glen organic tomato sauces next to the Del Monte and Contadina. Put the Barbara's natural breakfast cereals next to Kellogg's and Post. And stick the soymilk in the area with the dry and canned milk, rather than relegating it to a "health foods" aisle. Better yet, position the soymilk in the refrigerator case, next to the fresh cow's milk.

Natural Foods Stores versus Conventional Stores: Which Is Best?

You may want to shop at both. Many people find that they purchase certain items at one store and others at another store. For instance, you may shop at a natural foods store to buy such foods as frozen vegetarian entrees, specialty baking mixes, whole-grain pasta and breakfast cereals, and your favorite brand of soymilk by the case. Then you might shop at a conventional store for such items as toilet paper, fresh produce, and toothpaste.

Of course, you can usually buy everything at one store or the other. It all depends on your individual preferences. Some people buy everything at a natural foods store, including nonfood items, since they're usually more environmentally friendly. One factor that might make a difference in where you shop is your access to large natural foods superstores. You'll find them in larger cities, and prices may be better and the variety greater than in cities that have only small stores.

Try Ethnic Markets

Ever feel like shaking things up a little? Getting tired of looking at the same old items on the same old grocery store shelves? Stopping at an ethnic market might just give your imagination a jump start.

They're usually off the beaten track, hidden away in a strip center or on the other side of town. They're typically small, sometimes musty and a little unkempt, with ethnic-style music playing in the background. The sights and smells may be different than those to which you are accustomed. That's all part of the fun of it.

There are different types of ethnic grocery stores—Indian, Asian, Mexican, Middle Eastern, Kosher, and many more. Each one carries foods and ingredients that are commonly eaten in those cultures but are frequently difficult to find in mainstream American stores.

Helpful Hint

If you've never before set foot in a natural foods store, now's the time to do it. You may not shop there for all of your groceries and supplies, but you should take a look at the many vegetarian specialty items and other great choices that are available. Things are changing in regular supermarkets, but it will still be years before some products finally make it from the natural foods venue to neighborhood grocery stores. Why wait?

In Indian stores, for instance, you'll be amazed to see the many types of lentils that you can buy—red, orange, yellow, brown, and so on. You may find small, skillet-sized pressure cookers used in India to quick-cook dried beans and lentils. You'll find unusual spices and a variety of Indian breads.

In Asian stores, you'll find vegetables such as some Chinese greens that are shipped to the store from overseas but which aren't typically found in American stores. You'll find unusual condiments.

In all of these stores, you'll see a wide range of traditional foods, many of which are vegetarian or just different and can be incorporated into your vegetarian menus at home. More than anything, a trip to one of these types of stores may inspire you to sample foods of another culture and to expand your own repertoire of choices.

Co-Ops

Many communities have neighborhood *food cooperatives*, or *food co-ops*. A co-op is a group that has been organized to purchase foods in volume for distribution to its members, usually at a reduced cost. Costs are reduced because of the power of the group to buy in volume, so larger groups may be able to get better prices than smaller groups. Co-ops frequently emphasize natural foods products, and the arrangement can be especially helpful in small towns where people don't have access to large natural foods stores with good variety and competitive prices.

Membership rules vary from one co-op to the next. Some co-ops expect their members to contribute a certain number of hours to helping unload trucks, bag groceries, and distribute groceries. Others don't require that you work but give an additional discount to those who donate their time.

To find a co-op in your area, call your local vegetarian society or ask around among your friends.

Mail Order

Another alternative for people who don't have time to shop or can't find certain food items in their local stores is to shop via mail-order catalog. (A few sources are listed in Chapter 26, "Getting Educated About Everything Vegetarian.") These catalogs often offer such products as *textured vegetable protein* (TVP) in a variety of forms, vegetarian mixes, unusual grains, and other vegetarian specialty products.

Let's Go Shopping!

So you're ready to hit the stores. Almost.

What's Your Shopping Style?

Veggie Talk

Textured vegetable protein or **TVP** is made from soy flour that has been denatured by compressing the soy fibers. It's usually sold in granules that resemble ground beef when rehydrated. It can also be sold in chunks that have the texture and appearance of chunks of meat when rehydrated.

We don't really have to make a science out of shopping. Write a list, get in the car, and go.

But not everyone likes to shop from a list. It's not that they aren't organized. It's just that they like less structure. That's fine. I, on the other hand, am guaranteed to forget the one item that I actually made the trip to buy. So I carry a list, even if it only contains two items.

People have different shopping styles, just like they have different personalities. Some people like to plan their week's meals, draw up a corresponding shopping list, and buy only what they need to make the meals they've planned. Other people prefer the casual approach, walk up and down the aisles, and put whatever strikes their fancy into their basket. At home, they decide what they're having for dinner based upon what they feel like making and the supplies they have on hand.

When you've made a change in your eating habits and are developing new eating skills, it can actually be advantageous to do some planning ahead of time and shop from a list. Planning ahead will give you more control over your meals. Keep that in mind, but do what works best for you.

Some Shopping Tips to Take or Leave

Before you head for the store, I'll leave you with a few more pearls of shopping wisdom:

➤ Rotate the stores where you shop to avoid getting into a rut. Go to your neighborhood supermarket this week, try the one across town next time, and stop at the farmer's market when you can. Hit the natural foods store for hard-to-find items, and occasionally take a trip to an ethnic market for inspiration and the odd spice or vegetable.

➤ If you can tolerate lists, keep a running list of items you need taped to the refrigerator door. When you notice that you're low on something, add it to the list. When you're ready to go shopping, grab the list and go.

➤ If you have a problem with buying too many junk foods, eat before you leave for the store. If you're hungry, you'll be more likely to buy impulsively.

➤ If you have a problem with buying the same things over and over again and are in a rut, go to the store hungry. You'll see things with a different eye and may break out of your rut and buy some new foods.

➤ There are no hard and fast rules. If you don't like tofu or alfalfa sprouts, don't buy them.

About the Lists

The grocery lists that follow are only a suggestion of what you might buy to stock your vegetarian kitchen. You can adapt them to suit your individual preferences. If you like them just the way they are, you may want to photocopy them. Make enough copies to last you for a few months. Tape a fresh list onto the door of your refrigerator after each shopping trip. Check off items that you need or add any that aren't listed. There are separate lists for items that you buy weekly and items that you'll buy less often.

The lists show vegan options wherever eggs or dairy products are listed. You might have to look for some of these products at a natural foods store if your local supermarket doesn't carry them. While supermarkets frequently carry soymilk these days, they typically don't stock soy yogurt and soy cheeses, for example.

Weekly Vegetarian Shopping Lists

The foods on this list have to be purchased more frequently, since they are perishable and will keep in your refrigerator for only a week or two before spoiling.

❑ **Fresh Fruit** (especially locally grown, in season)
- ❑ apples
- ❑ apricots
- ❑ bananas
- ❑ blueberries
- ❑ cantaloupe
- ❑ cranberries
- ❑ grapefruit
- ❑ grapes
- ❑ guavas
- ❑ honeydew
- ❑ kiwi
- ❑ lemons
- ❑ limes
- ❑ mangoes
- ❑ nectarines
- ❑ oranges
- ❑ peaches
- ❑ pears
- ❑ pineapples
- ❑ plums
- ❑ strawberries
- ❑ watermelon

❑ **Prepared Fresh Fruits**
- ❑ chilled, bottled mango or papaya slices, pineapple chunks, fruit salad
- ❑ fresh juices: orange, grapefruit, tangerine, apple cider
- ❑ packaged, cut fruits

❑ **Fresh Vegetables** (especially locally grown, in season)
- ❑ asparagus
- ❑ bean sprouts
- ❑ beets
- ❑ bell peppers

Also Need:

- ❑ bok choy
- ❑ broccoli
- ❑ Brussels sprouts
- ❑ cabbage
- ❑ carrots
- ❑ celery
- ❑ collard greens
- ❑ corn
- ❑ cucumbers
- ❑ kale
- ❑ leeks
- ❑ mustard greens
- ❑ onions
- ❑ potatoes

❑ **Prepared Fresh Vegetables**
- ❑ fresh herbs: basil, dill, mint, rosemary, sage, thyme
- ❑ fresh vegetable juices: carrot, carrot/spinach, beet
- ❑ packaged, cut vegetables and mixed greens

❑ **Fresh Pasta** (made without eggs for vegans/lacto vegetarians)

❑ **Fresh Deli Items**
- ❑ four-bean salad
- ❑ fresh marinara sauce
- ❑ fresh pizza (with marinara sauce and veggie toppings; try without cheese)
- ❑ fresh salad dressings (olive oil or fat-free)
- ❑ fresh salsa
- ❑ hummus

❑ **Skim milk or Soymilk**

❑ **Nonfat Yogurt or Soy Yogurt**

❑ **Nonfat Cheese or Soy Cheese**

❑ **Eggs** (use whites only, or use commercial vegetarian egg replacer)

❑ **Fresh Tofu** (or aseptically packaged)

❑ **Breads** (especially whole-grain)
- ❑ bread sticks
- ❑ English muffins
- ❑ French bread
- ❑ German whole-grain
- ❑ Italian bread
- ❑ multigrain
- ❑ oatmeal
- ❑ pita pockets
- ❑ pumpernickel
- ❑ rye
- ❑ sourdough
- ❑ whole-wheat

❑ **Rolls** (especially whole-grain)
- ❑ garlic knots
- ❑ hard rolls
- ❑ hoagie rolls
- ❑ Kaiser rolls
- ❑ onion
- ❑ pumpernickel
- ❑ rye
- ❑ whole-wheat

❑ **Bagels** (any kind except egg for vegans/lacto vegetarians)

❑ **Other Bread Products**
- ❑ corn tortillas (not fried)
- ❑ flour tortillas (especially whole-wheat)
- ❑ fresh, whole-wheat pizza crust
- ❑ low-fat, whole-grain muffins

Monthly Vegetarian Shopping Lists

You can shop for these items less often, since they keep for a long time in your cupboard, refrigerator, or freezer.

❏ **Cupboard Staples**

❏ *Canned Goods*
- ❏ applesauce
- ❏ artichoke hearts
- ❏ bean salad
- ❏ beans (canned or dry): vegetarian baked beans, garbanzo, black, pinto, kidney, navy, split
- ❏ fruits: apricots, pineapple, peaches, pears, mandarin oranges, grapefruit, cranberry sauce, fruit cocktail,
- ❏ pasta sauces
- ❏ peas, lentils, black-eyed peas
- ❏ soups: lentil, vegetarian, vegetarian split pea, tomato
- ❏ sloppy Joe sauce
- ❏ tomato sauce and paste
- ❏ vegetables: green beans, peas, carrots, asparagus, corn, tomatoes
- ❏ vegetarian refried beans

❏ *Snacks and Treats*
- ❏ baked potato chips and baked tortilla chips
- ❏ bean dip
- ❏ canned pumpkin and fruit pie fillings
- ❏ flat breads (including matzo) and bread sticks
- ❏ fruit toppings: prune, cherry, apricot
- ❏ low-fat granola bars
- ❏ popcorn (bag kernels or low-fat microwave)
- ❏ rice cakes and popcorn cakes
- ❏ tapioca and flan (made with nonfat milk or soymilk)
- ❏ whole-grain, low-fat toaster pastries
- ❏ whole-grain cookies
- ❏ whole-grain crackers

❏ *Herbs and Spices*
- ❏ basil, bay leaves, cinnamon, cumin, curry powder, dill, vegetable bouillon, garlic, ginger, paprika, pepper, others:
_____

❏ *Natural Sodas*

❏ *Water*
- ❏ club soda
- ❏ plain or flavored mineral waters
- ❏ plain or flavored seltzer waters

❏ *Bottled Fruit Juices and Blends*
- ❏ sparkling cider, sparkling grape juice

❏ **Dry Items**
- ❏ couscous (whole-grain if available)
- ❏ dried bean flakes
- ❏ dry cereals (whole-grain): raisin bran, shredded wheat, bran flakes, others:
_____

- ❏ hot cereals (whole-grain): oatmeal, whole-wheat, mixed grain
- ❏ other grains: barley, millet, bulgur wheat, kasha, amaranth, spelt, teff, quinoa, kamut
- ❏ pasta (eggless for vegans/lacto vegetarians)
- ❏ rice: basmati, jasmine, brown, wild, arborio
- ❏ textured vegetable protein (TVP)
- ❏ vegetarian egg replacer
- ❏ whole-grain bread, pancake, and all-purpose mixes, and other whole-grain mixes:
_____

- ❏ whole-wheat flour; other flours:
_____

❏ *Soup Mixes or Cups*

❏ *Vegetable Oil Spray*

❏ *Flour Tortillas*

❏ *Corn Tortillas*

❏ *Tofu* (aseptically packaged)

❏ *Soymilk* (aseptically packaged)

❏ *Condiments*
- ❏ chutney
- ❏ fat-free mayonnaise
- ❏ fat-free salad dressings
- ❏ fruit preserves and conserves

- ❑ fruit-only or low-sugar spreads
- ❑ grape leaves in brine
- ❑ hoisin sauce
- ❑ honey (for nonvegans)
- ❑ horseradish mustard
- ❑ jams and jellies
- ❑ ketchup
- ❑ low-fat marinades and BBQ sauce
- ❑ mustard
- ❑ natural, butter-flavored sprinkles (for nonvegans)
- ❑ pickles and pickle relish
- ❑ salsa
- ❑ spicy brown bean sauce
- ❑ stir-fry sauces
- ❑ sun-dried tomatoes
- ❑ syrups, molasses
- ❑ sweet-and-sour sauce
- ❑ vinegar: balsamic, herbed, fruited, malt, rice
- ❑ others:

❑ *Bottled Vegetable Juices*
- ❑ tomato, V-8, borscht, carrot

❑ *Herbal Tea*

❑ *Dried Fruits*
- ❑ apples
- ❑ apricots
- ❑ blueberries

Also Need:

- ❑ cherries
- ❑ currants
- ❑ dates
- ❑ figs
- ❑ mixed fruits
- ❑ prunes
- ❑ raisins

❑ **Freezer Staples**

❑ *Frozen Bagels* (eggless for vegans and lacto vegetarians)

❑ *Muffins and Dinner Rolls*

❑ *Frozen Waffles and Pancakes*

❑ *Frozen Pasta* (eggless for vegans and lacto vegetarians)

❑ *Frozen Juices*
- ❑ apple
- ❑ cranberry raspberry
- ❑ grape
- ❑ grapefruit
- ❑ lemonade
- ❑ limeade
- ❑ orange
- ❑ pineapple orange
- ❑ tangerine orange
- ❑ others:

❑ *Frozen Entrees*

❑ *Meat Substitutes*
- ❑ burger crumbles
- ❑ meatless "bacon"
- ❑ meatless "sausage" links and patties
- ❑ vegetarian burger patties
- ❑ vegetarian hotdogs

❑ *Frozen Novelties*
- ❑ frozen juice bars
- ❑ Italian ices
- ❑ nonfat frozen yogurt and nonfat yogurt bars (for nonvegans)
- ❑ paletas
- ❑ Popsicles
- ❑ rice-based ice cream
- ❑ sorbet
- ❑ tofu ice cream

❑ *Frozen Egg Substitute* (for lacto ovo vegetarians, only, since the product is primarily egg whites) or use *commercial powdered vegetarian egg replacer* (no animal products)

❑ *Frozen Fruit*
- ❑ berry mixtures
- ❑ blueberries
- ❑ cherries
- ❑ mixed fruit
- ❑ peaches
- ❑ pineapple
- ❑ red raspberries
- ❑ strawberries

❑ *Frozen Vegetables*
- ❑ broccoli
- ❑ carrots
- ❑ cauliflower
- ❑ cut corn
- ❑ green beans
- ❑ green peas
- ❑ lima beans
- ❑ mixed vegetables
- ❑ spinach
- ❑ stir-fry mixes
- ❑ others:

The Least You Need to Know

➤ There's no legal definition for the term "natural foods."

➤ Natural foods stores carry some exceptional products that may not be found in regular supermarkets.

➤ Shop for groceries in a variety of places, including supermarkets, natural foods stores, ethnic markets, and farmer's markets or roadside stands. Co-ops and mail order may work well for people who don't have access to large natural foods stores.

➤ Shopping from a list and planning some meals in advance can be helpful to people who have changed their eating style and are trying to master new meal planning skills.

Part 5
Meal Planning Made Easy

Helen Nearing was a pioneering homesteader in New England from the early 1930s until her death a few years ago. In her cookbook, Simple Food for the Good Life *(Delacorte Press, 1980)—the jacket of which states that the book is "intended for the use of people of moderate fortune who do not affect magnificence in their style of living"—Ms. Nearing writes:*

> *It has been said (and probably by a good cook) that there are two kinds of people in the world: those who are good cooks and those who wish they were good cooks. I hold there is a third category: those who are not good cooks and who couldn't care less.*

You don't have to be a good cook to eat well. You don't even have to enjoy preparing meals to eat healthfully.

The chapters that follow will show you how easy it can be to plan tasty, nutritious, satisfying vegetarian meals with a minimum of fuss.

Chapter 18

A Daily Vegetarian Food Guide

In This Chapter

➤ A simple, daily food guide

➤ What's a serving and how many do I need?

➤ Choosing the best foods

➤ Making room for dairy and eggs

➤ Squeezing in sweets and treats

You shouldn't need a degree in nutrition to be able to plan your own nutritious vegetarian meals. You also shouldn't have to wield a calculator to balance your intake of essential nutrients.

Sure, eating well takes some degree of care and awareness of the principles of good nutrition. While you're in the learning stages, a "cheat sheet," like the one included in this chapter, can be reassuring.

This chapter presents a simple daily vegetarian food guide to help you plan meals and to remind you of the types of foods you should be including in your diet regularly. The guide also appears on the reference card in the front of this book. Tear it out and tape it to your refrigerator door if you'd like a visual cue to keep you on track.

A Simple, Daily Vegetarian Food Guide

Use the food guide that follows to help you plan meals. It will help you keep the following points in mind:

➤ In addition to a good diet, a health-supporting lifestyle also includes regular physical activity, plenty of fluids, and plenty of fresh air and sunshine (with precautions taken to prevent excessive exposure to the sun).

➤ The foundation of a healthful diet is whole grains, legumes, fruits, vegetables, nuts, and seeds.

➤ Sweets, dairy products, eggs, and vegetable oils are not necessary for anyone and should be limited, since excessive consumption of these foods is associated with health problems or displaces more important foods from your diet.

*Vegetarian Food Guide
Pyramid*

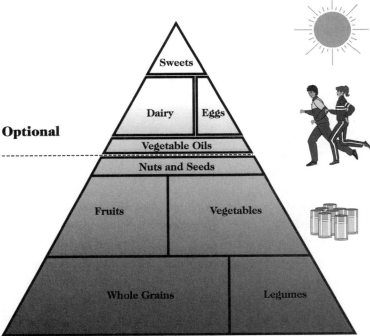

Used with permission of the Third International Congress on Vegetarian Nutrition and Loma Linda University.

How Many Servings Do I Need?

The number of servings you need from each of the food groups represented in the food guide will vary depending upon many factors, including your age, how physically active you are, what type of vegetarian diet you follow, and your size. A good way to approach meal planning is just to look at the types of foods shown below the dotted line in the food guide and try to eat a mixture of these foods. Eat enough of them to meet your calorie needs. It's really that simple.

If your calorie needs are high, eat a greater number of servings of any of the foods in the guide but especially those below the dotted line. If your calorie needs are low or you are trying to lose weight, eat less but not less than the minimum number of servings shown. If you are limiting your food intake, it's particularly important to include plenty of the foods below the dotted line. Remember, these foods are the foundations of a healthful diet.

The table that follows shows the daily number of servings you should aim for from each of the food groups in the pyramid, whether you are a vegan, lacto vegetarian, or lacto ovo vegetarian.

Heads Up!

If you're trying to lose weight, you'll need a deficit of about 3,500 calories a week to lose 1 pound per week. At the same time, you should be increasing your level of physical activity. If you can burn more calories through exercise, you won't have to cut your food intake as much. That's ideal, because if your calorie level is too low, it can be tough to get all of the nutrients you need. You want to lose weight, but you don't want to become malnourished while you're at it.

How Many Servings Do I Need?

Food Group	Servings	Serving Size
Whole grains	5–12	1 slice of bread
		1 oz. ready-to-eat cereal ($^3/_4$–1 cup)
		$^1/_2$ cup cooked grains, cereal, rice or pasta
Legumes	1–3	$^1/_2$ cup cooked dry beans, lentils, or peas
		$^1/_2$ cup tofu, soy products, or textured soy protein
		1 cup soy beverage (soymilk)
Vegetables	6–9	$^1/_2$ cup cooked vegetable
		1 cup raw vegetable or salad
		$^3/_4$ cup vegetable juice

continues

How Many Servings Do I Need?   (continued)

Food Group	Servings	Serving Size
Fruits	3–4	1 medium fruit: apple, banana, or orange
		1/2 cup chopped, cooked, or canned fruit
		3/4 cup fruit juice
		1/4 avocado
		10 olives
Nuts and seeds	1–2	1 oz. almonds, walnuts, seeds, (1/4 cup)
		2 Tbsp. nut butter such as peanut butter
Vegetable oils	4–7	1 tsp. vegetable oil
Dairy	0–2	1 cup milk or yogurt (low-fat or nonfat)
		1 1/2 oz. cheese (low-fat)
		1/2 cup ricotta cheese (part skim)
Eggs	0–1	Limit yolks to three per week
Sweets	limit	1 tsp. sugar, jam, jelly, honey, or syrup

Used with permission of the Third International Congress on Vegetarian Nutrition and Loma Linda University.

Choosing Breads, Cereals, Pasta, and Other Grain Products

When you choose grain products, keep some general rules of thumb in mind:

➤ Choose whole grains as often as possible. Whole-grain products contain more dietary fiber and usually contain more vitamins, minerals, and phytochemicals.

➤ It's okay to occasionally eat refined grain products, such as Italian bread, most bagels, French bread, and others. When you do, try to buy products that are enriched (though most bakery products are not).

➤ Eat a variety of different types of grains including oatmeal, wheat, rye, barley, millet, quinoa, rice, amaranth, and many others.

Some more tips for using grains creatively include:

➤ Many grains can be eaten hot or cold. For instance, rice is good hot with steamed vegetables or vegetarian chili, or it can be eaten cold in rice pudding or vegetarian-style sushi.

➤ Mixtures of different grains can be delicious. Examples are seven-grain hot cereal and multigrain breads and rolls.

➤ Cooked grains keep well in the refrigerator. When you cook grains such as rice, buckwheat, barley, and others, make more than you need. Store the remainder in the refrigerator and reheat it to eat with other foods such as cooked beans, vegetable gratins, bean burritos, and bean tacos.

➤ Some grains take a long time to cook on the stovetop. To save time, you can often bring a pot of water to boiling, add the uncooked grain, turn off the heat, and take the pot off the stove. Let the grain soak for an hour or two until the water has been absorbed.

Heads Up!

"Diet" breads are often advertised as having only 40 calories per slice and target people who are watching their weight, playing on the myth that breads are fattening. Ordinary whole-grain breads are not particularly high in calories and are a nutritious part of your diet. You'd be better off cutting down on fat to save calories or exercising a little longer, rather than cutting back on your consumption of bread. The only reason to eat "diet" breads or thinly sliced breads is if you happen to like them better than the regular kind.

Choosing Foods

Food Groups	Foods to Choose
Whole grains	Select whole-wheat or whole-grain products
	Cereals: wheat, rice, corn, oats, millet
	Grain products: bread, pasta, tortillas
Legumes	Beans: pinto, navy, limas, soy, garbanzo
	Peas: split peas, lentils, black-eyed
	Soy products: tofu, soy beverages (soymilks), textured vegetable protein
Nuts and seeds	Includes butters and spreads
	Use raw, in cooking or dry roasted
Vegetables	Includes all vegetables: leafy green, starchy
Fruits	Includes all fruit; emphasize whole fruit rather than juice

continues

Choosing Foods (continued)

Food Groups	Foods to Choose
Vegetable oils	Emphasize those high in monounsaturates such as olive, sesame, and canola
	Limit tropical oils (coconut, palm kernel, palm oil) and avoid hydrogenated fats
Dairy	Emphasize nonfat or low-fat products
	If dairy is not included, women, adolescents, children, and the elderly need to ensure adequate sources of calcium and vitamin D
Eggs	Limit eggs or use egg whites only
Sweets	Eat in moderation

Used with permission from the Third International Congress on Vegetarian Nutrition and Loma Linda University.

Choosing Vegetables

When you choose vegetables, keep the following points in mind:

➤ Whether you buy them fresh, frozen, or canned, you can't go wrong with vegetables. They're all nutritious.

➤ Some vegetables are nutritional superstars. These include deep yellow, orange, or red vegetables, as well as dark green vegetables. These vegetables are especially rich sources of vitamins A and C, iron, and calcium. Examples include sweet potatoes, red and green bell peppers, broccoli, kale, tomatoes, and carrots. Eat them often.

➤ *Cruciferous* vegetables are also particularly good choices because they are rich in phytochemicals that may protect your health. Examples include some of the dark-green vegetables such as broccoli and kale, as well as bok choy or Chinese cabbage, kohlrabi, and cauliflower.

➤ If you cook vegetables, expose them to heat for as short a time as possible to help preserve their nutrient content.

➤ If you have trouble getting enough calories on a vegetarian diet, eat more cooked vegetables and fewer bulky, raw vegetables.

➤ Eat large servings of vegetables. One-cup servings are a great idea.

➤ Buy locally grown vegetables in season when you can. You'll support local farmers, and fresh foods that don't have to be shipped long distances are more nutritious than foods that have to travel across the country to get to your table.

Good ways to work more vegetables into your diet include:

➤ Buying some prepared vegetables such as stir-fry mixes, peeled baby carrots, and ready-to-eat mixtures of salad greens. You may pay more, but the convenience is worth the price if it helps you to eat more of these foods.

➤ Buy an electric steamer and use it to steam potatoes, sweet potatoes, carrots, onions, and any other favorite cooked vegetables. Just wash the vegetables, cut into chunks, and toss into the steamer. Set the timer, go back to your work, and there's nothing left to do until the vegetables are ready. No watching the stove or fiddling with the microwave oven.

➤ Serve fresh vegetables with a variety of dips, including hummus, low-fat salad dressings, black bean dip, or salsa.

➤ Chop or grate vegetables finely and blend them into marinara sauce for pasta, or toss with cooked pasta and olive oil for pasta primavera.

➤ Grate fresh vegetables and use them to fill pita pockets along with a scoop of tofu salad, hummus, or a sprinkling of grated cheese.

Veggie Talk

Cruciferous vegetables, which are full of health-protecting phyto-chemicals, are in the cabbage family. The family includes broccoli, bok choy or Chinese cabbage, Brussels sprouts, kale, collard greens, turnip greens, mustard greens, turnips, cauliflower, kohlrabi (a white root vegetable), daikon, radishes, watercress, and arugula (a peppery tasting green). Choose these often.

The Last Bite

Fresh produce contains only a fraction of the amount of pesticides and herbicides that are found in animal products, because environmental contaminants accumulate more heavily in the animals' tissues. A vegetarian diet gives added protection against environmental contaminants because dietary fiber from plant matter helps to move contaminants through the body quickly, so there's less time for contaminants to be in contact with the lining of the intestines. However, you can remove some pesticide residues by washing produce with dish soap and water or using special produce rinses available in stores. You can also buy organically grown produce.

Choosing Fruits

When you choose fruits, remember:

➤ Buy locally grown fruits in season when you can, because they're fresher and more nutritious than foods that are shipped long distances.

➤ You can't go wrong with fruits and 100 percent fruit juices. They're all nutritious.

➤ Choose plenty of deep yellow, orange, or red fruits such as papayas, mangoes, apricots, peaches, and oranges. These are the nutritional superstars that are particularly rich in vitamins A and C and other phytochemicals.

➤ Try to eat two pieces of fresh fruit every day.

➤ If you are watching your weight, choose fresh fruits more often than dried fruits or fruit juice, which have considerably more calories for the same volume.

➤ Wash fresh fruits with dish soap and water or use a commercial produce rinse to remove pesticide residues if you are going to eat the peel.

Heads Up!

Even though you don't plan to eat the peel, be sure to wash the outsides of melons, grapefruit, and other fresh fruits before slicing them. If you don't, you may drag any bacteria or contaminants that may be present on the surface into the interior edible portion of the fruit. In some cases, these bacteria can cause sickness.

Some good ways to work more fruit into your diet includes:

➤ Keep a bowl of fresh fruit on your kitchen table or counter. Keep a variety of fruit on hand.

➤ When fresh fruits have been sitting untouched for several days, cut them up and make a fruit salad.

➤ Serve sliced fruit with meals. Use slices of apple and pear as garnishes on a plate, add chunks of fruit to salads, and serve fresh or cooked fruits for dessert.

➤ Occasionally cut up fruit and store it in an airtight container in the refrigerator on the top shelf. Somehow, fresh fruit can be more appealing when it's already cut up for you, and you're more likely to think of it if it's the first thing you see when you open the refrigerator to hunt for a snack.

Choosing Legumes and Meat Substitutes

Here are some general rules of thumb for choosing legumes and meat substitutes:

➤ You can't go wrong with beans, peas, or lentils of any kind.

➤ Feel free to use canned beans. For less sodium, rinse them with water in a colander before using.

➤ Buy organically grown canned and dry beans when it's feasible, but the regular kind are fine too.

➤ When you compare meat substitutes such as veggie burgers, hotdogs, and breakfast "meats," choose the ones that are lowest in sodium and fat and the highest in dietary fiber.

Some good ways to include more legumes in your diet:

➤ Add a can of any kind of bean to a pot of soup.

➤ Serve bean salads with meals. Marinated black beans with corn and diced red peppers make a colorful side dish to serve with sandwiches. Try a four-bean salad made with green beans, wax beans, dark red kidney beans, and garbanzo beans.

➤ Serve bean chili and onions over a vegetarian hotdog on a bun.

➤ Use mashed pinto beans or black beans as the base for a variety of bean dips that can be seasoned with different herbs and spices. Serve bean dips with raw vegetables, tortilla chips, or toasted pita bread wedges brushed with olive oil and minced garlic.

➤ Serve a variety of bean soups often as accompaniments to meals. Good choices are navy bean soup, lentil soup, minestrone soup with white kidney beans, split-pea soup with diced carrots, and black bean soup topped with minced onions.

The Last Bite

A number of products are made from soybeans, including tofu, tempeh, soy nuts, canned soybeans, soymilk, textured vegetable protein, and others. All of these are good choices, and when they replace meat and high-fat dairy products in your diet, they can dramatically reduce your intake of saturated fat and cholesterol.

About Nuts and Seeds

Nuts and seeds sometimes get a bad rap because they're so high in fat. The truth is, they *are* high in fat and they're concentrated sources of calories. So, anyone who is watching his or her weight should use them sparingly. A sprinkle here and there is fine. For instance, adding a tablespoon or two of sunflower seeds or pumpkin seeds to a salad adds flavor and crunch. A dash of slivered almonds adds flavor and nutrition to a plate of green beans. Using seeds or nuts in this way is not a problem.

On the other hand, people who have trouble getting enough calories on a bulky, vegetarian diet can add seeds and nuts to their meals for extra calories. Seeds and nuts are full of vitamins and minerals and phytochemicals that are beneficial to your health, so as long as you keep in mind the extra calories they contain, there's no reason not to eat them.

Heads Up!

Buy unsalted seeds and nuts when you have a choice to keep your sodium intake down. It's also better to eat seeds and nuts raw or dry roasted rather than cooked in additional oil.

If You Use Dairy Products or Eggs...

If you eat dairy products, use only nonfat dairy products such as milk, cheese, yogurt, and frozen desserts. If you are vegan or otherwise don't eat dairy products at all, be sure that you eat plenty of plant sources of calcium and that you get enough vitamin D from sunshine or other sources.

If you eat eggs, limit the yolks. There's no exact science to figuring out how many egg yolks are too many for any individual, but the fewer the better, generally speaking. If you eat eggs, you're better off using the whites only. Of course, there are many good egg substitutes, some of which have already been mentioned in previous chapters. (More substitution ideas are included in Chapter 20, "Recipe Magic!")

Finding Room for Sweets, Treats, and Other Extras

The term "moderation" is widely used to mean "just enough but not too much." How much is too much? To many people, "moderation" means "less than the other guy eats," and too often, it means that anything goes.

Heads Up!

Beer, wine, and liquor are vegetarian, but you should limit your consumption of alcoholic beverages. Some health organizations recommend that adults limit alcoholic beverages to the equivalent of one mixed drink, one beer, or one glass of wine per day, but others recommend that everyone abstain. All agree that less is better.

As Robert Pritikin, director of the Pritikin Longevity Centers, said, "In this country, we're dying of moderation."

Coming from the point of extremes (extremely high intakes of fat, cholesterol, sugar, salt, and so on) typical of many people's diets, the term "moderation" can lose its meaning. So how can you put your finger on how much dessert or candy or any other treat you can have and still have a healthful vegetarian diet?

The best way to say it is that you can have treats in moderation, but let's define moderation.

When sweets such as honey, jam, jelly, syrup, sugar, and so on are used as condiments—a teaspoon here and there to flavor your foods—they are generally not a concern and can be used on a daily basis. As long as you aren't using half the jar, it's doubtful that you could be eating too much.

On the other hand, when sweets are eaten in the form of desserts and snacks, too much can displace more nutritious foods from your diet. So, in the case of desserts and sweet snacks, one serving a day is a reasonable goal. If you are trying to lose weight, you might want to limit yourself to less—one serving every few days or once a week.

The same goes for junk foods such as chips and candies. Aim for not more than one serving of any of these each day. In other words, one serving of either a sweet dessert or snack or a junk food snack or treat. (Not one serving of each!)

The Least You Need to Know

➤ You can use the food guide included in this chapter and on the reference card in the front of this book to help guide your daily food choices.

➤ The foundation of your diet should be whole grains, legumes, fruits, vegetables, seeds, and nuts.

➤ If your calorie needs are greater, eat more servings from the various food groups, especially those below the dotted line on the food guide pyramid.

➤ If your calorie needs are less or you are trying to lose weight, eat less food but not less than the minimum number of recommended servings.

➤ Sweets and other treats can be worked into your diet regularly as long as they don't displace too much of the more nutrient-dense foods.

Chapter 19

When There's No Time to Cook: Quick and Easy Meals and Snacks

In This Chapter

➤ Tips for getting meal planning under control

➤ Ideas for quick and easy meals and snacks

➤ Fix-and-freeze ideas and make-ahead meals for the weekend cook

➤ Sample menus

You don't have to be a professional chef to fix adequate vegetarian meals. You don't even have to impress your friends. All you have to do is satisfy yourself (and your family—maybe).

Are you already a gourmet cook? Yes? Then you probably need no reassurance that you'll be just as adept at fixing vegetarian masterpieces once you've figured out what you want to make. Which won't take long, since you're already skilled and creative.

On the other hand, you may be one of the rest of us—just regular people who somehow manage to put together reasonably appealing meals most of the time. Sometimes we even do it with a little flair. But most of the time, we're talking whipping meals together in 30 minutes or less, with the emphasis on less.

This chapter is for anyone who needs a little head start or a leg up in planning meals. There's some good-sense advice about ways to simplify meal preparation, and there are plenty of mix-and-match sample menus to give you some ideas of where to begin. You can use them and modify them until you feel confident enough to begin creating your own.

Please note that you won't need recipes to make many of the foods on these menus. In cases where you may not know how to make the item listed, any number of vegetarian cookbooks will contain a similar recipe. For example, you can find recipes for vegetarian chili, vegetarian lasagna, lentil soup, and eggless French toast in many vegetarian cookbooks.

A list of some popular vegetarian cookbooks is provided in Chapter 26, "Getting Educated About Everything Vegetarian."

Helpful Hint

Make a list of your favorite vegetarian foods and post it somewhere in the kitchen (behind a cabinet door is a good place). Some may be foods that are favorites even for non-vegetarians, such as macaroni and cheese, grilled-cheese sandwiches, vegetarian pizza, and bean burritos. You can refer to your list when you can't think of something vegetarian to make for lunch or dinner.

Rise and Shine: Breakfast Time

Okay, so you may not be a breakfast eater. How about a very early lunch?

Really, eating breakfast is an excellent way to fire up your gray cells. Boost your blood sugar with a good, high-carbohydrate meal first thing in the morning, and you'll function better for the rest of the day than you would without it.

What's more, if you are a breakfast eater, you'll find that there couldn't be an easier vegetarian meal to prepare.

Breakfast Pointers

When you think about what you want to fix for breakfast, consider the following:

➤ There's nothing wrong with having leftovers from last night's dinner, cold pizza, cold Chinese take-out, or a bowl of soup for breakfast. Nobody said that breakfast had to be cereal or toast.

➤ A glass of juice and a bowl of cereal is a substantial breakfast. So is a couple of pieces of toast and a banana. Breakfast doesn't have to be particularly creative, and it doesn't have to be a five-course meal. But it can be if you want it to be. Mandarin crepes with seasonal fresh berries would be a fabulous vegetarian breakfast if you had the time and inclination.

➤ Since a vegetarian breakfast can consist of exactly what a nonvegetarian would ordinarily eat for breakfast, it's a good meal to serve when you are entertaining nonvegetarian guests. You could serve freshly squeezed orange juice and French toast with apple compote and warm maple syrup, for example. Everyone would be happy, and no one would know the difference.

➤ You can also modify a traditional breakfast to be vegetarian or vegan. For instance, for a meal consisting of juice, pancakes, and sausage, you could substitute vegetarian sausage for the regular sausage, and the meal would be essentially the same. Instead of a breakfast consisting of scrambled eggs, bacon, toast, juice, and coffee, you could serve scrambled tofu, vegetarian bacon, toast, juice, and coffee.

➤ If you like cold cereal in the morning, try mixing two or three varieties in the same bowl for a change of pace.

➤ Just as leftovers from yesterday's dinner can be a fine breakfast, breakfast foods can be a great change of pace for lunch or supper or a late night snack. So, don't feel guilty if you like a bowl of cereal for dinner now and then, or even once a week. It's okay.

Helpful Hint

Surprise your family and friends with a delicious breakfast juice blend of freshly squeezed orange juice mixed with fresh carrot juice. Experiment to find the ratio of orange to carrot juice that you prefer, but a 50:50 blend is good. You can use orange juice concentrate instead of fresh orange juice if need be, but fresh carrot juice tastes much better in this drink than canned carrot juice. If your supermarket doesn't carry fresh carrot juice (check the deli area), you'll need a high-speed blender or juicer to make your own.

A Week of Breakfasts

The sample menus that follow represent a range of ideas for healthful vegetarian breakfasts. They've all been planned without animal products so that they're appropriate for any type of vegetarian. If you'd prefer to use dairy products or eggs in some cases, just substitute them for the vegan option in the menu. For example, if soymilk is listed, you can substitute skim milk, or if tofu scrambler is listed, feel free to use scrambled eggs. Realize, though, that the nutritional analyses will be different if you make changes.

Another detail that you may notice is that I've used fortified orange juice and soymilk wherever those foods are listed. That's just a nod to the fact that many people—especially vegans—will have trouble meeting the recommended levels of intakes of calcium without including substantial amounts of high-calcium foods, supplements, or fortified foods in their diets. If you use dairy products regularly, you may opt not to use fortified juice or soymilk.

Breakfast One

³/₄ cup calcium-fortified orange juice

2 slices of eggless French toast (made with whole-grain bread, bananas, vanilla, and soymilk)

¹/₂ cup sliced apple compote, lightly sweetened (with sugar or any sweetener, corn syrup, etc.)

4 Tbsp. warm maple syrup

Hot beverage

Calories (Kcal): 724	Sodium (mg): 509.5
Protein (gm): 10	Iron (mg): 6
Total fat (gm): 5	Calcium (mg): 508
Saturated fat (gm): 0.5	Zinc (mg): 1.5
Cholesterol (mg): 0	Vitamin B12 (µg): 0.5
Dietary fiber (gm): 9	

Breakfast Two

¹/₂ cup prune juice

1 cup cooked oatmeal with cinnamon, brown sugar, and raisins

1 cup fortified vanilla soymilk

Hot beverage

Calories (Kcal): 491	Sodium (mg): 103
Protein (gm): 13	Iron (mg): 5
Total fat (gm): 5.5	Calcium (mg): 416
Saturated fat (gm): 0.5	Zinc (mg): 2
Cholesterol (mg): 0	Vitamin B12 (µg): 1
Dietary fiber (gm): 4	

Breakfast Three

$^1/_2$ grapefruit

2 slices multigrain toast with 1 tsp. soy margarine and 1 Tbsp. raspberry preserves

$^3/_4$ cup bran flakes

1 cup calcium-fortified soymilk

Hot beverage

Calories (Kcal): 489

Protein (gm): 15

Total fat (gm): 9.5

Saturated fat (gm): 1

Cholesterol (mg): 0

Dietary fiber (gm): 11

Sodium (mg): 671.5

Iron (mg): 11

Calcium (mg): 432

Zinc (mg): 5

Vitamin B12 (µg): 3

Breakfast Four

$^3/_4$ cup calcium-fortified orange juice

$^3/_4$ cup scrambled tofu

$^1/_2$ cup hash brown potatoes

2 slices whole-wheat toast brushed with olive oil

Hot beverage

Calories (Kcal): 588

Protein (gm): 28

Total fat (gm): 29

Saturated fat (gm): 7

Cholesterol (mg): 0

Dietary fiber (gm): 8

Sodium (mg): 343.5

Iron (mg): 16

Calcium(mg): 593

Zinc (mg): 3

Vitamin B12 (µg): 0

Breakfast Five

³/₄ cup grapefruit juice

Whole bagel with 2 Tbsp. soy cream cheese

Banana

Hot beverage

Calories (Kcal): 443.5

Protein (gm): 10

Total fat (gm): 12

Saturated fat (gm): 3

Cholesterol (mg): 0

Dietary fiber (gm): 3

Sodium (mg): 284.5

Iron (mg): 2

Calcium (mg): 44

Zinc (mg): 1

Vitamin B12 (µg): 0.1

Breakfast Six

³/₄ cup calcium-fortified orange juice

¹/₂ cup mixed fruit compote

1 bran muffin

Hot beverage

Calories (Kcal): 289

Protein (gm): 5

Total fat (gm): 5

Saturated fat (gm): 1

Cholesterol (mg): 0

Dietary fiber (gm): 5

Sodium (mg): 177

Iron (mg): 2

Calcium (mg): 56

Zinc (mg): 1

Vitamin B12 (µg): 0.1

Breakfast Seven

³/₄ cup freshly squeezed orange juice

1 cup hot whole-grain cereal with 1 Tbsp. chopped dates and 2 Tbsp. brown sugar

1 cup calcium-fortified vanilla soymilk

1 slice multigrain toast with 1 tsp. strawberry jam

Hot beverage

Calories (Kcal): 421

Protein (gm): 14

Total fat (gm): 5

Saturated fat (gm): 0

Cholesterol (mg): 0

Dietary fiber (mg): 4

Sodium (mg): 780

Iron (mg): 3

Calcium (mg): 216

Zinc (mg): 2

Vitamin B12 (µg): 1

A Week of Light Meals

The light meal menus that follow can be used for lunches, snacks, or light suppers.

You may notice that the sodium levels of some of the menus are extremely high. This is because canned soups and canned beans are included in the data base used in the analyses of the menus. In a few cases, sodium levels are 1,000 milligrams to 1,500 milligrams in a meal. They're a dramatic example of how much sodium prepared convenience foods add to your diet.

You can cut the sodium content of these meals in half or more by doing the following:

➤ Make your own soups, using minimal or no added salt.

➤ Buy reduced-sodium soups. Many natural foods brands are much lower in sodium than conventional store brands.

➤ Rinse canned beans before using them.

Light Meal One

6 baby carrots with salsa

Hummus sandwich on 2 slices cracked-wheat bread with ¹/₄ cup hummus, sliced tomato, and alfalfa sprouts

³/₄ cup vinaigrette coleslaw

Water with lemon

Calories (Kcal): 431.5

Protein (gm): 14

Total fat (gm): 15

Saturated fat (gm): 2

Cholesterol (mg): 0

Dietary fiber (gm): 9

Sodium (mg): 1,044

Iron (mg): 4.5

Calcium (mg): 139

Zinc (mg): 1

Vitamin B12 (µg): 0

Light Meal Two

Bean burrito with 1 flour tortilla, chopped tomatoes, lettuce, onions, $^1/_4$ cup rice, and 2 Tbsp. salsa

Orange slices

Herbal iced tea

Calories (Kcal): 371

Protein (gm): 14

Total fat (gm): 4

Saturated fat (gm): 1

Cholesterol (mg): 0

Dietary fiber (gm): 4

Sodium (mg): 651

Iron (mg): 4

Calcium (mg): 174

Zinc (mg): 2

Vitamin B12 (µg): 0

Light Meal Three

1 cup black bean soup topped with minced onions

Mixed green salad with tomato slices and spicy vinaigrette dressing

Sourdough roll with 1 Tbsp. balsamic vinegar and 2 tsp. olive oil

Water with lemon

Calories (Kcal): 394

Protein (gm): 12

Total fat (gm): 18

Saturated fat (gm): 3

Cholesterol (mg): 0

Dietary fiber (gm): 4

Sodium (mg): 1,522

Iron (mg): 4

Calcium (mg): 84

Zinc (mg): 2

Vitamin B12 (µg): 0

Light Meal Four

Vegetarian burger on a Kaiser roll with lettuce and tomato

$^1/_2$ cup sweet corn and red bean salad

$^1/_2$ cup home fries

Herbal tea

Calories (Kcal): 465

Protein (gm): 23

Total fat (gm): 12

Saturated fat (gm): 4

Cholesterol (mg): 0

Dietary fiber (gm): 10

Sodium (mg): 823

Iron (mg): 5

Calcium (mg): 138

Zinc (mg): 2

Vitamin B12 (µg): 0

Light Meal Five

1 cup of split-pea soup with minced carrot

Pesto (1 tsp.) and tomato sandwich on whole-wheat toast

$^3/_4$ cup fresh fruit salad

Water with lime

Calories (Kcal): 433

Protein (gm): 16

Total fat (gm): 9

Saturated fat (gm): 2

Cholesterol (mg): 0

Dietary fiber (gm): 7

Sodium (mg): 1,329

Iron (mg): 5

Calcium (mg): 81

Zinc (mg): 3

Vitamin B12 (µg): 0

Light Meal Six

$^1/_2$ cup grapefruit sections

Tofu salad ($^1/_2$ cup) sandwich on 2 slices marble rye bread

$^1/_2$ cup three-bean salad

Herbal iced tea

Calories (Kcal): 260

Protein (gm): 9

Total fat (gm): 7

Saturated fat (gm): 1

Cholesterol (mg): 0

Dietary fiber (gm): 5

Sodium (mg): 529

Iron (mg): 2

Calcium (mg): 108

Zinc (mg): 1

Vitamin B12 (µg): 0

Light Meal Seven

1 cup vegetarian chili

Corn muffin (3-inch diameter)

Apple, sliced

Hot beverage

Calories (Kcal): 496	Sodium (mg): 1,051
Protein (gm): 21	Iron (mg): 7
Total fat (gm): 6	Calcium (mg): 150
Saturated fat (gm): 1	Zinc (mg): 2
Cholesterol (mg): 0	Vitamin B12 (µg): 0
Dietary fiber (gm): 19	

A Week of Main Meals

Use these menus for dinner or a heavier mid-day meal.

The sodium content of the main meals that follow can be reduced by following the same instructions given earlier for light meals.

Main Meal One

Tempeh sloppy Joe (1/2 cup filling) on a whole-grain bun

2 ears of corn on the cob

3/4 cup cooked kale with minced garlic and sesame seeds

One pear, sliced

Water with lemon

Calories (Kcal): 650	Sodium (mg): 680
Protein (gm): 29	Iron (mg): 14
Total fat (gm): 13	Calcium (mg): 306
Saturated fat (gm): 2	Zinc (mg): 5
Cholesterol (mg): 0	Vitamin B12 (µg): 0
Dietary fiber (gm): 21	

Main Meal Two

Mixed baby greens with chopped walnuts and raspberry vinaigrette dressing

6 oz. vegetable lasagna

Multigrain roll

1 cup mixed berries

Water with lime

Calories (Kcal): 479	Sodium (mg): 1,292
Protein (gm): 30	Iron (mg): 3
Total fat (gm): 14	Calcium (mg): 85
Saturated fat (gm): 1	Zinc (mg): 1
Cholesterol (mg): 0	Vitamin B12 (µg): 0
Dietary fiber (gm): 6	

Main Meal Three

$^3/_4$ cup sweet and sour cabbage

1 cup stir-fried vegetables and bean curd (tofu) over

1 cup steamed white rice

$^1/_2$ cup sautéed Chinese greens

One orange small, sliced

Hot beverage

Calories (Kcal): 440	Sodium (mg): 121
Protein (gm): 12	Iron (mg): 5
Total fat (gm): 6	Calcium (mg): 311
Saturated fat (gm): 1	Zinc (mg): 1
Cholesterol (mg): 0	Vitamin B12 (µg): 0
Dietary fiber (gm): 11	

Main Meal Four

$^1/_2$ cup hummus appetizer with 6 pita wedges and several raw vegetable sticks

2 stuffed cabbage rolls made with garbanzo beans, steamed rice, raisins, lemon juice, and seasoning

$^3/_4$ cup cooked mixed vegetables

2-inch piece of baklava (made with honey alternative if vegan)

Hot beverage

Calories (Kcal): 695	Sodium (mg): 1,135
Protein (gm): 32	Iron (mg): 6
Total fat (gm): 20	Calcium (mg): 175
Saturated fat (gm): 1	Zinc (mg): 2
Cholesterol (mg): 0	Vitamin B12 (µg): 0
Dietary fiber (gm): 8	

Main Meal Five

Mixed green salad with ripe strawberry halves and poppyseed dressing

2 bean tacos

³/₄ cup seasoned rice (or alternative cooked grain for a change of pace)

³/₄ cup steamed broccoli

¹/₂ cup vanilla pudding

Hot beverage

Calories (Kcal): 602	Sodium (mg): 994
Protein (gm): 24.5	Iron (mg): 8
Total fat (gm): 10	Calcium (mg): 471
Saturated fat (gm): 1	Zinc (mg): 4
Cholesterol (mg): 0	Vitamin B12 (µg): 0
Dietary fiber (gm): 11	

Main Meal Six

1 cup minestrone soup

2 cups fettuccine tossed with steamed mixed vegetables, garlic, and 1 tsp. olive oil

¹/₂ cup sautéed spinach

2-inch chunk of Italian bread

Large wedge of cantaloupe

Water with lemon

Calories (Kcal): 429	Sodium (mg): 1,436
Protein (gm): 17	Iron (mg): 6
Total fat (gm): 8	Calcium (mg): 255
Saturated fat (gm): 1	Zinc (mg): 2
Cholesterol (mg): 0	Vitamin B12 (µg): 0
Dietary fiber (gm): 10	

Main Meal Seven

Black bean burger on a multigrain bun with red onion

³/₄ cup steamed, fresh, green beans with slivered almonds

³/₄ cup roasted red potatoes with olive oil, minced garlic, and parsley

¹/₂ cup peach crisp

Hot beverage

Calories (Kcal): 557	Sodium (mg): 465
Protein (gm): 25	Iron (mg): 5
Total fat (gm): 9	Calcium (mg): 169
Saturated fat (gm): 1	Zinc (mg): 2
Cholesterol (mg): 0	Vitamin B12 (µg): 0
Dietary fiber (gm): 11	

Anytime Snacks

A snack may have to be nonperishable and portable enough to pack in a briefcase, purse, gym bag, or backpack. On the other hand, it may be nothing more than leftovers from dinner earlier in the day, or a glass of soymilk and a couple of cookies grabbed in the middle of the night during a wee-hours fit of the munchies.

So, your choice of a snack may vary depending upon the circumstances. You've got lots of options, though. A few ideas are listed below to get you started. See how many more you can add to the list yourself. The snacks in this list range from about 100 to 300 calories each:

➤ Soymilk and fruit smoothie

➤ Cookies and soymilk

➤ Graham crackers and milk

➤ Bowl of cereal and milk

➤ Half of a sandwich

➤ Soy yogurt

➤ Bran muffin

➤ Low-fat popcorn

➤ Bagel with jelly

➤ Soup cup with whole-grain crackers

➤ Bowl of three-bean salad

➤ English muffin or toast with jam

➤ Baby carrots with hummus dip or salsa

➤ Baked tortilla chips with black bean dip

➤ Fresh fruit

➤ Frozen banana

➤ Frozen fruit bar

➤ Bean burrito

➤ Bean taco

➤ Bowl of fruit salad

➤ Bowl of rice pudding

➤ Freshly picked strawberries topped with vanilla ice cream (nonfat or rice- or soy-based)

➤ Oatmeal cookies

➤ Fig Newtons

The Last Bite

A mid-morning or mid-afternoon snack can be a good strategy for many people. A snack can help stave off a headache, especially if it's been more than three hours since you last ate a meal and if another meal is still a few hours away. A snack can also help boost your energy level when there's going to be a long stretch of time between meals. A snack can even help prevent you from overeating. For example, a light snack just before leaving work or school in the late afternoon can take just enough of the edge off your hunger so that you don't eat everything in sight when you arrive home.

For the Sunday Cook

Planning ahead can help you gain control over meals. That's especially important when you're working on changing your eating behavior. If you're new to a vegetarian diet, meal planning may be easier for a while if you think about the next day's meals the day before. That way, you'll help to avoid a last-minute crunch when you're tired and hungry and can't think of something to fix. You might even have time to prepare part of the meal the night before—a salad or a sandwich filling, for instance.

One effective way of planning ahead is to prepare a few foods that can be stored in the refrigerator for several days or in the freezer and are available to take out and use whenever you need them.

Set aside a couple of hours one day a week to fix a few meal items for the coming weeks. Since some of those foods can be frozen, over time you'll build up a good supply of ready-made foods to have on hand for times when you're too tired or busy to cook a complete meal.

Refrigerator Helpers

Lots of foods can be fixed ahead of time and kept in the refrigerator until you need them. Some will keep for only a few days, such as fresh fruit and vegetable salads. Others, such as some dips and grain-based salads, may last a little longer—several days to a week. Still, having a salad or a sandwich filling or two on hand can be a tremendous help when it comes time to put dinner on the table. Who wants to wash and peel vegetables and toss a salad when they get home from work? Sometimes it's all you can do to fix a quick pasta dish or sauté some vegetables for a stir-fry.

Here's a list of a few salads that will keep two or three days in the refrigerator:

➤ Cucumber and tomato salad (best if eaten within two days)

➤ Three-bean salad

➤ Greek salad (best if eaten within two days)

➤ Mixed fresh fruit salad (add bananas just before serving)

➤ Mixed berry salad

➤ Melon salad

➤ Winter salad with apples, pears, raisins, chopped figs, and cinnamon

➤ Green bean and boiled potato salad

➤ Coleslaw

These dips and salads will keep for several days to a week in the refrigerator:

➤ Tabouli salad

➤ Wheat berry with cranberries salad

➤ Hummus

➤ Rice pilaf

➤ Marinated vegetable salad (broccoli, cauliflower, mushrooms, carrots)

➤ Broccoli salad (broccoli, sweet onions, dried cherries, sunflower seeds, soy mayonnaise)

➤ Black bean dip or spread

➤ Pinto bean spread (refried beans)

➤ Potato salad

Fix-and-Freeze Head Starts

It's also nice to have a few things in the freezer—casseroles, soups, main dishes, breads, and muffins—that can be taken out as needed. Of course, since they're frozen, they'll keep for several weeks until you use them.

You can freeze bread products, such as pancakes, waffles, cookies, and muffins. Store them in small batches or single servings so that you can take out only what you need for a few days at a time. If you freeze pancakes, put a layer of waxed paper between each so that they don't stick together and are easier to separate.

Other foods that freeze well include:

➤ Vegetarian chili

➤ Soups

➤ Lasagna

➤ Grain and vegetable casseroles

➤ Stuffed shells or manicotti

➤ Grapes and bananas (Peel bananas first. These make great frozen snacks or you can use the frozen bananas for smoothies.)

➤ Fresh berries and melon balls

➤ Spinach pie

➤ Tofu quiche

➤ Fruit crisps and pies

The Least You Need to Know

➤ Vegetarian meals don't have to be fancy, and you don't have to be a great chef to fix a tasty and satisfying meal.

➤ Breakfast is the easiest vegetarian meal to fix, because most breakfast foods are already vegetarian.

➤ Taking an hour or two once a week to fix several batches of food, including salads, sandwich fillings, muffins, cookies, casseroles, soups, or an entree, can give you a terrific head start on meals throughout the week.

➤ Some make-ahead foods can keep in the refrigerator for a few days to a week, and others can keep in the freezer for several weeks. Store them in small batches and take them out as needed.

Recipe Magic!

When I think about vegetarian substitutions for animal products in recipes, I immediately think of Gilligan, the Skipper, palm trees, deserted islands, and big coconut cream and banana cream pies.

You may not want to admit it publicly, but surely you remember the TV show *Gilligan's Island*. As a kid, I was intrigued by those pies and wondered how the castaways managed to make them without eggs, butter, and milk. Okay, they had coconut milk. No eggs or butter, though. And those pies looked so good.

In this chapter, I'll let you in on the secret to making all of your favorite foods without using any animal products whatsoever. (Of course, some vegetarians eat dairy products and eggs and won't care to work those ingredients out of recipes. However, vegans and anyone who wants to lower their intake of saturated fat and cholesterol may find this information useful.)

Cookbook Logic

You may not have known that you didn't need eggs, milk, or butter to make your favorite desserts, because standard cookbooks didn't give you any other choices.

Think about it. Your old *Betty Crocker* and *Joy of Cooking* call for animal products in nearly every baked good or dessert recipe they contain. Cookies, cakes, pies, quick breads—they all call for eggs, milk, and butter. What holds a meatloaf together? Eggs, of course. How do you make French toast? With eggs and milk, naturally.

It's our tradition. In our culture, animal products play a major role in nearly every meal we eat. They are incorporated into nearly every recipe. Even the standards by which many foods are judged are dependent upon animal product ingredients for the qualities that have come to be considered desirable.

For example, a pie crust or biscuit is supposed to be flaky and tender. How does it achieve that texture? By the use of lard (or more recently, hydrogenated shortening). If you used vegetable oil instead, the crust or biscuit would not be as flaky. Similarly, if you used soymilk and mashed bananas in place of milk and eggs to make French toast, you'd get delicious French toast, but it wouldn't be quite the same as the French toast to which you may be accustomed. The color and flavor would be a little different.

So, when you make substitutions for animal ingredients in recipes, the qualities of the finished product may be different from those made with animal products.

If you want to substitute nonanimal ingredients in your favorite traditional recipes, you will probably be on your own in figuring out how much of each ingredient to use. Unless you're using a vegan or vegetarian cookbook in which the recipes have already been tested, you'll have to fiddle around with regular recipes yourself until you hit on the ingredients that work best and the proper amounts.

In many cases, there are several different foods that can substitute for the same animal product in a recipe. You'll need to experiment to find the one that gives you the best result. The information that follows in this chapter will help guide you in working the animal products out of nonvegetarian or nonvegan recipes and give you a sense of where to start.

Replacing Eggs in Recipes

How many times have you wanted to bake a batch of cookies, only to find that you're missing a vital ingredient, such as eggs?

Bet you didn't know that those eggs weren't so vital. If you had known that you could substitute any number of other foods for the eggs in your recipes, you wouldn't have had to waste a minute running to the store.

Eggs perform a number of different functions in recipes, including binding other ingredients together, leavening, affecting texture, and affecting color (such as in a sponge cake or French toast). So your choice of a substitute will depend upon how well it can perform the function needed. In some cases, the effect of the eggs in the recipe is so slight that you can leave the eggs out altogether, not replace them with anything else, and not even notice that they're missing.

In this section, we'll look at some of the foods that can be used to replace eggs in recipes.

Removing Eggs from Baked Goods

In baked goods, eggs are usually used for *leavening*, or lightness, and to act as a binder. The type of baked good determines whether or not you can leave the eggs out entirely and not replace them, or whether you need another ingredient to perform the function of the eggs in the original recipe.

For example, in baked goods that are relatively flat and don't need a lot of leavening, such as cookies and pancakes, you can oftentimes get away with leaving out the eggs and not replacing them. That's particularly true when the original recipe calls for only one or two eggs. In recipes that call for more eggs, the eggs probably play a much greater role in leavening or binding, and you'll find that the recipe fails if you don't replace them.

In baked goods that are lighter and have a fluffier texture, you'll want to replace eggs with an ingredient that provides some lift. Try any of the following to replace one whole egg in a recipe:

➤ ¹/₂ of a small, ripe, mashed banana. This works well in recipes in which you wouldn't mind a banana flavor, including muffins, cookies, pancakes, and quick breads.

Veggie Talk

Eggs can provide **leavening** or lift to baked goods and help to make them lighter in texture. In some recipes, eggs are beaten or whipped, incorporating air into the product and decreasing the product's density.

Helpful Hint

If you omit the eggs in a recipe and don't replace them, you might want to add a tablespoon or two of additional liquid—soymilk, fruit juice, water, and so on—for each egg omitted, just to help the product retain its original moisture content.

➤ ¹/₄ cup of any kind of tofu, blended with the liquid ingredients in the recipe. If you use "lite" tofu, you'll reduce the fat and calories in the finished product.

➤ 1¹/₂ tsp. of a commercial vegetarian egg replacer, such as Ener-G Egg Replacer, mixed with 2 Tbsp. of water. This product is a combination of vegetable starches and works wonderfully in virtually any recipe that calls for eggs. It's sold in a 1 pound box in natural foods stores.

➤ ¹/₄ cup of applesauce, canned pumpkin or squash, or pureed prunes. These fruit or vegetable purees may add a hint of flavor to foods. If you want a lighter product, also add an extra ¹/₂ tsp. of baking powder to the recipe, since using fruit purees to replace eggs can make the finished product somewhat denser than the original recipe.

➤ 1 heaping Tbsp. soy flour or bean flour mixed with 1 Tbsp. water.

➤ 2 Tbsp. cornstarch beaten with 2 Tbsp. water.

➤ 1 Tbsp. finely ground flax seeds whipped with ¹/₄ cup water.

Egg-Free Binders in Casseroles, Loaves, Burger Patties, and Main Dishes

In foods such as vegetable and grain casseroles, lentil loaves, vegetarian burger patties, and other foods in which the ingredients need to stick together, you need an ingredient that acts as a binder. Eggs traditionally serve that function in nonvegetarian foods such as meatballs, meatloaf, hamburgers, and many casseroles, but there are plenty of alternatives for people who want to omit the eggs.

In the substitutions that follow, you'll find that you have to experiment a bit to determine just the right amount of an ingredient to serve the purpose in a specific recipe. A good starting point with most recipes is 2 or 3 tablespoons of any of the ingredients listed, or a combination of them, to replace one whole egg. If the original recipe calls for two eggs, start with 4 to 6 tablespoons of egg substitute.

Some of the ingredients listed may affect the flavor of the finished product too, so consider that when you decide which ingredients to use to replace the eggs. For instance, if you add sweet potato to a burger patty, you may be able to taste it, whereas if you mix some into a casserole, it may be more disguised by the other ingredients. On the other hand, the extra flavor that some of these ingredients add may be a nice change of pace.

To replace eggs that act as binders in recipes, try any of the following. Begin with 2 or 3 tablespoons for each egg replaced and adjust the amount as needed. When working with dry ingredients such as arrowroot or cornstarch, some recipes may work best if you mix the dry ingredient with water, vegetable broth, or another liquid (about 1¹/₂ tsp. dry ingredient to 2 Tbsp. water). Moist foods such as casseroles and some vegetarian loaves may not require the additional moisture.

➤ ¹/₄ cup any kind of tofu, blended with 1 Tbsp. flour

➤ Tomato paste

➤ Arrowroot starch

➤ Potato starch

➤ Cornstarch

➤ Ener-G Egg Replacer (1¹/₂ tsp. mixed with 2 Tbsp. water for each egg replaced)

➤ Flour (whole-wheat, unbleached, oat, or bean flours)

➤ Finely crushed bread crumbs, cracker meal, or matzo meal

➤ Quick-cooking rolled oats or cooked oatmeal

➤ Mashed potatoes, mashed sweet potatoes, or instant potato flakes

Egg Replacers for Sandwich Fillings and Scrambled Eggs

Tofu can stand in for eggs in all sorts of recipes. Usually it's invisible as an ingredient, but sometimes it appears simply as an egg imposter. For instance:

➤ You can use chopped firm or extra firm tofu in place of egg whites in recipes for egg salad sandwich filling. Just make your favorite egg salad recipe, but use chopped tofu instead of hard-boiled eggs. You can even use soy mayonnaise instead of regular mayonnaise for a vegan version.

➤ Add chopped firm tofu to mixed green salads or spinach salad in place of chopped, hard-boiled eggs. You can also add chopped or minced tofu to bowls of Chinese hot and sour soup.

➤ Make scrambled tofu instead of scrambled eggs for breakfast. Natural foods stores stock "tofu scrambler" spice packets, and you may also see them in the produce section of your regular supermarket, next to the tofu. Vegetarian cookbooks also give recipes for making scrambled tofu. The recipes usually include turmeric to give the tofu a yellow color similar to scrambled eggs.

You can also use scrambled tofu to fill pita pockets or as a sandwich filling on hoagie rolls.

Replacing Milk and Other Dairy Products in Recipes

It's not nearly as tricky to replace dairy products in recipes as it is to replace eggs. The dairy products that you're most likely to find in recipes are milk, yogurt, sour cream, butter, and cheese. There are good nondairy alternatives that can easily be substituted for all of these.

Helpful Hint

Soymilk is generally more nutritious than any of the other milk alternatives, such as rice milk, almond milk, and others. Fortified soymilk has extra calcium, vitamins A, D, and B12 too. If you use substantial amounts of a milk alternative, fortified soymilk is usually the best choice in terms of nutrition.

Heads Up!

If you try soymilk for the first time and don't care for it, give it a second chance and try another brand. Soymilk varies in flavor considerably from one brand to the next. You may have to taste three or four before you find your favorite. Most of the soymilk sold in the United States and Canada is made from whole soybeans, so it has a bit of a beany aftertaste, which some people find pleasant but others don't like. If you object to the mild bean flavor, you may prefer a flavored soymilk to plain. Soymilk grows on you. If you use it for a while, you'll probably grow to love it.

Milk Replacers

Cow's milk can be replaced in recipes by soymilk, rice milk, potato milk, nut milks, or oat milk. Just substitute any of these milk alternatives cup for cup for cow's milk.

Soymilk is made by grinding soybeans that have been soaked and cooked. The soymilk is pressed out of the beans. A similar process is used to make other kinds of milk substitutes.

Plain and vanilla flavors (as opposed to carob) are the most versatile, since the mild flavors blend in with just about any recipe. I use vanilla-flavored soymilk exclusively, and it's worked well in any recipe I've ever made. Some people, however, prefer to use plain soymilk in savory recipes such as some main dish sauces and soups. They use vanilla soymilk in sweeter dishes, such as puddings, custards, on cereal, in baking, and for smoothies. Carob soymilk is also delicious in some smoothies and puddings.

Soymilk, rice milk, almond milk, oat milk, and blends of soy and rice milk can all be found in shelf-stable, aseptic boxes in natural foods stores, and many brands are now carried at regular supermarkets too. Potato milk is sold in natural foods stores in powdered form. Some soymilk is still sold in powdered form too. Most people find the liquid soymilk to be more palatable and much more convenient, though.

Yogurt and Sour Cream Replacers

If you prefer not to use dairy yogurt, you'll find soy-based, plain and flavored yogurts at the natural foods store. They're delicious. Natural foods stores also sell soy-based sour cream. Nutritionally, the biggest advantage to both of these products is that they contain no cholesterol and far less saturated fat than their dairy counterparts. Some soy yogurts also contain active cultures, just like many dairy yogurts.

You can use soy yogurt and sour cream in most of the same ways that you used the dairy versions, including baking, in sauces and dips, and to eat "as is." Since they sometimes separate when they're heated in a pan on the stove, they may or may not work in certain sauce recipes. Most of the time, however, you'll find you have no problems substituting them for dairy yogurt and sour cream.

Cheese Replacers

Full-fat dairy cheeses are loaded with saturated fat and cholesterol, but many people find that the nonfat varieties are short on flavor (they taste like plastic) and don't melt. For anyone who wants to avoid dairy cheeses, there are a several nondairy alternatives on the market.

Cheese alternatives are usually sold in natural foods stores—only a few regular supermarkets carry them at this time—and are usually soy- or nut-based. They come in a variety of flavors and types, such as mozzarella style, jack or cheddar style, and others. Parmesan style cheese and cream cheese are also widely available in natural foods stores. Most taste reasonably good, and they are free of cholesterol and much lower in saturated fat than their dairy counterparts.

They don't all melt as well as regular, full-fat dairy cheeses, but they generally melt better than nonfat dairy cheeses. That's due, in part, to the fact that they tend to be high in fat, albeit vegetable fat. The sodium content of cheese alternatives varies. Some are higher, some are lower, and some are about the same as their dairy counterparts.

Experiment with cheese replacers to find the brands you like the best and the varieties that work best in your recipes. Most cheese substitutes do well as an ingredient in a mixed dish, such as a casserole, in which the cheese doesn't have to stand alone but is mixed throughout the dish. Cheese substitutes, including nonfat dairy cheeses, melt better this way too.

Nutritional yeast works well as a substitute for Parmesan cheese on casseroles, salads, baked potatoes, popcorn, and pasta. It has a savory, cheesy flavor. You'll find it in natural foods stores.

Heads Up!

Save money at many supermarkets and natural foods stores: Buy soymilk (or other milk alternatives) by the case. Since the aseptic packages can keep for several months in your cupboard, you may find it convenient to buy one or two cases at a time. There are usually 12 boxes to a case, and many stores will give you 10 percent off each case.

Helpful Hint

Make your own nondairy buttermilk by adding 2 teaspoons lemon juice or vinegar to 1 cup soymilk.

Heads Up!

Full-fat and even low-fat cheeses can add a substantial amount of saturated fat and cholesterol to your diet. Consider using some soy- or nut-based cheeses in place of some of the dairy cheese that you eat.

Butter Replacers

Soy margarine is available at natural foods stores. It's free of casein and other dairy by-products that other brands of margarine usually contain. So, soy margarine can be used by vegans.

Helpful Hint

You can make your own nondairy substitute for ricotta cheese or cottage cheese. Mash a block of tofu with a fork and mix in a few teaspoons of lemon juice. You can use this "tofu cheese" to replace ricotta cheese or cottage cheese in lasagna, stuffed shells, manicotti, Danish pastries, cheese blintzes, and many other recipes.

Veggie Talk

Trans fatty acids are vegetable fats that have had their chemical compositions changed through a method of processing that hardens the vegetable oil into a form that can hold the shape of a stick. Trans fatty acids are associated with a greater incidence of coronary artery disease.

In terms of your health, though, it's even better if you switch to olive oil for as many uses as possible. For instance, instead of spreading margarine on your bread and vegetables, it would be healthier to brush your foods with a little olive oil (use a pastry brush).

That's because the vegetable oils used to make all forms of margarine, including soy margarine, have been chemically altered, resulting in a form of fat that scientists call *trans fatty acids*. If you consume trans fatty acids, you'll increase your risk for coronary artery disease even more than you do when you use butter.

If health is your only consideration in choosing a fat, olive oil, followed by other vegetable oils, is by far the best form of fat to use. Butter is better than margarine, even though it is high in saturated fat. If you choose to use margarine, choose the brand that is lowest in saturated fat. Check the food label, and choose a brand that contains not more than 1 gram of saturated fat per serving.

Replacing Meat in Recipes

Some vegetarian dishes are originals—they've been meatless from the start, and they don't cry out for a meat-like ingredient. Some good examples include falafel (a Middle Eastern food made with deep-fried chick-pea balls, often served in pita pockets), mutter paneer (an Indian dish), lentil or black bean soup, spinach pie, ratatouille (a spicy vegetable dish), pasta primavera, and many, many more.

Other dishes were made with a meat-like ingredient in mind. Without meat—or a suitable substitute—they're lacking something. Examples include chili, burgers (a burger without the burger is just a bun), sloppy Joes, and recipes that call for chunks of meat, such as stews and stir-fries.

Some meat products are stand-alone traditions—hotdogs, hamburgers, sausage, cold cuts, and bacon, for instance. Believe it or not, there are some very good imposters to replace even these. Whatever the recipe, you've got lots of choices when it comes to replacing the meat.

Tofu and Tempeh

People often talk about tofu and tempeh as if they're bookends and go together like a matching pair. The fact is, they look and taste very different, and their functions in recipes vary too.

Tofu is a smooth, creamy food, and it has very little flavor or odor. It picks up the flavor of whatever it's cooked with. It blends well, so it can be used to replace dairy products in sauces, dips, puddings, fillings, and a host of other recipes. As we've already discussed, it can also replace eggs in many recipes too. Tofu is extremely versatile.

When tofu is used as a meat substitute, it's usually cut up into cubes and stir-fried (extra-firm tofu works best for this), or it's marinated and cooked in slabs or chunks. If it's frozen first, then thawed, tofu develops a chewy texture that resembles meat.

Tempeh is more limited in its usefulness, since it's made with whole soybeans and can't be blended the way that tofu can be to make foods that have a smooth or creamy texture. But it can be crumbled, and many people use crumbled tempeh to make such foods as tempeh sloppy Joes, tempeh mock chicken salad, and tempeh chili.

Tempeh can also be used in ways that meats are more traditionally used. For instance, strips or blocks of tempeh can be grilled, barbecued, baked, and broiled. Chunks of tempeh can be used with vegetable pieces for shish kebob. Chunks of tempeh can also be used to make stews, casseroles, and other combination dishes.

Helpful Hint

Use about $^7/_8$ cup of vegetable oil to replace 1 cup of butter in recipes. This substitution may not work as well in recipes for baked goods as it does in other recipes, so you may need to experiment to find the recipes that work best.

Helpful Hint

Cream soups can be made without milk or cream. Just puree some cooked potato with vegetable broth and mix it into the soup. You can use pureed soft tofu the same way. Blend the soft tofu with a little vegetable broth, then mix it into the soup. Works wonderfully.

Seitan

Seitan is a chewy food made from wheat *gluten*, or wheat protein. You can buy mixes for seitan at natural foods stores, but most people find it far more convenient to buy it ready-made. It's usually found in the refrigerated section of the natural foods store.

One of the best ways to sample seitan is at a Chinese or Thai restaurant where you can try it prepared in different ways. It can take different forms, but it's often served in chunks or strips in a stir-fry. Seitan dishes are absolutely scrumptious. Many people get totally hooked on the stuff (me included). But you may have to go to a restaurant in a big city to find it. Since seitan is relatively unfamiliar to most Westerners, you aren't likely to find it in small town and even medium-sized-city restaurants. You'll usually see it in big-city Asian restaurants where the menu is fairly extensive.

Textured Vegetable Protein

Textured vegetable protein (TVP) canreplace the ground meat in taco and burrito fillings, sloppy Joe filling, and in spaghetti sauce. You can toss a handful into a pot of chili and not be able to tell the difference between the TVP and ground meat. Buy it frozen in bags at supermarkets or dried in small bits or chunks in boxes, bags, or in bulk at natural foods stores.

Heads Up!

At Chinese restaurants, when the menu lists "bean curd" dishes, it means that these dishes are made with tofu. Bean curd is another name for tofu.

TVP is much more widely used in Great Britain and Western Europe than it is in the United States and Canada, and it's been sold overseas in natural foods stores, especially in bulk, longer than it has here. British vegetarian cookbooks, for instance, are more likely to call for TVP in recipes than are American or Canadian cookbooks. That may be changing, now that interest in TVP is growing and manufacturers are "mainstreaming" it in regular supermarkets.

Bulgur Wheat

Bulgur wheat is rolled, cracked wheat. It has a nutty flavor, and it can be used in some of the same ways that TVP is used. For example, you can toss a handful of bulgur wheat into a pot of chili and get much the same effect as you would if you used TVP. It absorbs the liquid in whatever it's cooked with and has the appearance of ground meat and a chewy texture.

Veggie Talk

The word **seitan** is pronounced *SAY-tan* as opposed to the erroneous and more snicker–eliciting *Satan*. Seitan is an Asian food made from wheat **gluten**, which is the protein portion of wheat.

Veggie Burgers, Franks, Cold Cuts, and Breakfast Meats

You don't have to miss a good old-fashioned burger, chili dog, BLT, pancake and sausage breakfast, or bologna sandwich when you go vegetarian. There are vegetarian versions of all of these meats.

Like soymilk, you may need to try several different brands of each until you hit on a favorite. But these products are generally very good-tasting, and in texture and appearance they often look very much like their meat counterparts.

You can use these products in all the same ways you used the meat versions. Crumble vegetarian bacon onto a spinach salad, add franks to your beans, have a sausage biscuit, or make yourself a submarine sandwich with cold cuts. You can have a cheeseburger or a chili dog (made with TVP chili and onions!).

Replacements for Gelatin

Vegetarian sources of gelatin are usually made from sea vegetables and are available in natural foods stores. Agar is one form, and it's made from red algae. Natural foods stores carry plain and fruit-flavored powdered vegetarian gelatin. These products can be used in the same ways that commercial gelatin found in regular supermarkets is used.

Helpful Hint

If you use vegetarian gelatin in recipes in which regular gelatin is usually liquefied then added to cold ingredients, you may need to change the process a bit. If the recipe doesn't turn out well using the original method, try blending the vegetarian gelatin into cold liquid first, then bringing the liquid to a boil. Vegetarian gelatin may begin to set immediately, so you'll need to add the rest of the recipe's ingredients right away.

The Least You Need to Know

➤ Standard cookbooks depend heavily on milk, eggs, and butter in their recipes. All of these animal products can be replaced by plant-based ingredients.

➤ Eggs can often be replaced in recipes, depending upon their function in the recipe, by substituting mashed bananas, tofu, fruit purees, commercial vegetarian egg replacer, soy flour, bean flour, cornstarch, or finely ground flax seeds mixed with a little water, as well as arrowroot starch or potato starch, tomato paste, cooked oatmeal, mashed potatoes, and many other foods.

➤ Milk and other dairy products can be replaced in recipes by substituting soymilk and other milk alternatives, soy cheese, soy yogurt, soy sour cream, olive oil, or soy margarine.

➤ Meats can be replaced in recipes by substituting tofu, tempeh, seitan, textured vegetable protein, bulgur wheat, or by using meat alternatives such as vegetarian burgers, hotdogs, cold cuts, and breakfast meats.

Chapter 21

Holidays and Entertaining

In This Chapter

➤ Adopting new traditions for holidays and special occasions

➤ Considerations in planning a successful vegetarian meal for guests

➤ Keys to preparing for the event

➤ Ways to enhance the presentation of the food

➤ Creating a pleasing setting for your meal

If you're a new vegetarian, you may be a little apprehensive the first few times you have family, friends, or business associates over to your home for holiday meals and special occasions. That's understandable. You've changed your way of eating, and your old menus may not fit anymore. Now you've got to plan a new menu. You'd like to fix a nice vegetarian meal, but you want to ensure that your guests will like the food as much as you do.

Holidays can be especially tough, since so many people associate specific animal foods with various holidays, and those foods are as much a part of the holiday tradition as any other part of the observance. For some people, Thanksgiving just isn't Thanksgiving without the turkey. Easter means ham, and they drink eggnog at Christmastime. Maybe your family has always celebrated anniversaries or birthdays with a steak.

Can Passover be Passover without traditional foods made with eggs? Thanksgiving without the turkey? All possible. All you need is a little imagination, a bit of know-how, and a room full of hungry guests. This chapter will help you get started.

A New View

If a vegetarian diet is new to you, planning vegetarian meals for special occasions and holidays, or just entertaining guests in your home, will require you to put yourself in a different frame of mind. You'll need to acquire a new mindset about what holiday meals look like and how to set a table without making meat the centerpiece.

To do that, a little creativity helps. So do some good-sense strategies.

Create New Traditions

We expect turkey on Thanksgiving and ham for Easter dinner because they're traditions. We've simply done it that way for so long that those specific foods have become associated with those specific occasions. The food and the occasion seem to be inextricably linked.

But they're not. Not necessarily.

You can easily create new traditions, and you can even do it without forgoing all memories of the way it used to be. The first few times you serve vegetarian dishes in place of the old animal-product dishes, it may seem a little odd to you or to some of your guests. But if you leave other components of the celebration in place, the change won't seem so drastic.

Thanksgiving dinner is a great example. Let's say that in your family, Thanksgiving dinner has always meant turkey with stuffing, mashed potatoes, green beans, candied sweet potatoes, a mixed green salad, dinner rolls, fruit salad, and pumpkin pie for dessert. How could you modify that meal to make it vegetarian?

Actually, very easily. The vegetarian version of a Thanksgiving dinner doesn't have to be much different at all. Replace the turkey with a meatless entree, and leave everything else the same.

For instance, in place of a turkey, you might serve a large, baked squash stuffed with an apple-cinnamon-nut filling or any number of favorite stuffing recipes. Stuffed squash is very much in keeping with the spirit of a late autumn meal, it makes an eye-catching centerpiece, and it tastes good.

Other options:

> ➤ Serve a tofu "turkey." Some people use a seasoned tofu mixture to make a loaf in the shape of a turkey. It's baked and may be served with stuffing on the side.

Helpful Hint

There are times when it may also work well to entertain guests at a restaurant rather than in your home. That's especially true if you think that peoples' food preferences may be difficult to accommodate. At a restaurant, everyone can choose what they like.

➤ Serve a lentil loaf, a cheese and nut loaf, or a hearty casserole as the main dish.

➤ Serve small, individual stuffed pumpkins as the main course.

➤ Serve a different favorite entree, such as a vegetable lasagna or spinach pie. Fix something that takes more time to make and that you perhaps don't make every week, so that it seems more special.

Choose any of these options or think of another, but in planning the meal, also include the foods that you've always associated with that occasion that happen to be meatless or that can be modified to make them vegetarian.

No matter what the holiday or special occasion, it helps to take the point of view that you are creating new traditions. What's new today, with time, will become tomorrow's tradition. You'll look forward to it just as you did the turkey, ham, or any other meat or animal product.

Modify Traditional Recipes

There's no need to scrap all of your favorite holiday foods just because they aren't vegetarian. Many of them can simply be modified. Use the information provided in Chapter 20, "Recipe Magic!" to make the recipe substitutions. Soy margarine, soymilk or other milk alternatives, and egg replacers can be used to bake holiday cakes and cookies. You can work the meat, dairy products, and eggs out of recipes for side dishes, casseroles, breads, and other foods too.

Coleslaw can be made with a vinaigrette dressing instead of mayonnaise, or you can use soy mayonnaise to make both coleslaw and potato salad. Use vegetarian bacon to make German potato salad or to add "bacon" bits to a salad. Use pureed soft tofu to make cream soups. Pumpkin pie filling can also be made using tofu instead of eggs and milk.

Challah (a rich Jewish egg bread) can be made with vegetarian egg replacer instead of real eggs. Even mincemeat pie filling can be made without the meat. You'll find lots of good recipes for all of these foods in the cookbooks that are listed in Chapter 26. "Getting Educated About Everything Vegetarian."

Helpful Hint

There's no rule that says you must have an entree at meals. Another option for adapting holiday meals or meals for entertaining is to simply not have a specific entree at all. Instead, serve several interesting dishes, such as casseroles or gratins, quiches or savory pies, along with salads, breads, and desserts. Chances are good that no one will miss that piece of meat they're used to.

Peruse Vegetarian Cookbooks

Many vegetarian cookbooks have an ethnic theme. They emphasize foods from one or more cultures in which meatless foods are a tradition. For example, they may contain lots of recipes for foods of Middle Eastern origin, or they may emphasize vegetarian pasta dishes. These can be great resources for planning special meals.

Helpful Hint

Many large cities have caterers that specialize in vegetarian cooking. Some restaurants will also cater. Depending upon your budget and time constraints, having a special meal catered can be very convenient. Most caterers will set up the meal at your house using their own equipment, or you can arrange to pick up the food at their place of business and serve it yourself. Some upscale supermarkets also provide this service.

On the other hand, if you want vegetarian versions of traditional American recipes, you can find those too. Scores of vegetarian cookbooks give recipes for hearty soups, chili, macaroni and cheese, potato salad, coleslaw, pumpkin pie—you name it—all made without animal products.

Go to the library and check out cookbooks that interest you. If you find a few that are especially good, go to a bookstore and buy them (you can also shop by catalog and on-line). Some vegetarian cookbooks even provide menus and suggestions for holiday meals and entertaining.

Observe Other Vegetarians

Take opportunities to share meals for special occasions and holidays with other vegetarians. It can be helpful to see what others serve. Many local vegetarian societies hold covered-dish get-togethers, restaurant gatherings, or catered events for holidays. Oftentimes they're held a week or two before the actual holiday date, since many people have family obligations then.

Planning Is Important

Never underestimate the value of planning when you're entertaining. If you have any anxiety at all about serving a vegetarian meal to your guests, taking some time to plan ahead will boost your confidence and increase the likelihood that your event will be a success.

Choose a Theme

Sit down when you're relaxed and have a few minutes to yourself, and think about what kind of meal you'd like to serve. If it's late summer and corn on the cob, tomatoes, and melons are in season, maybe you'd like to serve a simple, informal summer meal featuring fresh, locally grown produce. If it's wintertime, you might want to fix a hearty grain and vegetable casserole and serve it with a green salad and some good bread.

Try to visualize the meal that you'd like to serve, including the types of foods you think your guests would enjoy, the degree of formality you prefer, and the setting. Begin to look for a theme or overall mood you'd like to create with the meal.

Keep Your Guests in Mind

If your guests are vegetarians themselves, they're probably familiar with many different types of vegetarian dishes and will like whatever you serve. If they're not, you might want to serve "crossover" foods that are enjoyed by vegetarians and nonvegetarians alike. These are foods that don't scream "meatless" to a nonvegetarian.

For a cookout, you could serve:

➤ Veggie hotdogs and veggie burgers cooked on a grill

➤ Baked vegetarian beans with veggie franks

➤ Potato salad or coleslaw made with soy mayonnaise

➤ Corn on the cob

➤ Chips and salsa

➤ Watermelon

➤ Oatmeal cookies

➤ Lemonade or herbal iced tea sweetened with fruit juice

For a Super Bowl party, you could serve:

➤ Vegetarian pizza

➤ Cut vegetables and a variety of chips with salsa and/or black bean dip

➤ Fruit salad

➤ Brownies

➤ Beverages

For a more formal meal, you might serve vegetable lasagna, spaghetti, pasta primavera, stuffed shells or manicotti filled with cheese, or a tofu mixture as a main course. You could serve bean chili with cornbread and a salad, or a hearty lentil or bean soup with a salad and a loaf of good bread.

Brainstorm other foods that happen to be vegetarian that your guests would find familiar and satisfying. You'll probably find that it's not hard to fix a vegetarian meal that is made up of foods that most people know and enjoy.

Think Ethnic

Many of the vegetarian foods that nonvegetarians like are ethnic.

Most people like bean burritos, bean tacos, nachos, Chinese stir-fry vegetable dishes, Italian pasta dishes, and Greek spanakopita or spinach pie. Look through ethnic vegetarian cookbooks for ideas. Planning a meal with an ethnic theme can be fun. If the foods are new to your guests, they may enjoy trying something different. When

Helpful Hint

If you're serving a meal with an ethnic theme, consider ordering out for part of the meal. For example, you might order a take-out Chinese soup and egg rolls for four, then fix a vegetable stir-fry to go with it at home. Ordering out for part of the meal can cut down substantially on the amount of time and work for you. Plus, there are some ethnic foods that are hard to make at home and never seem as good unless they're made by the experts!

your meal has an ethnic theme, it can also be simpler to plan, because side dishes and accompaniments are easier to "match."

For example, you might serve a mixed green salad, black bean soup, hard rolls, and vegetable paella for a meal with a Spanish theme. You could serve green papaya salad, a vegetable curry over jasmine rice, and hot jasmine tea for a meal with a Thai theme. Check bookstores, catalogs, and on-line resources for more good ethnic vegetarian cookbooks.

Spread Out the Work

Even a fairly simple holiday meal or dinner party can be a time-consuming affair. If you can break the task down into parts, you'll see that much of the preparation can be staggered over several days leading up to your event. If you can get much of the work done ahead of time, you'll be less stressed the day of your meal and will be in better shape to handle any minor glitches that may crop up.

A few days to a week before your meal, you can:

➤ Wash and iron tablecloths and napkins

➤ Polish silver

➤ Set out any decorations that you're going to use

➤ Bake and freeze some desserts, such as cookies or cake layers

➤ Pick out music

➤ Draw up a grocery list and buy any supplies that aren't perishable

A day or so before the meal, you can:

➤ Pick out and chill wine if it's being served

➤ Buy fresh fruits or vegetables and other perishable groceries

➤ Prepare any parts of the meal that can keep in the refrigerator for a day, such as marinated salads, salad dressings, casseroles, and so on

On the day of the meal, start early in the day washing, chopping, and trimming vegetables, assembling salads and appetizers, and setting the table. Buy fresh flowers (or pick them from your garden) the day of the event. Spread the work out over the course of the day, rather than waiting until a few hours before. In the two or three hours before your guests arrive, you'll want to be putting last-minute touches on the table, getting some last-minute meal items together, and watching any foods that may be in the oven or on the stove. You'll also want time to shower and change your clothes so that you'll feel refreshed before your guests arrive.

Presentation Counts

Some people will tell you that they don't care about how foods look. They care only about how they taste. Don't believe them. Appearances do count.

Foods that are presented with a flair—with an eye to aesthetics, neatly arranged in appealing bowls and platters, with a garnish—look like they're going to taste good. It's important to pay attention to presentation.

Any of the following embellishments can make your dishes look lovely:

➤ Garnishes such as slivers or twists of fresh fruits (oranges, lemons, limes, apples, or strawberries); edible flowers; sprigs of fresh herbs; a black olive; cherry tomato halves; a handful of sweet potato chips or a pickle wedge

➤ A doily placed on a plate under the dessert

➤ A charger or liner (a large, often contrasting, plate upon which the smaller dinner plate is placed)

➤ A sprinkling of grated cheese, chopped parsley or cilantro, or a dusting of cinnamon, powdered sugar, or cocoa

➤ A dab of chocolate sauce, raspberry or vanilla sauce, or cheese sauce. You can drizzle the sauce over the food itself or in a zigzag pattern over the plate before arranging the food on top

Heads Up!

If you make your food look good, people will expect it to taste good too. They'll go into the meal with a positive attitude. That's especially important when people are trying foods with which they may not be familiar. If you're serving a vegetarian meal to friends, it pays to "put your best food forward."

Put some thought into the dishes and bowls in which you serve your food too. Colorful fruit and vegetable salads can be stunning when served in a clear glass or crystal bowl. Hearty stews and casseroles look nice served in rustic pottery bowls.

Set the Mood

In addition to making your food look good, give some attention to the setting of your meal.

Remove distractions. Turn off the television. Put on some pleasant music but not so loud that people can't hear themselves talk.

Dim the lights if it's evening, and light some candles. Have some fresh flowers nearby or on the table. Your table should be neat and not too cluttered. Use place mats if you aren't using a tablecloth. An interesting quilt or Oriental rug can make a nice tablecover for a change of pace.

The Least You Need to Know

➤ The vegetarian foods that you serve for holidays and special occasions in place of traditional animal products may become new traditions over time.

➤ Many foods that are served for holidays and special occasions are already vegetarian.

➤ Many traditional recipes that contain animal products can be modified to make them vegetarian or vegan.

➤ Take some time to think through your meal and plan. If you are serving non-vegetarian guests, it may help to serve vegetarian foods with which they are already familiar.

➤ Begin to prepare for your event a week or so before the date. Spread out the tasks over several days to make your workload more manageable.

➤ Appearances count. If your food is presented nicely in an inviting setting, it will be received more favorably by your guests.

Part 6
Taking the Show on the Road

It's one thing to be a vegetarian in your own home, where you can choose the foods you have on hand and what you fix for meals. It's quite another when you're a guest at someone else's home, when you're traveling, or when you're eating out. You lose a measure of control once you leave home, and most of the time you're surrounded by a society for which a vegetarian lifestyle is not the norm.

Dealing with the nonvegetarian world and handling the situations that can come up when you're away from home takes a special set of skills that vegetarians acquire over time and with experience. The chapters that follow provide some insights into being a vegetarian away from home, whether you're visiting relatives or friends, traveling by land, sea, or air, eating in a school cafeteria or at the office, or looking for meatless meals at restaurants.

Chapter 22

Veggie Etiquette

In This Chapter

➤ How to be a gracious dinner guest

➤ Securing a vegetarian meal at weddings, banquets, and other events

➤ Dating a nonvegetarian

➤ Making a good impression at business luncheons

It's one thing to maintain a vegetarian lifestyle at home. It's another to do it away from home with style and grace.

It shouldn't be different for vegetarians, but it is. Remember: Vegetarian diets are outside our culture. That means that your eating style—especially if you are vegan—is at odds with the ways of most everyone else you'll meet. True, that's changing. People are more health conscious, and more people are aware of the environmental and ethical advantages of a vegetarian diet. But the vast majority still eat meat, and you're the one that will have to do most of the adapting when you're out with them socially.

This chapter will focus on some common situations for which you'll need to develop skills in relating to nonvegetarians. You'll become more comfortable with these situations as you have more experience with them.

The Dinner Invitation

Being invited to a nonvegetarian's home for dinner is one of the most common and most stressful events that many vegetarians encounter. How you approach the situation depends upon the degree of formality of the occasion and how well you know your host.

Tell Your Host the Truth

You're a vegetarian. Out with it.

Find the right moment to tell your host that you're a vegetarian, but do say something. If the invitation comes by phone, the best time to say something is at the time that you get the invitation. Something as simple as, "Oh, thanks, I'd love to come. By the way, I'd better tell you that I'm a vegetarian. You don't have to do anything special for me—I'm sure I'll find plenty to eat—but I just didn't want you to go to the trouble of fixing meat or fish for me."

The chances are good that your host will ask if you eat spaghetti or lasagna or some other dish that he or she is familiar with serving and thinks will suit your preferences. If your host suggests a shrimp stir-fry, you can also nip that one in the bud by letting him know that your don't eat seafood (if you don't). In that case, it would also be a good time to toss out a few more suggestions of foods you do eat, or you could reassure your host that you'll be fine with extra servings of whatever vegetables, rice, potatoes, salad, and other side dishes are served.

Helpful Hint

If you think that you may have trouble finding something you can eat at your host's home, have a snack before you leave home. That way, you won't be starving if you find that there isn't much to eat.

If you get an invitation to dinner by mail, through a spouse or partner, or in some other indirect way, you have two choices. You can show up for dinner and eat what you can, or you can call your host, thank her for the invitation, and mention that you're a vegetarian. If you've been invited as the guest of the invitee (your spouse, partner, or date), you might want that person to call the host on your behalf. Feel the situation out and do what feels most appropriate and comfortable.

It may feel a bit awkward at first, but telling your host that you're a vegetarian up front may be less uncomfortable than showing up for dinner and finding that there's nothing you can eat, or finding that something special has been made for you that you have to decline.

It may make some people a little nervous when you say that you're a vegetarian. Most people who invite guests to dinner want them to enjoy the food and have a good time, and they may not be as familiar with what a vegetarian will and won't eat. It's important to reassure your host that you'll be fine so that he won't worry too much. On the other hand, most people appreciate knowing ahead of time that you won't be eating the meat or fish. It saves them from preparing something that won't be eaten and is therefore possibly wasted. It also saves everyone the embarrassment of scurrying to find something for you to eat. And it also saves you from being stuck in a situation where the rice is cooked with chicken stock, the salad is sprinkled with bacon, the appetizer is shrimp cocktail, and steak is the main course. It can be a bit conspicuous if all you have on your plate is a dinner roll.

Tell your host that you're a vegetarian.

Offer to Bring a Dish

Another way to handle dinner invitations is to offer to bring a dish that you and everyone else can share. This works best in casual situations when you know your host or the setting is going to be relatively informal. You might not feel as comfortable suggesting this, for instance, if you are being invited to a formal company function at the home of someone with whom you don't interact regularly. In that case, bringing your own food could look tacky.

Offer, but don't push. If you tell your host that you're a vegetarian and she sounds worried or unsure about how to handle it, you might say something like: "If you'd like, I'd be happy to make my famous vegetable paella and saffron rice for everyone to try."

If your host bites, great. If she brushes the suggestion aside, just consider your job done and leave it at that. Reassure her that you think you'll be fine eating the salad and side dishes that don't contain meat or seafood and that you're looking forward to coming.

Helpful Hint

Someday, it may happen that you've told your host that you're a vegetarian, and they've tried to fix a meal that you can eat but have "missed." For example, they may have prepared a gelatin mold salad, used eggs in the baked goods, put bacon on the salad, or served the salad with Caesar dressing. What should you do? Be the best actor that you can be and just eat whatever you can of the other parts of the meal. Make your plate look as full as you can so that your host doesn't feel as though you don't have enough. Assure your host that you're fine. You won't starve. Enjoy the company, then eat when you get home.

If You Choose to Stay Mum

If you decide for whatever reason not to tell your host in advance that you're vegetarian, then downplay the fact during the meal or stay undercover. Pointing out that you can't eat the food will make everyone uncomfortable and may put a damper on the evening. Your host may feel bad and even ask why you didn't say something sooner. Eat what you can. If you have to ask about ingredients in the food or you have to say that you can't eat something because it's not vegetarian, be sure to play down any inconvenience, and reassure your host that you'll be just fine with what there is.

Weddings and Banquets and Such

It's much easier to manage invitations to weddings, banquets, and other functions at which there will be lots of people and where the food is served from a buffet line. Even if a sit-down meal is served, the food is usually catered by a hotel or restaurant. You may find it much easier to speak to hotel or restaurant staff about getting a vegetarian meal than you would be asking the host directly.

At a Private Home

If the function happens to be held at a private residence, you can follow the advice given earlier for dinner invitations. Since the occasion is likely to involve a greater number of guests, it's likely that more food will be served, and even more likely that your host won't have to do anything special for you. You'll probably find plenty of foods that you can eat.

At a Hotel, Country Club, Community Hall, or Restaurant

If the event is planned at a hotel, country club, community center, or restaurant, call ahead and ask to speak with the person in charge of food service. You don't have to say anything to your host. It's perfectly fine to speak to the chef or caterer and request a vegetarian or vegan entree as a substitute for whatever the other guests will be served. It would be very unusual if there would be an extra charge to the host for an alternate dish, but if you are worried, you can ask to be sure.

Be clear about what you can and can't eat. For example, if you eat no meat, fish, or poultry, be sure to say so. If you don't, you may end up with fish or chicken, since "vegetarian" may mean "no red meat" to some people. You might ask about how other items will be prepared. For instance, if Caesar salad is being served, see if a salad with a different dressing can be set aside for you (and remind the kitchen that you don't eat bacon on your salad). Be sure to note whether or not you eat dairy products or eggs. If you aren't explicit, and you're vegan, you may end up with egg pasta, an omelet or quiche, grated cheese on your salad, or cheese lasagna.

Heads Up!

If you're a dinner guest at a non-vegetarian's home, it's a major faux pas to carry on about the evils of meat. Even if another guest eggs you on and attempts to engage you in an earnest discussion or debate about the merits of vegetarianism, resist the temptation to participate. To do otherwise is just uncouth.

Helpful Hint

If you call the restaurant or hotel kitchen to request a vegetarian meal for an event, feel free to suggest a dish that you know you can eat and that the kitchen is likely to be able to make. For example, most kitchens have the ingredients on hand to make pasta primavera or a large baked potato topped with steamed vegetables. They're simple to fix too. They can also be preferable to that ubiquitous steamed vegetable plate.

When the meal is served and the waiter arrives at your table, quietly mention that you have a vegetarian meal ordered. If the waiter whisks a regular plate of food under your nose before you can say a word, let the food sit there until you can flag the waiter down again to request your meal.

Buffet Lines

If the meal is served as a buffet, you may not even need to mention to your host that you're a vegetarian unless you think there's a chance that the menu will be limited. If the meal is served at a restaurant or hotel, it's very likely that the menu will include a wide variety of dishes and plenty of foods that you can eat.

If you are vegan, however, it may still be wise to phone ahead and ask about the menu, just to be certain that there will be some dairy- and egg-free choices for you. You may find that you'll need to ask for some rice, pasta, or vegetables to be set aside for you if everything on the buffet line is going to be doused with butter or cream sauce. They might even be able to make a suitable dish for you and serve it to you at your seat.

The Dating Game

If your date is also a vegetarian, you're off to a good start. All you'll have to worry about is whether you're in the mood for Mexican or Thai or Ethiopian food. Even if you're a lacto ovo vegetarian and he's a vegan, at least you're simpatico. You'll work it out.

On the other hand, if your date is not a vegetarian, it's best to broach the subject early on. You don't have to make a big deal out of the fact that you don't eat meat, but it's probably best to mention that fact sooner rather than later, and probably before you get together for a meal.

The Last Bite

Vegetarian singles groups are active in some cities. Check with your local vegetarian society to see if such a group exists in your area. You might also check some of the resources listed in Part 7, "Veggie Survival Strategies." These groups plan restaurant outings, outdoor activities, and other events with the needs and interests of singles in mind.

So, will your mixed relationship survive? Could you live with a nonvegetarian? Be married to one? What about children—would you raise them vegetarian or not?

These are weighty questions for many vegetarians. It's a good idea to think about them and begin to formulate some answers, even though your ideas might change after you've met someone and are in a relationship.

But some vegetarians won't even date a nonvegetarian. (Kiss someone with greasy cheeseburger lips? No way!) Would you? If you restrict yourself to dating only fellow vegetarians, you may find yourself spending many a Saturday night alone in front of the television. After all, you're one of only 1 percent of the population, and only a fraction of that number is on the market for dating.

If you did begin dating a nonvegetarian, would you expect that person to stop eating meat eventually? What would the ground rules be if you decided to live together or get married? Would you have meat in the house? Cook two different meals, or each fend for yourselves? What would you do if you had nonvegetarian guests over for dinner—serve them meat or not? How would you resolve the conflict if you and your partner had different views about what to do?

Can you live and let live, or would you need your partner to see things as you do and maintain a vegetarian lifestyle with you? This question is especially important if your vegetarianism is rooted in ethical beliefs or attitudes. It's more difficult to compromise when your personal philosophy is at issue. You'll have to decide whether there's room in your life for someone who marches to a different drummer than yourself. Some vegetarians will find it harder to connect with a partner who doesn't share the same sensitivities. If it doesn't matter now, it may later. You don't have to arrive at any hard and fast conclusions about these issues today, but if you've never faced them before, it's a good idea to begin thinking about them.

Heads Up!

If you go into a relationship with a person who is not a vegetarian, be sure that your expectations about that person's future eating style are realistic. It's old-fashioned advice, but it's not out-of-date: Don't expect people to change. If you think you can change someone, you may be in for a disappointment. Be ready to accept that person as he or she is if you want the relationship to survive. A change in lifestyle is a very personal decision and one that each person must make on his or her own. You may be motivated to live the way you do, but your partner may not share the same conviction and possibly never will.

On the Job

Your success at the office is partly dependent upon how well you blend into the culture of the organization. If your job involves entertaining clients or meeting with colleagues over lunches and dinners, your eating habits will be on display for all to observe. The manner in which you conduct yourself, then, if you're a vegetarian, will mark you as sensible and health conscious or eccentric and difficult to please. It may be an asset or a liability, depending upon how you play it.

This may matter more in some work settings than in others. An advertising agency or marketing department within a company, for instance, is likely to be comfortable with creative people who do things differently and may be better able to tolerate an "eccentricity." It may be more important for you to appear compatible with your peers if you're in a more conservative line of work such as finance or banking.

The Last Bite

Why should you care about what your coworkers think about your eating habits? You should care because the perception that you are a social standout may negatively affect your chances of getting a promotion or a choice job opportunity. If you play your cards right, however, you can turn the difference in your lifestyle into an asset that will reflect positively on you and enhance the company's impression of you.

Putting Your Best Foot Forward: The Job Interview

First impressions count. In job interviews, you want your prospective employer and colleagues to focus on your skills and ideas, rather than on the fact that you don't eat meat. When they reflect on their meeting with you, you want them to think about how well you'll fit into their environment and about how your unique set of abilities will be an asset to their organization.

Job interviews often involve lunching with your prospective employer and colleagues. If that happens, there's no need to hide the fact that you're a vegetarian. At the same time, it's best not to make a big deal of it. Just approach the subject in a confident, matter-of-fact way.

Do your best to downplay any inconveniences due to your diet. When you're on a job interview, it's common for the people interviewing you to choose the restaurant where you'll eat, so you may not have an opportunity to steer them to a restaurant with lots of vegetarian choices. If that happens, size up your menu options as quickly as possible. It's fine to ask the waiter whether the soup is made with chicken stock or a beef base or if the beans contain lard. But if you do, make it as low-key as you can. If the answer is affirmative, have an alternative choice in mind so that you don't hold up the table's order while you struggle to find another choice.

You might also have a standby in mind, in case you have trouble finding something on the menu. For example, if the restaurant serves pasta, it's usually easy for the kitchen to whip up pasta tossed with olive oil, garlic and vegetables, or served with a marinara sauce. If you find yourself at a steak house, take a baked potato, salad, and vegetable side dishes.

Make Your Lifestyle a Business Asset

The best way to handle your dietary difference is to present yourself with confidence and your diet in a matter-of-fact way. Let your coworkers view you as being sensible and health conscious, a virtue that would reflect upon you positively in most business settings. Even if your coworkers have a vague sense that you may be motivated by ethical or political ideals, remain above it all and keep your views to yourself.

Whatever you do, don't allow yourself to be sucked into silly conversations or debates about the political or ethical issues relating to vegetarianism. Certainly these subjects have merit, but you'll be a loser if you bring them up in a business setting. You may find that some of your officemates won't be able to resist prodding you a bit, especially if they think that they can elicit an emotional reaction out of you or instigate an argument. Don't fall for it. Don't engage them. If you do, you'll be branded a standout, a radical, or worse. You'll be the loser, not them. All of your opinions may be valid, but the work setting is not the best place to air them unless you're prepared to accept the consequences. Unfortunately, this is just a fact of life. You might as well be realistic about it.

Helpful Hint

You may find yourself at a job interview being served a catered luncheon in a conference room. If you're served a ham sandwich, eat what you can from your plate and leave the rest. No explanation is necessary unless someone asks why you've left the food. In that case, all you have to say is, "I don't eat ham." You might also reassure your host that you'll be fine, that you aren't particularly hungry, or whatever sounds appropriate to you. The key is not to make a big deal out of the fact that they served you meat and you aren't eating it.

The Least You Need to Know

➤ If you're invited to someone's home for dinner, it's best to tell your host ahead of time that you're a vegetarian.

➤ At weddings, banquets, and other catered functions at hotels, country clubs, and restaurants, it's fine to phone ahead and request that a vegetarian entree be prepared for you.

➤ If you're invited out to dinner on a date, let your date know that you're a vegetarian. It may be possible to suggest a few restaurants at which you'll know you'll have some choices.

➤ It's generally not realistic to think that you can change another person, so give some thought ahead of time to what your expectations will be of a partner who is not vegetarian.

➤ In work settings, it may be best to keep your vegetarianism low-key. Don't permit yourself to be sucked into counterproductive debates or arguments about the merits of a vegetarian lifestyle.

Chapter 23

Restaurant Dining and Other Venues

In This Chapter

➤ Where to find the best vegetarian options at restaurants

➤ What to order when the menu isn't veg friendly

➤ How to sidestep hidden animal ingredients

➤ Getting good food at school

➤ Finding vegetarian choices in the company cafeteria

In the land of 16-ounce steaks, chicken halves, and pint-sized servings of vegetables, it's finally becoming quite easy to find vegetarian entrees on restaurant menus. It's even becoming somewhat easier to find vegetarian options in the workplace, in schools, and of course vegetarian options are ubiquitous on college campuses.

Still, you'll need to have a few tricks up your sleeve to find a satisfying vegetarian meal away from home. This chapter covers some of the strategies and know-how that seasoned vegetarians rely on when they go out to eat.

Natural Foods and Vegetarian Restaurants

Many natural foods stores have a cafe tucked away in a corner of the store in which you can get a quick bite to eat. Some carry cold salads and ready-made sandwiches, and others have a more extensive menu including a soup and salad bar, hot foods, and baked goods. Natural foods store cafes are popular places for many people to pick up a take-out meal for lunch during the work week and for dinner on the way home from work.

Vegetarian restaurants, on the other hand, can run the gamut from raw foods or macrobiotic eateries and homey little vegetarian hideaways to large metropolitan restaurants that stay packed during business hours. Many serve foods with an ethnic bent such as Indian or Middle Eastern, and some blend various ethnic cuisines.

The Last Bite

Small and mid-sized cities frequently do not have a totally vegetarian restaurant. If they have a so-called vegetarian restaurant, it's often a restaurant that serves chicken and fish as well as some meatless entrees. Outside of large metropolitan areas, it can be hard to find enough of a customer base to keep a totally vegetarian restaurant in business. It's easier to find vegetarian restaurants on the West Coast or in large cities on the East Coast than in other parts of the country.

Vegetarian restaurants often have an "alternative" feel to them—an earthy atmosphere that is usually quite casual. They tend to serve foods made with natural ingredients. For instance, you're likely to find brown rice served instead of white rice, and breads—even desserts such as cookies and pie crusts—tend to be made from whole grains. Some may be flagged as vegan. You'll find raw sugar on the table, and the menu will offer natural soft drinks, herbal teas, dishes made with tempeh and tofu, and menu items made with minimally processed ingredients. You may find soymilk on the menu too. All of these features—as well as a rustic, homey atmosphere—give many vegetarian restaurants a distinctive personality that sets them apart from other restaurants.

Helpful Hint

For a listing of vegetarian restaurants in your area, check out *Vegetarian Journal's Guide to Natural Foods Restaurants in the U.S. and Canada* (Avery Publishing Group), which is updated regularly. It's available at bookstores or by calling the Vegetarian Resource Group at (410) 366-8343.

Great Vegetarian Choices at Other Restaurants

If you live in a major metropolitan area, you can eat at a vegetarian restaurant every time you go out to eat. If you live anywhere else, you'll need to rely on the meatless options served at regular restaurants, or you can go ethnic.

When the Choice Is All-American

The good news forvegetarians is that the restaurant industry has gotten the word that a sizable percentage of the population wants meatless foods when they eat out. Not all of these folks are vegetarians per se, but they see vegetarian menu choices as being more healthful.

Even some of the most traditional of restaurants have responded by adding at least one or two vegetarian options to their menus. Many have added veggie burgers to their menus, since burgers are so familiar and popular (most supermarkets carry them now). It's also not uncommon to see a vegan option now and then, although it may not be labeled as such. An example is pasta primavera tossed with olive oil and garlic and made with egg-free noodles.

When the Choice Is Ethnic

Many cultures worldwide have vegetarian traditions, such as India and China. Not everyone in these countries is vegetarian, but many are, and everyone—vegetarian or not—is familiar with the concept and the foods.

Others, such as countries of the Mediterranean, the Middle East, and parts of Latin America, have some traditional foods that happen to be vegetarian, despite the fact that their diets rely heavily on meats and other animal products. For example, in the Middle East, lamb is eaten in large amounts, while falafel, spanakopita, and hummus, which happen to be vegetarian, are also traditional favorites.

What you order when you eat out at an ethnic restaurant will depend upon what type of vegetarian diet you follow and how that restaurant prepares specific foods. In one Italian restaurant, for example, the eggplant Parmesan sandwich may contain cheese, and in another it may not. If you are vegan, you probably won't eat the spanakopita at a Greek restaurant, since it's usually made with cheese. On the other hand, you might be perfectly happy with a Greek salad (minus the feta cheese), some pita bread, and an order of boiled potatoes with Greek seasonings.

Wherever you eat, you'll need to ask the wait staff for specifics about how the food is prepared, especially if you're vegan. One restaurant's baked ziti in marinara sauce may be vegan while another's may come to the table smothered in melted mozzarella unless you request otherwise. In the following table, you'll find common vegetarian foods that are often served in a variety of ethnic restaurants.

The World in Your Backyard: Vegetarian Choices at Selected Restaurants

At Italian restaurants, try:

Fresh vegetable appetizers with or without mozzarella cheese (antipasto)

Mixed green salads

Minestrone soup, lentil soup, or pasta e fagioli (pasta with beans)

Foccacia

Italian bread with olive oil or flavored oil for dipping

Vegetable-topped pizzas (with or without cheese)

Pasta primavera

Spaghetti with marinara sauce

Pasta with olive oil and garlic

Other pasta dishes tossed with vegetable combinations

Italian green beans with potatoes

Cappuccino or espresso

Italian ices

Fresh fruit desserts

At Mexican restaurants, try:

Gazpacho

Bean nachos

Mixed green salads

Tortilla chips with salsa

Bean soft or regular tacos

Bean tostadas

Bean burritos

Spinach burritos or enchiladas

Cheese enchiladas

Bean chalupas (fried tortilla layered with beans, lettuce, tomato, guacamole, and beans)

Chile rellenos (cheese-stuffed green pepper, usually batter-dipped and fried, topped with tomato sauce)

Flan (custard dessert made with milk and eggs)

At Chinese restaurants, try:

Vegetable soup or hot and sour soup

Vegetarian spring rolls or egg rolls

Sweet and sour cabbage (cold salad)

At Chinese restaurants, try:

Vegetable dumplings (fried or steamed)

Minced vegetables in lettuce wrap

Sesame noodles (cold noodle appetizer)

Sautéed greens

Steamed rice

Chinese mixed vegetables

Broccoli with garlic sauce

Vegetable lo mein

Vegetable fried rice

Szechwan-style green beans or eggplant

Tofu family style

Other tofu and seitan (or gluten) dishes

Fortune cookies (usually contain eggs)

Fresh orange slices

At Indian restaurants, try:

Dal (lentil soup)

Cucumber and yogurt salad

Chutney

Steamed rice

Chapatti, pappadum, naan, roti (Indian breads)

Samosas and pakoras (vegetable-filled appetizers)

Muttar paneer (tomato-based dish made with cubes of cheese and peas)

Vegetable curry

Palak paneer (spinach-based dish)

Other entrees, some based on lentils, chick peas, and vegetables

Fresh fruit

Rice pudding

At Ethiopian restaurants, try:

Mixed green salad

Injera (large, round, flat, spongy bread—tear off small pieces with which to pinch bites of food from a communal tray)

Variety of bean, lentil, and vegetable-based dishes served directly on a sheet of injera on a tray or platter

continues

The World in Your Backyard: Vegetarian Choices at Selected Restaurants (continued)

At Middle Eastern restaurants, try:

Hummus

Spinach salad

Dolma (stuffed grape leaves)

Baba ghanouj (a blended eggplant appetizer)

Fattouche (minced fresh green salad)

Tabouli salad (wheat salad)

Spinach pie

Lentil soup

Falafel plate or sandwich (chick-pea patties)

Vegetarian stuffed cabbage rolls (filled with rice, chick-peas, and raisins)

Halvah (sesame dessert)

Muhallabia (ground rice pudding; contains milk but no egg)

Ramadan (cooked, dried fruit with nuts, often served with cream and nutmeg)

Middle Eastern lemonade

The Last Bite

Fast-food restaurants usually have a limited number of vegetarian options, but some have several. Some choices: pancakes with syrup, muffins, mixed green salad, bean burrito (you can order it without the cheese), bean soft taco or regular taco, bean tostada, beans and cheese side dish, veggie burger (or ask for the cheeseburger, hold the meat, or a tomato sandwich on a bun), baked potato with toppings from the salad bar, veggie wrap sandwich, or a big salad from the salad bar.

When the Restaurant's Not Veg Friendly

There are going to be times when there's virtually nothing on the menu for a vegetarian. Some fast-food restaurants and truck stops are good examples—the baked beans contain pork, the biscuits are made with lard, the vegetables are cooked with bacon, and the staff just chuckles and looks incredulous when you ask if there's anything vegetarian on the menu. You're stuck.

In most cases, though, there are plenty of choices. You just have to get creative. With a little practice, this will become a relatively simple matter for you.

If you find yourself at a restaurant with limited vegetarian options, try some of these tried-and-true ideas for hunger prevention and possibly even a very good meal:

➤ At finer restaurants, peruse the menu for interesting side dishes that may be served with meat entrees. You may be able to combine some of them into a vegetarian plate that will be the envy of everyone else at your table.

➤ If the restaurant serves baked potatoes, ask for one as your entree. You can top it with items from a salad bar if the restaurant has one. Try adding broccoli florets, salsa, black olives, sunflower seeds, or whatever looks good to you.

➤ Combine several appetizers and/or side dishes to create a vegetarian plate. For example, you might order a mixed green salad, a bowl of gazpacho, an order of stuffed mushrooms, and an appetizer portion of grilled spinach quesadilla.

➤ Take a good look at meat-containing entrees and determine whether they can be prepared as vegetarian dishes instead. For instance, a pasta dish mixed with vegetables and shrimp could easily be made without the shrimp. A club sandwich might be able to be fixed with grilled portabello mushroom, avocado, cheese, or tomato slices instead of the meat. This is most likely to work at restaurants where the food is made to order.

> **Helpful Hint**
>
> When a restaurant isn't veg friendly, scan the menu to get an idea of the ingredients they have on hand. In many cases, you can ask for a special order using ingredients used to make other menu items. For example, if the restaurant serves spaghetti with meat sauce, you know they have pasta. The tomato sauce may already be mixed with meat, but they may have vegetables on hand for side dishes. Ask for pasta made with olive oil and garlic and whatever vegetables they can add. If all else fails, you can usually ask for a baked potato and a salad, or a salad and a tomato sandwich on whole-wheat toast. Be creative.

More Tips for Restaurant Survival

If you want to find a good meal and avoid disappointments when you go out to eat as a vegetarian, you need to be aware of some of the realities of the restaurant industry. The good-sense suggestions that follow will make it easier for you to get what you need.

➤ Finer restaurants are in a better position to accommodate special requests. They tend to prepare their menu items to order. Family restaurant chains are less likely to be able to help you out, since many of their menu items are already prepared. They might not be able, for instance, to cook the rice without chicken stock—it may have been made in a large batch the day before—or to fix the pasta without meat in the sauce.

➤ When you speak with restaurant staff about your order, be clear about what you would like. For instance, instead of just saying, "I'm a vegetarian," explain specifically what you do and do not eat. Let the wait staff know if dairy and eggs are okay, or if you don't want your foods flavored with chicken broth or beef broth.

➤ If you have plans to go to a restaurant that is unfamiliar to you, try to get a copy of the menu ahead of time. If you have a fax machine, ask them to fax you a menu. Look it over and call the restaurant to discuss options if needed. You can also ask to speak with the chef and ask for recommendations.

➤ Given enough notice, finer restaurants are usually happy to prepare a special meal for you. Give them a day or two notice, if possible.

➤ Be reasonable about special requests, especially if you can see that the restaurant is very busy. If it's a Friday or Saturday night and the place is packed, make your requests as simple as possible.

➤ Ask questions about how the food is prepared *before* you order. If you prefer to avoid cream, butter, grated cheese, anchovies, and other animal products, check to be sure that these ingredients aren't added to the food, rather than sending the food back once it comes to the table with the offending ingredient.

➤ Ask your server whether your special request will increase or decrease the cost of the meal.

Heads Up!

Be aware of cooking terms that can be clues that a menu item contains an animal product. For example, "au gratin" usually means that the food contains cheese, "scalloped" means that the food contains cream, "sautéed" can mean that the food is cooked with oil or butter, and "creamy" usually means that the item is made with cream or eggs.

Sidestepping Animal Ingredients

Unless you know you're at a restaurant where everything served is vegetarian or vegan, you'll need to be on the lookout for hidden animal ingredients in foods that you order. Some foods are more suspect than others. For instance, the beans in Mexican restaurants are notorious for containing lard. If you think the beans taste a little unusual, you may well be tasting an animal ingredient. Likewise, those flaky biscuits and pie crusts that you've been eating at your favorite diner may be made with lard. Ask your server to check with the cook or read the ingredient label if the food comes from a package or can.

The table that follows lists some of the foods that may contain animal ingredients. There are many others. Remember to be assertive and ask questions *before* you order so that you're not disappointed when the food comes to the table and you don't have to send food back.

Don't Ask—Don't Tell? Hidden Animal Ingredients in Restaurant Food

Food	Likely Culprits
Refried beans	Lard
Flour tortillas	Lard
Biscuits, pie crust	Lard
Bean soup	Bacon
Split pea soup	Ham
Caesar salad	Anchovies in the dressing
Stir-fry	Oyster sauce
Greek salad	Anchovies on top
Steamed rice	Chicken stock
Sautéed vegetables	Chicken stock (fatback or salt pork is often used in the South)
Green beans	Bacon
Cooked greens	Fatback or salt pork is often used in the South
Potato salad	Bacon if German-style potato salad; eggs
Spinach salad	Bacon; eggs
Baked beans	Pork

Also note that most baked goods are made with eggs and/or dairy products, that many vegetables and other menu items may be seasoned with butter, and that cream, cheese, or eggs may be added to creamy-style foods and foods served with a sauce.

Teaching Johnny About Good Food? School Lunch

Finding satisfactory vegetarian options in elementary and high school cafeterias can be difficult, though the situation is slowly improving. For now, the reality is that many vegetarian kids have to bring food from home if they want a good meal at school.

If your child has to take a bag lunch to school, vary the contents. Some good choices include small, aseptic cartons of vanilla- or carob-flavored soymilk or fruit juice, small boxes of raisins, single-serving containers of pudding or canned fruit, fresh fruit, peanut butter or almond butter sandwiches, hummus in a pita pocket, peeled baby carrots with salsa or hummus to dip, muffins, whole-grain cookies, bagels, graham crackers, and granola bars (try natural product brands). If your child is old enough to operate a microwave oven and has access to one at school, soup cups and hot cereal cups are also convenient and come in many varieties. If your child has access to a refrigerator, you can also pack a tofu-salad sandwich, pasta salad, yogurt, and other perishable items.

Read more about ways that vegetarian children can find suitable meals at school in Chapter 10, "Kids' Stuff or Adults Only? Vegetarian Diets for Children and Teens."

The Last Bite

Most college and university campuses offer vegetarian choices on their menus these days, and many offer them at every meal. Requests for vegetarian foods are common, and colleges and universities do not have to adhere to the kinds of regulations that elementary schools have to follow in menu planning. So, vegetarian college students generally have a much easier time finding something to eat at school.

At the Company Cafeteria

Isn't it nice to be an adult? Nobody is standing over you making sure that you take two servings from the meat group anymore. You don't have to take the milk, either.

Company cafeterias vary considerably in what they offer employees. Some employ their own cooks or chefs who prepare foods on-site, and others contract with a food service company to provide the meals. The food can range from burgers and fries to more sophisticated sandwiches and salads. Some companies offer more, some less.

The nice thing is, you probably don't care anymore if someone looks at you cross-eyed because you've taken a bag lunch to work. In some ways, you can use some of the same strategies in dealing with meals at work as you do with your kids' meals at school.

➤ If a weekly menu is available, plan ahead of time which days you'll eat the company's food and which days you'll bring your own from home. On some days, you might take an item or two from the company cafeteria and supplement it with a piece of fruit from home.

➤ If you are having difficulties dealing with meals at work, arrange a meeting with the person in charge of food service. See if there is any room for them to provide choices that meet your needs.

➤ You may not be the only one at your work site that would like more meatless choices. Even the nonvegetarians may want meatless options from time to time. See if you can recruit some others to lend support to your request.

The Least You Need to Know

➤ It's easier to find vegetarian restaurants in large metropolitan areas than in most small and mid-sized cities, unless they're college towns.

➤ Restaurants everywhere are serving more meatless entrees. Ethnic restaurants are often a good bet for finding vegetarian foods.

➤ If a restaurant's not veg friendly, try piecing a meal together from appetizers, side dishes, or ingredients from other menu items.

➤ It's best to phone ahead if you want the restaurant to prepare something special for you, especially on a Friday or Saturday night when most restaurants are busy.

➤ Colleges and universities are likely to offer vegetarian entrees daily, but elementary schools are way behind the times and vegetarian foods are difficult to obtain.

➤ If your choices at school or work are limited, look at the menu ahead of time and plan to supplement your meal with foods from home on days when there are no acceptable vegetarian choices.

Chapter 24

Staying Vegetarian from Sea Level to 35,000 Feet

In This Chapter

➤ Why travel poses a special challenge to vegetarians

➤ Strategies for traveling by car or by foot

➤ What to expect on cruise ships

➤ Air travel and how to make the most of it

Traveling puts many people into "survival mode" where meals are concerned. You're off your home turf. You've got less control over meals, you may be in unfamiliar surroundings, and you have to contend with the challenges that a change in your normal routine can bring. That can put you at risk of eating poorly, either because you can't find what you need or because you get trapped into eating foods that you ordinarily wouldn't eat.

Traveling makes you more vulnerable to impulsive food choices. You're also more susceptible to the "I'm on vacation so I'm entitled to eat whatever I want to" mentality, which can be especially problematic for frequent travelers.

For vegetarians, avoiding meat and possibly other animal products requires a set of skills that takes time and experience to acquire. In this chapter, I'll help you get started by explaining some of the ways in which you can improve your chances of getting what you need when you're on the road (or on the sea or in the air).

You're on the Road Again

If you want something to eat when you're traveling by car, you're usually limited to whatever is near the exit off the highway. Your choices are likely to be a family chain restaurant or a truck stop.

A better choice—especially if you travel by car a lot—is to pack a cooler or bag of food to take along with you in the car. Take your own food, and you're likely to:

➤ *Save time.* You won't have to stop to eat a meal, unless you want to take the time for a picnic along the way. If you eat in the car while you're en route, you'll have to stop only for stretch breaks, to fill up with gas, and to use the restroom. (If you're the driver, be careful that whatever you are eating doesn't cause enough of a distraction from driving to endanger you or others on the road.)

➤ *Save money.* Food that you take from home is likely to cost less than food that you eat at a restaurant.

➤ *Eat more healthfully.* Let's face it: Planning ahead helps to ensure that you eat well. You'll also be less likely to eat junk out of desperation if you have trouble finding vegetarian options on the road.

Helpful Hint

Many people fall into the trap of thinking that a bag lunch has to have a main course, which usually means a sandwich. Not so. Your bag-lunch meal can be much more interesting—and you won't run out of ideas as fast—if you mix and match odds and ends instead, such as muffins, bagels, fresh fruit, left-overs, instant soup cups, and so on.

The following list will give you some ideas of handy vegetarian foods that you can pack in a cooler or bag to take along with you in the car. You can add to the list yourself by giving some thought to foods that you have in your cupboard and refrigerator that might travel well.

Cooler and Brown-Bag Buddies

Individual aseptic packages of soymilk (buy carob-flavored for a change of pace)

Small cans or aseptic packages of fruit juice

Bottles of mineral water or flavored seltzer water

Bagels

Peanut butter or almond butter sandwiches on good bread

Fresh fruit

Baby carrots, peeled

Instant soup cups (or chili, rice and beans, lentils and beans). Mix with hot water from the coffee maker at a gas station/food mart

Instant hot cereal cups (get hot water at gas station/food mart)

Cooler and Brown-Bag Buddies

Snack-sized cans of fruit or applesauce

Homemade, whole-grain quick breads, muffins, and cookies

Graham crackers

Individual boxes of dry breakfast cereal with soymilk or rice milk

Deli salads

Hummus sandwiches

Tofu salad sandwiches

If you like to take trips by bicycle, or if you hike, you'll need to pack foods that are light and portable and don't require refrigeration. Dried fruit and nut mixtures, small containers of soymilk or fruit juice, crackers and peanut butter, and fresh fruit are good choices. You can munch during the day while you're active, then pile on the calories that you need when you stop for the night and have time to prepare a meal or have dinner at a good restaurant.

Cruisin'

If it's been a whilesince you've been on a cruise, stand informed: Today's cruise ships are spas on the waters, with a wide selection of all types of food, including healthful options. Therefore, food is not a problem for most people, unless you buckle under the temptations of five-course meals and rich desserts. After all, even fat-free calories count, and on cruise ships, the kitchen never seems to close.

As for any vegetarians on board, they're usually in luck. It's more common now for cruise ships to see vegetarian passengers, and most can accommodate them.

Some cruise lines have separate menus for health-conscious people, or they flag specific entrees and menu items as being "healthy." In many cases, that means meatless. If meat is included in the dish, it's often something that can be left out of meals that are cooked to order. For example, a pasta dish mixed with vegetables and seafood can easily be made without the seafood.

If you do find that the menu choices on a particular day don't include enough options for you, handle the situation the way you would at a better restaurant. Explain your needs to your server or the chef and ask for a special order. If possible, let the

Helpful Hint

If you have concerns about whether a cruise line will be able to accommodate your food preferences, have your travel agent request information about meals and get sample menus for you to examine. You can also call the cruise line's customer services office yourself and ask for more details.

kitchen know what you want the day before, especially if the ship is going to be serving a large number of people in that sitting (for the captain's dinner, for instance).

In lieu of or in addition to sit-down meals, cruise ships are known for their elaborate buffets. The sheer volume and variety of foods served make it easy for most vegetarians to find enough to eat. You'll have to sidestep the gelatin salads, and vegans may have to bypass items made with cream or mayonnaise. But think of it this way: The foods with those ingredients are the ones that give other people traveler's remorse after the vacation when they get on the scale and see the pounds they've gained. You can sit smug and satisfied with your fresh tropical fruit salads, rice and pasta and vegetables, and good breads, and have just as much fun.

Flying Friendly Vegetarian Skies

It's easy enough to order a vegetarian meal when you fly. Just call the airline's reservations desk at least 24 hours before your flight to make your request, or make the request at the time that you make your flight reservations. Ask the agent if meals or snacks are scheduled to be served on any of the flights. If so, say that you'd like to request vegetarian meals. The agent should ask what type of vegetarian meal you'd prefer. If he or she doesn't ask, be sure to say something if you prefer no eggs and/or dairy.

Experienced vegetarian travelers know about other special meal options too. They also know when to anticipate problems with their meal service, and they know how to handle problems when they arise. You will too, with a little coaching and some practice.

Of course, flying isn't just about in-flight meals. You'll need some tips for dealing with airport food between flights as well.

How to Order a Vegetarian In-Flight Meal

Airlines are cutting back on meal service, especially on shorter flights. So don't be too surprised if the next time you fly, you discover that you won't be served anything more than peanuts and a beverage.

On many short flights, a beverage and a handful of peanuts or pretzels is all that may be served, whereas a few years ago passengers would have been served a snack. Flights on which passengers may once have been served complete meals are now being serviced with a light snack instead.

Some airlines give passengers an opportunity to make special requests for their snacks as well as their meals, whereas some permit only special requests for full meals.

On domestic flights, most airlines offer several options for vegetarians. They typically include:

➤ Lacto ovo vegetarian meal

➤ Vegetarian meal, no eggs or dairy (some airlines also use the term "vegan")

➤ Fruit plate

Fruit plates can be a great idea for any traveler. If you've never ordered one before, consider it the next time you fly. They're light, and they provide a good way to get some fresh fruit into your diet when you're traveling—fresh foods are often few and far between, causing many people's diets to suffer.

On some flights, the crew will have a list of passengers who have ordered special meals, and they may identify you as you are taking your seat, or they may ask you to ring your flight attendant call button just before they begin meal service. On other flights, you'll get served a regular meal unless you speak up and tell the flight attendant that you've ordered a vegetarian meal.

On international flights, you may have even more options.

On airlines that fly to the Orient, you may be offered "Asian vegetarian" or "Indian vegetarian" meals, which may include vegetable stir-fries, curried vegetables, and other traditional entrees. Some airlines designate the Indian option as "Hindu." You can specify whether you want the meal to include dairy (and eggs) or not. These special meals can be a nice change of pace from the standard airline issue.

When You Don't Get What You Ordered

As any frequent flyer will tell you, ordering a vegetarian meal doesn't ensure that you'll get it.

That isn't always the airline's fault. Sometimes a last-minute change of aircraft can mean that the meals meant for your flight aren't on that plane. If you miss a flight and have to take an alternate, you won't get the meal that you special ordered. If you

Helpful Hint

The airline representative will probably inform you of meals scheduled to be served when you reserve your flights, but you can always ask to be sure. You can also put in a standing order for vegetarian meals with your travel agent or corporate travel office if they routinely handle your reservations.

Heads Up!

If you are seated near the back of the plane, you may want to ring your call button early in the meal service to let the attendants know that you are expecting a vegetarian meal. That's to ensure that they don't give it away before they get to you. That can happen if someone asks for a vegetarian meal despite not having ordered one (and the flight attendant doesn't check the name on the meal), or when the airline hasn't loaded enough of a particular special request onto the aircraft.

upgrade your ticket to first class just before you board your flight, your vegetarian meal may be back in coach and you may have another (maybe better) menu from which to choose in first class. Your flight attendant can usually retrieve your meal from coach if you still want it.

If you find yourself stuck with a ham sandwich instead of your vegetarian meal, there are a few things that you can do:

Heads Up!

If you have a particularly long travel day and want to be extra sure that your vegetarian meal has been ordered, you may want to phone the airline a day or two before you leave, just to reconfirm that the request has been noted. This is especially important if you've made a schedule change, because the agent may not have carried your meal request over to your new reservations.

➤ Eat what you can of the meal that you have been served. Picking the meat off a sandwich and eating the rest of it isn't an option for many vegetarians, nor is pushing the sausage away from the stack of pancakes that it's been leaning against. But your only other option may be peanuts and tomato juice, so if you're really hungry, you may at least be able to eat the salad or crackers.

➤ Ask your flight attendant for cookies, crackers, nuts, pretzels, or juice. If your flight attendant knows that you haven't received your special order, he or she should be able to help you out with some extra snacks or beverages.

➤ Pull out the reserves (fresh fruit, a bagel, a sandwich) that you might have taken along in your carry-on bag "just in case."

Planning for Mishaps

You know what they say about best-laid plans. Missed connections happen, and airlines make mistakes. There's always a good probability that you won't get the special meal you ordered.

For that reason, it's a good idea to eat a full meal before you leave home. If you don't have time or if you're going to be traveling all day, pack a few small items in your carry-on bag to hold you if you miss a meal or can't get something that suits your needs.

In the Terminal

You may find yourselfroaming the airport terminal during a lengthy layover and decide to stop for a meal or a snack. Or you might even have to grab something to go if you're hungry, you're racing to catch a flight, and

Heads Up!

If you are traveling internationally, you may not be able to take fresh fruits and vegetables back and forth between countries. Instead of packing fresh foods in your carry-on bag, take small containers of aseptically packaged soymilk or fruit juice, packaged crackers, pretzels, nuts, trail mix, or dried fruit.

you know that the flight won't be offering meal service. If so, your food choices will vary considerably, depending upon the size and location of the airport.

At worst, you'll be stuck with vending machines and newsstands selling candy, packaged cookies and crackers, and maybe some nuts. That's the disadvantage of small airports, although the trade-off is an easy time getting to your connecting gate. At larger airports, you may find several full-service restaurants, cafeterias, and food stands with a huge variety of food choices.

At larger airports with a wide range of places to eat, the restaurants are essentially the same as those outside the airport. Ethnic restaurants (Mexican, Chinese) have the most options for vegetarians, and one or two others may serve veggie burgers. In some airports on the West Coast, you'll find juice bars, and on the East Coast you'll find bagel stands that sell New York–style bagels and bowls of fresh fruit salad, both good choices for anyone.

The table that follows lists some vegetarian food options that can be found at most airports.

Helpful Hint

Many hotels have bowls of fruit at the check-out desk. Before you leave your hotel, pick up a piece and stow it in your carry-on bag. If you don't find fruit at your hotel, buy a piece or two in the airport terminal at a food stand or cafeteria. Fruit is good to have on hand in case you get hungry while you're traveling, and it's a good source of dietary fiber and other nutrients that tend to be neglected when people travel.

Airport Food Options for Vegetarians

Food Service	Your Choice
Newsstands	Packaged cookies, crackers, pretzels, nuts, and trail mix
Food stands	Frozen yogurt, soft pretzels, nuts, fresh fruit and fruit salad, bagels, fruit juice, bottled water, trail mix, muffins, popcorn, pizza
Cafeterias	Mixed green salads, bagels, fresh fruit, fruit salads, fruit juices, bottled water, yogurt, frozen yogurt, muffins, pizza, French fries
Restaurants	Bean burritos, bean tacos, bean tostadas, mixed green salads, vegetable stir-fry, veggie burgers, vegetarian pizza, vegetarian-style sandwiches, and many others, depending upon the restaurant
Airline clubs or lounges	Hot and cold beverages including coffee, tea, fruit juices, soft drinks, bottled water, cookies, crackers, nuts, and bagels

The Least You Need to Know

➤ You're better off packing a cooler or bag of food to take from home when you travel by car.

➤ Cruise ship buffets usually have a lot for vegetarians to choose from, or you can ask your server for a special request at sit-down dinners.

➤ Make a request for vegetarian meals and snacks at the time you make your plane reservations.

➤ There are many reasons that you may not get the vegetarian meal you requested on a flight. Plan ahead!

Part 7
Veggie Survival Strategies

You're on your way! Now here are some more smart ways to hone your new skills, reinforce and expand on what you've learned, and challenge your increasingly sophisticated taste buds.

The remaining two chapters in this book offer some important parting shots of advice and a comprehensive listing of valuable resources.

Best wishes!

Chapter 25

Getting Involved in the Veg Scene

In This Chapter

➤ Why get involved?

➤ What to expect from local and national vegetarian organizations

➤ How to find community groups that can help you

➤ Businesses worth checking out

Now comes the fun part—putting your new-found knowledge into practice and reaching out to interact with other vegetarians.

Not that you have to reach out to anyone, of course. You may be quite content to do your own thing all by yourself. But if you are curious and inclined to investigate some of the resources available out there, you'll find some good sources of additional support and information.

This chapter will introduce you to some of the linkages with the wider vegetarian world that you might find particularly valuable or interesting. You'll find that there's a wide range of individuals and groups who practice a vegetarian lifestyle. They have different reasons for their vegetarianism, different outlooks, approaches, interests, and different things to offer you.

As you explore these resources, don't be surprised to find some of them weird and others wonderful. It's similar to experimenting with new foods—you'll find some duds and some new favorites. Likewise, what appeals to you may not be the same as what appeals to someone else. Investigate, stick with what you like, or move on to something else.

Why Bother Getting Involved?

Even people who are highly motivated find that they face challenges when they make the switch to a vegetarian lifestyle. That stems largely from the fact that vegetarian lifestyles are outside our culture—our society's not veg friendly, for the most part. Yes, it's changing. But in the meantime, there are numerous skills that you'll need to practice in order to be reasonably comfortable getting along. Making connections with other vegetarians and vegetarian and veg-friendly groups can be a good way to get support.

Helpful Hint

When nonvegetarians try to provoke you with questions such as "If you're a vegetarian, why are you wearing leather?" or "How do you know that plants don't feel pain?" it can be helpful to ask other vegetarians for suggestions about how to respond if you're unsure. Local and national vegetarian groups are happy to coach you on how best to handle such needling.

Getting to know other vegetarians can also be good for your emotional well-being. When your lifestyle is at odds with the norm, you can sometimes feel isolated. Having a network of like-minded others can help you feel more confident and comfortable. It can help you gain some perspective on problems when they arise. Observing other vegetarians can also help you to see the many ways in which people practice vegetarianism.

Connecting with Local Vegetarian Groups

If you live in a large metropolitan area, it's very likely that there's a local vegetarian organization operating close by. If you live in a mid-sized city, it's also quite possible that there's a vegetarian group in your area. If you live in a small town, don't give up hope until you've checked around. It takes only one interested person to get a group started, and you may be surprised to learn that there's a vegetarian group alive and well in your little town. Local vegetarian organizations are thriving in some of the most unlikely places.

Uh, What Exactly Is a Local Vegetarian Group?

Local vegetarian organizations come in all shapes and sizes. Some are affiliated with churches such as the Seventh-day Adventist Church, and some are affiliated with other philosophical, environmental, or political movements or groups. However, the vast majority are simply organized and run by people drawn together by nothing more than their desire to follow a vegetarian lifestyle.

In fact, the members of local vegetarian organizations often have little in common with each other outside of their common interest in vegetarianism. They may include Republicans, Democrats, Libertarians, and Socialists as well as accountants, artists, doctors, computer programmers, plumbers, construction workers, financial analysts, dental hygienists, nutritionists, teachers, Christians, Jews—and so on. You may find that you enjoy getting together with this group of people occasionally just because it is so diverse and because you might not otherwise have gotten to know some of the members.

Local vegetarian organizations usually meet once a month or every other month in a particular location that can range from someone's house to a church community room or a room in the local library or other public place. Some groups even meet at restaurants.

Helpful Hint

You don't necessarily have to be a vegetarian to join a local vegetarian organization or attend meetings. Some people attend just because they're interested and want to learn more.

What Goes on at Meetings?

Groups vary in what they do when they meet. Most group meetings are strictly social events and revolve around a potluck or covered dish dinner. Every member brings a dish or beverage to share with the others. Many groups ask that members bring a note that describes the dish and labels it vegan, lacto, or lacto ovo vegetarian. Nonmembers (and nonvegetarians) can usually attend, but some groups ask that people who attend without bringing a dish pay a nominal fee—typically $3 to $5 per person.

At some meetings, groups sponsor a speaker. The speaker may be a nutritionist or physician who discusses the health and nutrition aspects of vegetarian diets, or she might be an environmentalist or local activist who speaks on a relevant issue.

Most meetings have an informal agenda of some sort. The president or presiding member may update the group about the status of the group's activities, such as hosting a booth at a local health fair, compiling a cookbook as a fundraiser, or local news of interest to members.

Some groups publish newsletters, and many sponsor special meetings or events around particular holidays or observances, such as Thanksgiving, the Fourth of July, or World Vegetarian Day on October 1st. Restaurant gatherings are also popular events.

The Last Bite

Attending meetings of a local vegetarian society can be a nice way to sample a variety of vegetarian foods and to discuss vegetarian issues with like-minded and sympathetic individuals. Many people form long-term friendships with other members, some of whom they may never have met otherwise. Vegetarian societies often meet at Seventh-day Adventist or Unitarian churches or at the homes of vegetarian society members. You may also read about upcoming meetings in the community events section of your local newspaper.

How Can I Find a Local Group?

There are several ways to locate a vegetarian organization in your area.

➤ *Ask the manager of your local natural foods store.* Vegetarian organizations often do business of one sort or another with local natural foods stores, so check with the manager to see if he or she can give you the name and phone number of a contact person. News of meetings may even be posted in the store's in-store newsletter, if there is one.

➤ *Call your local Seventh-day Adventist Church.* If a vegetarian group is active in your area, the chances are good that the church knows about it. The meetings may even be held in the church community room, although the group may not have any other connection with the church. Another good bet is to call a Unitarian Universalist Church—another likely spot for vegetarian society meetings.

➤ *Call a national organization* such as the Vegetarian Resource Group to see if they know of a group in your area.

➤ *Check your local newspaper* or alternative press paper for a mention of a vegetarian society meeting.

➤ *Ask your friends.* If your friends don't know of a local organization, maybe they know someone who does.

➤ *Check with the student affairs office* of a college or university in your area to see if there is a student vegetarian group on campus.

What Do National Groups Have to Offer?

Several national groups promote a vegetarian lifestyle.

National vegetarian organizations serve a function different from that of local groups, although both groups can be a good source of support for anyone adopting a vegetarian lifestyle.

Like local groups, national vegetarian organizations vary in many ways. However, they all tend to be more involved in advocacy issues on the national level as compared to local groups, which are more active in the city in which they are located. They may publish a newsletter or magazine that is distributed to a wide national audience, and they may sponsor conferences or other events that draw participants from around the country and even internationally. They tend to address issues of general concern and interest to vegetarians everywhere and to report on events that happen nationally.

The differences between national and local vegetarian organizations are like the differences between the national and local news on television. It's nice to have both. One gives a bigger picture; the other keeps you up on what's happening close to home.

Helpful Hint

If there is no vegetarian organization where you live, why not start one yourself? You may be surprised at how many people will want to join. The Vegetarian Resource Group (see Chapter 26, "Getting Educated About Everything Vegetarian") can provide you with materials to help you organize your own local group.

Other Community Groups

If your community doesn't have a local vegetarian society or if it's not your style to join such a group, there may be some other places where you can get support locally.

➤ *Alternative health care centers.* These may be billed as mind/body centers, complementary or integrative medicine centers, or holistic health centers. Some are affiliated with hospitals, and others are independent. If they have a nutrition component, with nutrition counseling, cooking classes, or tours of a local natural foods store, they may be helpful to you. However, more hospitals are jumping on the alternative-health bandwagon and are setting up mind/body centers, complementary or integrative medicine centers, and holistic health centers.

➤ *Cooking classes.* If your local community college, cooking supply store, or natural foods store offers cooking classes, you may be in luck. If they don't already offer classes on cooking with tofu and tempeh, vegetarian cuisine, Indian or Asian cuisine, or other subjects that interest you, request them. Schools and businesses will often add a course if there's a demonstrated interest in it.

➤ *Health fairs sponsored by the Seventh-day Adventist Church.* Seventh-day Adventist Churches often host health fairs at which you'll find a variety of resources concerning vegetarian diets. You don't have to be a church member to attend. In fact, the church typically advertises to the entire community and welcomes nonmembers.

➤ *Jewish community centers and YMCAs.* Check with area organizations such as these to see if they have any events or activities planned that relate to natural foods, cooking (ethnic, vegetarian, or soy foods, for instance), or other topics that may relate to vegetarianism.

➤ *Organic gardening clubs.* Some communities have organic gardening organizations, which may be of interest to some vegetarians and through which you might meet other vegetarians.

Heads Up!

If you seek out information about vegetarian diets from a nutritionist or other health care provider at an alternative health care center, be sure that the person is knowledgeable and qualified to discuss vegetarian nutrition with you. Most dietitians and other health care providers have little, if any, experience or knowledge about vegetarian diets and may not be in a position to counsel you properly. Be cautious. Ask about the practitioner's experience with vegetarian diets. If he or she begins talking about concerns about protein, a need for lots of supplements, or in other ways appears nonsupportive, say "thanks but no thanks" and look elsewhere for guidance. Traditionally trained health care personnel are often still learning when it comes to alternative health matters.

Add These Businesses to Your List

I've already mentioned that natural foods stores are a great place to go for vegetarian specialty products. If your community has a food co-op, it may be another good place to find vegetarian specialty products. You may be required to pay a refundable fee to join, or you may have to work at the co-op in order to be eligible for the biggest discount on products.

Mail-order is another option for anyone who lives in a community that doesn't have a co-op or natural foods store. (See Chapter 26 for more details.) Adventist churches often have stores in their communities where members can buy vegetarian specialty products. These stores are not always widely known outside of Adventist circles, but they sell some good products, and anyone is welcome to shop there. Call a local Adventist church or check your phone book. The store might be billed as an "Adventist book store," but it probably sells foods as well.

Become an Advocate for Good Food and a Vegetarian Lifestyle

It will be easier for all of us to get good vegetarian foods in schools, at supermarkets, and in restaurants if everybody makes it a habit to advocate for vegetarian alternatives.

On the national level, consumer advocacy groups such as the Vegetarian Resource Group, the Center for Science in the Public Interest, and Public Voice for Food and Health Policy lobby for change and urge their supporters to write letters to their elected officials and representatives to express their views on proposed legislation or regulation changes.

On the local level, you can speak to the manager of your neighborhood supermarket to request that the store carry certain food products, or you can talk with the chefs or owners of your area restaurants and encourage them to serve more vegetarian entrees. You might also meet with the food service manager at your child's school to express your interest in seeing more vegetarian options available on school menus.

The Least You Need to Know

➤ Tapping into community resources for vegetarians can help you feel more confident and comfortable as you adapt to a vegetarian lifestyle.

➤ Local and national vegetarian organizations can be terrific sources of information and practical assistance as you adopt a vegetarian lifestyle.

➤ Local alternative health care centers, complementary or integrative medicine centers, or holistic health centers may all be local sources of information and assistance for you in adopting a vegetarian lifestyle.

➤ Cooking classes offered through cooking supply stores or community colleges, health fairs sponsored by the Seventh-day Adventist Church, Jewish Community Center, or YMCA-sponsored events, and even organic gardening clubs are practical sources of information for you.

➤ Natural foods stores, food co-ops, and mail-order catalogs are good sources of vegetarian specialty products.

➤ It's important for vegetarians to advocate for more vegetarian options by requesting them at supermarkets, restaurants, and schools.

Getting Educated About Everything Vegetarian

Hopefully, this book has given you a solid introduction to all things vegetarian. The next step? Do it all over again. And again. And again.

Not necessarily the same book—just the same topics.

The reason? Let's face it, it takes most people several rounds before they absorb and understand a new subject well. Repetition is good. It helps us learn.

Besides, it's helpful to hear (or read, or view) the same subject matter presented differently by a variety of people or media. Sometimes, hearing the same information presented in a slightly different way is all it takes to make it "click."

The resources that are outlined in the next several pages are not an exhaustive listing of everything that is available. They're a sampling of some of those that I have found to be the best. There's no need to rush out and read or see or contact every one of them immediately. Move along at whatever pace seems appropriate for you, and choose those resources that sound the most interesting. You may prefer books to videos, or you might have an itch to dive right in to cookbooks and start experimenting with new recipes.

Helpful Hint

When it comes to adopting a vegetarian diet, there is a long list of resources and other sources of support from which to choose. It's perfectly fine to focus on those that seem the most fun or interesting to you at the moment. You're in this for the long haul. Do what feels comfortable to you.

Some people find that it's effective to get information from books, videos, and other sources for a while, then to switch gears and focus on such practical matters as eating out, cooking, and entertaining vegetarian style. They might do that by taking a cooking class, experimenting with vegetarian cookbooks, or getting more active with a local vegetarian society. Of course, there doesn't have to be any particular structure or plan to how you approach this. Some people simply do it all in bits and pieces as they feel like it and as opportunities present themselves.

The most important thing is to know where to go for great resources. Those that follow in this chapter will get you started.

Great Organizations to Get to Know

There are many great vegetarian organizations. Those that are listed here are simply a starting place. In fact, not all of the groups listed here are vegetarian organizations per se. Nevertheless, all of them are great resources for vegetarians.

Many states have vital, active local groups, and there are some other smaller, national organizations that are also good resources. If you request materials or attend conferences sponsored by the groups listed here, they will lead you to some of these other organizations.

> **Center for Science in the Public Interest**
> 1875 Connecticut Ave., N.W., Suite 300
> Washington, DC 20009-5728
> (202) 332-9110
> Web site: http://www.cspinet.org

CSPI is an independent nonprofit consumer advocacy organization that targets health and nutrition issues. It publishes the *Nutrition Action Healthletter* (10 issues per year). The group takes no paid advertising in its newsletter, and it accepts no government or industry funding.

National Center for Nutrition and Dietetics
The American Dietetic Association
216 W. Jackson Blvd., Suite 800
Chicago, IL 60606-6995
(800) 366-1655
Web site: http://www.eatright.org

NCND is the public education arm of the American Dietetic Association. If you call the toll-free consumer hotline, you'll have the option of listening to a recorded message about nutrition (changes regularly), you can speak to a registered dietitian about nutrition questions, you can get a referral to a dietitian using the association's referral service, and you can request association materials.

You'll find that the recorded messages are all funded by the food industry. My recommendation is to call the NCND for specific materials, including a copy of the association's position paper on vegetarian diets, and its brochure, "Eating Well—The Vegetarian Way." One copy of each is available free of charge.

North American Vegetarian Society
PO Box 72
Dolgeville, NY 13329
(518) 568-7970
E-mail: navs@telenet.net

NAVS sponsors the annual Summerfest vegetarian conference, usually held in upstate New York in July. This casual, family oriented conference draws an international crowd with diverse interests. Nonvegetarians are welcome. Summerfest is an excellent place to sample fabulous vegetarian foods, meet other vegetarians, attend lectures, and pick up materials from a variety of vegetarian organizations. The group also publishes *The Vegetarian Voice*, a newsletter for members.

Physicians Committee for Responsible Medicine
5100 Wisconsin Ave., N.W., Suite 404
Washington, DC 20016
(202) 686-2210
Web site: http://www.pcrm.org

PCRM is a nonprofit organization of physicians and others who work together to advocate for compassionate and effective medical practices, research, and health promotion. The group publishes the quarterly newsletter *Good Medicine*.

Vegetarian Nutrition Dietetic Practice Group
Division of Practice
The American Dietetic Association
216 W. Jackson Blvd., Suite 800
Chicago, IL 60606-6995
(800) 366-1655

The VN DPG is an interest group of the American Dietetic Association for dietitians and other members who are interested in vegetarian nutrition. The group publishes the quarterly newsletter, *Issues in Vegetarian Dietetics*, which is available by subscription even to people who are not members of the ADA. Fact sheets about various aspects of vegetarian nutrition are also available through the group.

The Vegetarian Resource Group
PO Box 1463
Baltimore, MD 21203
(410) 366-8343
E-mail: vrg@vrg.org
Web site: http://www.vrg.org

VRG is a nonprofit organization that educates the public about vegetarianism and the interrelated issues of health, nutrition, ecology, ethics, and world hunger. The group publishes the bimonthly *Vegetarian Journal* and provides numerous other printed materials for consumers (many printed in Spanish) free of charge or at a modest cost. All health and nutrition materials are peer reviewed by a team of physicians and/or registered dietitians. The organization also advocates for health and food policy changes.

Books

The titles that follow are sorted into two groups: general or comprehensive books about vegetarianism, and those that focus specifically on vegetarian diets for kids and teens. There are far too many to give a comprehensive listing here, so this is a sampling of the many good ones.

General and Comprehensive Books

Becoming Vegetarian. Vesanto Mellina, R.D., Brenda Davis, R.D., and Victoria Harrison, R.D. Book Publishing Company, Summertown, TN, 1995.

Being Vegetarian. Suzanne Havala, M.S., R.D., for the American Dietetic Association. Chronimed Publishing, Minneapolis, 1996.

Dr. Dean Ornish's Program for Reversing Heart Disease. Dean Ornish, M.D. Random House, New York, 1990.

Eat More, Weigh Less. Dean Ornish, M.D. HarperCollins Publishers, New York, 1995.

Good Foods, Bad Foods: What's Left to Eat? Suzanne Havala, M.S., R.D. Chronimed Publishing, Minneapolis, 1998.

The Natural Kitchen. Suzanne Havala, M.S., R.D. Berkley Publishing, New York, 1999.

Vegan Handbook. Debra Wasserman, M.A., and Reed Mangels, Ph.D., R.D. The Vegetarian Resource Group, Baltimore, 1996.

Vegetarian Times Vegetarian Beginner's Guide. Editors of *Vegetarian Times* magazine. Macmillan, New York, 1996.

The Vegetarian Way. Virginia Messina, M.P.H., R.D., and Mark Messina, Ph.D. Crowne Trade Paperbacks, New York, 1996.

For or About Kids and Teens

Dr. Spock's Baby and Child Care, Seventh Edition. Benjamin Spock, M.D., and Steven Parker, M.D. Pocket Books, New York, 1998.

A Teen's Guide to Going Vegetarian. Judy Krizmanic. Viking, New York, 1994.

Cookbooks

This list represents a small fraction of the number of good vegetarian and vegan cookbooks that are now on the market. Cookbooks are a matter of personal preference—some people like pretty pictures, some people want simple recipes, some want gourmet food, and others just look for spiral lay-flat bindings. You'll find the range on this list. It's an excellent starting point, but you might also want to go to your library or a bookstore and peruse the shelves for others that look appealing to you.

Note that I've included some cookbooks that contain recipes with high fat contents. Some of those listed include dairy products and/or eggs in the recipes too. I've included these cookbooks because they're considered classics and sentimental favorites among vegetarians. However, most of the titles on this list contain recipes that are low in saturated fat and cholesterol and/or are vegan.

The cookbook list is also divided into three groups: all-purpose cookbooks, cookbooks for children, and cookbooks for entertaining.

All-Purpose Cookbooks

The Complete Soy Cookbook. Paulette Mitchell. Macmillan, New York, 1998.

The Enchanted Broccoli Forest. Mollie Katzen. Ten Speed Press, Berkeley, CA, 1982.

Laurel's Kitchen Caring. Laurel Robertson. Ten Speed Press, Berkeley, CA, 1997.

Lean, Luscious and Meatless. Bobbie Hinman and Millie Snyder. Prima Publishing, Rocklin, CA, 1992.

The Meatless Gourmet: Easy Lowfat Favorites. Bobbie Hinman. Prima Publishing, Rocklin, CA, 1997.

Mollie Katzen's Vegetable Heaven: Over 200 Recipes for Uncommon Soups, Tasty Bites, Side-By-Side Dishes, and Too Many Desserts. Mollie Katzen. Hyperion, New York, 1997.

The Moosewood Cookbook. Mollie Katzen. Ten Speed Press, Berkeley, CA, 1977, 1992.

The New Laurel's Kitchen. Laurel Robertson, Carol Flinders, and Brian Ruppenthal. Ten Speed Press, Berkeley, CA, 1976, 1986.

The New Vegetarian Cuisine. Linda Rosenweig and the food editors of *Prevention* magazine. Rodale Press, Emmaus, PA, 1994.

The Peaceful Palate. Jennifer Raymond. Heart and Soul Publications, Calistoga, CA, 1992.

The Savory Way: High Spirited, Down-to-Earth Recipes from the Author of The Greens Cookbook. Deborah Madison. Bantam Books, New York, 1990.

Simply Vegan. Debra Wasserman and Reed Mangels, Ph.D. The Vegetarian Resource Group, Baltimore, 1994.

Soy of Cooking: Easy-to-Make Vegetarian, Low-Fat, Fat-Free & Antioxidant-Rich Recipes. Marie Oser. Chronimed Publishing, Minneapolis, 1996.

1,000 Vegetarian Recipes. Carol Gelles. Macmillan, New York, 1996.

Tofu Cookery, Revised Edition. Louise Hagler. Book Publishing Company, Summertown, TN, 1991.

The Uncheese Cookbook. Joanne Stepaniak. Book Publishing Company, Summertown, TN, 1996.

Vegetarian Cooking for Everyone. Deborah Madison. Broadway Books, New York, 1997.

The Vegetarian Hearth. Darra Goldstein. HarperCollins Publishers, New York, 1996.

Vegetarian Times Complete Cookbook. Editors of *Vegetarian Times* magazine. Macmillan, New York, 1995.

For Kids

Leprechaun Cake and Other Tales. Vonnie Crist and Debra Wasserman. The Vegetarian Resource Group, Baltimore, 1995.

Pretend Soup and Other Real Recipes: A Cookbook for Preschoolers and Up. Mollie Katzen and Ann Henderson. Tricycle Press, Berkley, CA, 1994.

For Entertaining

Table for Two. Joanne Stepaniak. Book Publishing Company, Summertown, TN, 1996.

Vegetarian Times Vegetarian Entertaining. Editors of *Vegetarian Times* magazine. Macmillan, New York, 1996.

Magazines and Newsletters

The following are a few of the publications that reliably offer practical and scientifically accurate information about vegetarian nutrition.

Issues in Vegetarian Dietetics
Vegetarian Nutrition Dietetic Practice Group
Division of Practice
The American Dietetic Association
216 W. Jackson Blvd., Suite 800
Chicago, IL 60606-6995
(800) 366-1655

This newsletter is produced primarily for dietitians with an interest in vegetarian nutrition. However, its articles and scientific references may be of interest to consumers as well.

Loma Linda University Vegetarian Nutrition and Health Letter
Loma Linda University
School of Public Health
1711 Nichol Hall
Loma Linda, CA 92350
(888) 558-8703

Vegetarian Nutrition and Health Letter is an eight-page newsletter published 10 times per year by the Loma Linda University School of Public Health.

Vegetarian Journal
The Vegetarian Resource Group
PO Box 1463
Baltimore, MD 21203
(410) 366-8343

The *Vegetarian Journal* is available by subscription and can also be found on many newsstands. It is published bimonthly and covers a range of practical matters of interest to vegetarians.

Vegetarian Times
PO Box 570
Oak Park, IL 60303
(708) 848-8100 or (800) 435-9610

Vegetarian Times magazine is a monthly magazine sold on newsstands everywhere.

Materials for Health Professionals

If you are a health professional—a doctor, nurse, dietitian, and others—and you would like more information about the health and nutrition aspects of vegetarian diets, the resources that follow are for you. Some lay people may also find these materials to be useful. Many of the materials listed previously are also appropriate for health professionals.

Brochures and Printed Materials

If you are speaking to groups or need reliable materials to hand out in your office to patients or clients, the American Dietetic Association's brochure, "Eating Well—The Vegetarian Way," is available in bulk for a fee. Check with the association sales department at (800) 877-1600 for information about prices.

The Vegetarian Resource Group has numerous brochures and handouts that are appropriate for use with groups and individuals, and most are available in bulk free of charge or for a nominal fee. Some are available in Spanish. The organization also has teaching plans, videos and audiotapes for loan, and numerous other materials. Contact the VRG at PO Box 1463 Baltimore, MD 21203; (410) 366-8343. The VRG can also arrange speakers for professional association meetings on such subjects as vegetarian diets for children, the health and nutrition aspects of vegetarian diets, how to integrate vegetarian entrees into food service, and others.

Books

Many of the books listed earlier are appropriate for health professionals. An additional resource is:

The Dietitian's Guide to Vegetarian Diets: Issues and Applications. Mark Messina and Virginia Messina. Aspen Publishers, Gaithersburg, MD, 1996.

This book is a comprehensive compilation of the scientific literature relating to vegetarian nutrition.

Journals and Newsletters

Issues in Vegetarian Dietetics (see previous listing under "Magazines and Newsletters").

The Loma Linda University Vegetarian Nutrition and Health Letter (see previous listing under "Magazines and Newsletters").

Vegetarian Journal (see previous listing under "Magazines and Newsletters").

Vegetarian Nutrition: An International Journal. Editor: Mark Messina, Ph.D. Managing Editor: Sharon Parkinson.

A new professional journal first published in 1997 and published quarterly thereafter by MCB University Press. For more information, contact Sharon Parkinson at sparkinson@mcb.co.uk or Mark Messina at markm@olympus.net.

Internet Resources

Sci-veg is an e-mail list devoted to the discussion of social and natural science topics relating to vegetarianism. Contact www.waste.org/sci-veg/.

The Least You Need to Know

➤ Repetition helps you learn, and reading the same material presented by different sources will help you learn and retain key concepts concerning a vegetarian eating style.

➤ Gain information from a variety of reliable sources, and move along at a pace that feels comfortable for you.

➤ Get your information from the sources that appeal to you most at the time. It's okay to start reading a book, put it aside for a while to try your hand at cooking for a change, then come back to the book later when you feel like it.

➤ There are some excellent vegetarian organizations that are a wealth of knowledge and support for people who choose vegetarian lifestyles.

➤ There are also many good books, countless cookbooks, videos, web sites, and other resources that you should investigate for more information.

Recommended Dietary Allowances and Dietary Reference Intakes

About Recommended Dietary Allowances and Dietary Reference Intakes

Recommended Dietary Allowances (RDAs) are levels of intake of essential nutrients that scientists deem to be adequate to meet the needs of practically all healthy people in the United States. The RDAs are established by the Food and Nutrition Board of the National Academy of Sciences.

Dietary Reference Intakes (DRIs) is a new term that is being used to refer to three different sets of reference values: Estimated Average Requirement, Recommended Dietary Allowance, and Tolerable Upper Intake Level. This new terminology reflects increases in scientific knowledge about human nutrition. By the year 2000, the Food and Nutrition Board hopes to have Dietary Reference Intakes established for all nutrients.

For now, DRIs have only been established for the nutrient groups listed in the following tables. Nutritionists will continue to use the RDAs for other nutrients, until the transition is complete. When it is, we'll not only have RDAs for nutrients, but we'll have additional information. The *Estimated Average Requirement* (EAR) is the intake of a nutrient that is estimated to meet the requirement of 50 percent of an age- and sex-specific group. In other words, at the EAR level, 50 percent of people would be getting enough of the nutrient, and 50 percent would not meet their needs.

The *Tolerable Upper Limit Level* (UL) means just what you'd guess: The UL is the maximum level of daily intake of a nutrient that is not likely to be unsafe for almost all of the people in the group for whom the UL was designed.

Table A.1 Food and Nutrition Board, National Academy of Sciences—Institute of Medicine Recommended Levels for Individual Intake, 1998, B Vitamins and Choline

Life-Stage Group	Thiamin (mg/d)	Riboflavin (mg/d)	Niacin (mg/d)[a]	B6 (mg/d)	Folate (µg/d)[b]	B12 (µg/d)	Pantothenic Acid (mg/d)	Biotin (µg/d)	Choline[c] (mg/d)
Infants									
0–5 mo	0.2*	0.3*	2*	0.1*	65*	0.4*	1.7*	5*	125*
6–11 mo	0.3*	0.4*	3*	0.3*	80*	0.5*	1.8*	6*	150*
Children									
1–3 yr	0.5	0.5	6	0.5	150	0.9	2*	8*	200
4–8 yr	0.6	0.6	8	0.6	200	1.2	3*	12*	250*
Males									
9–13 yr	0.9	0.9	12	1.0	300	1.8	4*	20*	375*
14–18 yr	1.2	1.3	16	1.3	400	2.4	5*	25*	550*
19–30 yr	1.2	1.3	16	1.3	400	2.4	5*	25*	550*
31–50 yr	1.2	1.3	16	1.3	400	2.4	5*	30*	550*
51–70 yr	1.2	1.3	16	1.7	400	2.4[d]	5*	30*	550*
>70 yr	1.2	1.3	16	1.7	400	2.4[d]	5*	30*	550*
Females									
9–13 yr	0.9	0.9	12	1.0	300	1.8	4*	20*	375*
14–18 yr	1.0	1.0	14	1.2	400[e]	2.4	5*	25*	400*
19–30 yr	1.1	1.1	14	1.3	400[e]	2.4	5*	30*	425*
31–50 yr	1.1	1.1	14	1.3	400[e]	2.4	5*	30*	425*
51–70 yr	1.1	1.1	14	1.5	400[e]	2.4[d]	5*	30*	425*
>70 yr	1.1	1.1	14	1.5	400	2.4[d]	5*	30*	425*

Life-Stage Group	Thiamin (mg/d)	Riboflavin (mg/d)	Niacin (mg/d)[a]	B6 (mg/d)	Folate (µg/d)[b]	B12 (µg/d)	Pantothenic Acid (mg/d)	Biotin (µg/d)	Choline[c] (mg/d)
Pregnancy (all ages)	1.4	1.4	18	1.9	600[f]	2.6	6*	30*	450*
Lactation (all ages)	1.5	1.6	17	2.0	500	2.8	7*	35*	550*

Note: This table presents Recommended Dietary Allowances (RDAs) in bold type and Adequate Intakes (AIs) in ordinary type followed by an asterisk (*). RDAs and AIs may both be used as goals for individual intake. RDAs are set to meet the needs of almost all (97 to 98%) individuals in a group. For healthy breast-fed infants, the AI is the mean intake. The AI for other life-stage groups is believed to cover their needs, but lack of data or uncertainty in the data prevent clear specification of this coverage.

[a] As niacin equivalents. 1 mg of niacin = 60 mg of tryptophan.

[b] As dietary folate equivalents (DFE). 1 DFE = 1 µg food folate = 0.6 µg of folic acid (from fortified food or supplement) consumed with food = 0.5 µg of synthetic (supplemental) folic acid taken on an empty stomach.

[c] Although AIs have been set for choline, there are few data to assess whether a dietary supply of choline is needed at all stages of the life cycle, and it may be that the choline requirement can be met by endogenous synthesis at some of these stages.

[d] Since 10 to 30% of older people may malabsorb food-bound B12, it is advisable for those older than 50 years to meet their RDA mainly by taking foods fortified with B12 or a B12-containing supplement.

[e] In view of evidence linking folate intake with neural tube defects in the fetus, it is recommended that all women capable of becoming pregnant consume 400 µg of synthetic folic acid from fortified foods and/or supplements in addition to intake of food folate from a varied diet.

[f] It is assumed that women will continue taking 400 µg of folic acid until their pregnancy is confirmed and they enter prenatal care, which ordinarily occurs after the end of the periconceptional period—the critical time for formation of the neural tube.

313

Table A.2 Food and Nutrition Board, National Academy of Sciences—Institute of Medicine Dietary Reference Intakes, 1997

Life-Stage Group	Calcium AIᵃ (mg/day)	Phosphorus RDAᵇ (mg/day)	Phosphorus AI (mg/day)	Magnesium RDA (mg/day)	Magnesium AI (mg/day)	Vitamin D AIᶜ,ᵈ (μg/day)	Fluoride AI (mg/day)
Infants							
0–6 mo	210		100		30	5	0.01
6–12 mo	270		275		75	5	0.5
Children							
1–3 yr	500	460		80		5	0.7
4–9 yr	800	500		130		5	1
Males							
9–13 yr	1,300	1,250		240		5	2
14–18 yr	1,300	1,250		410		5	3
19–30 yr	1,000	700		400		5	3
31–50 yr	1,000	700		420		5	4
51–70 yr	1,200	700		420		10	4
>70 yr	1,200	700		420		15	4
Females							
9–13 yr	1,300	1,250		240		5	2
14–18 yr	1,300	1,250		360		5	3
19–30 yr	1,000	700		310		5	3
31–50 yr	1,000	700		320		5	3
51–70 yr	1,200	700		320		10	3
>70 yr	1,200	700		320		15	3

Life-Stage Group	Calcium AI[a] (mg/day)	Phosphorus RDA[b] (mg/day)	Phosphorus AI (mg/day)	Magnesium RDA (mg/day)	Magnesium AI (mg/day)	Vitamin D AI[c,d] (μg/day)	Fluoride AI (mg/day)
Pregnancy							
≤18 yr	1,300	1,250			400	5	3
19–30 yr	1,000	700			350	5	3
31–50 yr	1,000	700			360	5	3
Lactation							
≤18 yr	1,300	1,250			360	5	3
19–30	1,000	700			310	5	3
31–50	1,000	700			320	5	3

[a] AI = Adequate Intake. The observed average or experimentally set intake by a defined population or subgroup that appears to sustain a defined nutritional status, such as growth rate, normal circulating nutrient values, or other functional indicators of health. AI is utilized if sufficient evidence is not available to derive an EAR. The AI is not equivalent to RDA. For healthy breast-fed infants, AI is the mean intake. All other life-stage groups should be covered at the AI value.

[b] RDA = Recommended Dietary Allowance. The intake that meets the nutrient need of almost all (97 to 98%) individuals in a group.

[c] As cholecalciferol. 1 μg cholecalciferol = 40 IU vitamin D.

[d] In the absence of adequate exposure to sunlight.

© Copyright 1997 by the National Academy of Sciences. All rights reserved.

Table A.3   Food and Nutrition Board, National Academy of Sciences—National

Designed for the maintenance of good nutrition of practically all healthy people in the United States

Age (Years) or Condition	Weight[b] (kg)	Weight[b] (lb)	Height[b] (cm)	Height[b] (in)	Protein (g)	Fat-Soluble Vitamins Vitamin A (µg RE)[c]	Fat-Soluble Vitamins Vitamin E (mgαTE)[d]	Fat-Soluble Vitamins Vitamin K (µg)
Infant								
0.0–0.5	6	13	60	24	13	375	3	5
0.5–1.0	9	20	71	28	14	375	4	10
Children								
1–3	13	29	90	35	16	400	6	15
4–6	20	44	112	44	24	500	7	20
7–10	28	62	132	52	28	700	7	30
Males								
11–14	45	99	157	62	45	1,000	10	45
15–18	66	145	176	69	59	1,000	10	65
19–24	72	160	177	70	58	1,000	10	70
25–50	79	174	176	70	63	1,000	10	80
51+	77	170	173	68	63	1,000	10	80
Females								
11–14	46	404	457	62	46	800	8	45
15–18	55	120	163	64	44	800	8	55
19–24	58	128	164	65	46	800	8	60
25–50	63	138	163	64	50	800	8	65
51+	65	143	160	63	50	800	8	65
Pregnant					60	800	10	65
Lactating								
1st 6 mo					65	1,300	12	65
2nd 6 mo					62	1,200	11	65

[1] Note: This table does not include nutrients for which Dietary Reference Intakes have recently been established

[a] The allowances, expressed as average daily intakes over time, are intended to provide for individual variations should be based on a variety of common foods in order to provide other nutrients for which human requirements

[b] Weights and heights of Reference Adults are actual medians for the United States, population of the designated from Hamill et al. (1979). The use of these figures does not imply that the height-to-weight ratios are identical.

[c] Retinol equivalents. 1 retinol equivalent = 1 µg retinol or 6 µg beta-carotene.

[d] α-Tocopherol equivalents. 1 mg d-α tocopherol = 1 α-TE.

[e] 1 NE (niacin equivalent) = 1 mg niacin or 60 mg dietary tryptophan.

Research Council Recommended Dietary Allowances[a], Revised 1989 (Abridged[1])

Vitamin C (mg)	Water-Soluble Vitamins						Minerals			
	Thiamin (mg)	Riboflavin (mg)	Niacin (mg NE)[e]	Vitamin B6 (mg)	Folate (µg)	Vitamin B12 (µg)	Iron (mg)	Zinc (mg)	Iodine (µg)	Selenium (µg)
30	0.3	0.4	5	0.3	25	0.3	6	5	40	10
35	0.4	0.5	6	0.6	32	0.5	10	5	50	15
40	0.7	0.8	9	1.0	50	0.7	10	10	70	20
45	0.9	1.1	12	1.1	75	1.0	10	10	90	20
45	1.0	1.2	13	1.4	100	1.4	10	10	120	30
	1.3	1.5	17	1.7	150	2.0	12	15	150	40
60	1.5	1.8	20	2.0	200	2.0	12	15	150	50
60	1.5	1.7	19	2.0	200	2.0	100	15	150	70
60	1.5	1.7	19	2.0	200	2.0	10	15	150	70
60	1.2	1.4	15	2.0	200	2.0	10	15	150	70
50	1.1	1.3	15	1.4	150	2.0	15	12	150	45
60	1.1	1.3	15	1.5	180	2.0	15	12	150	50
60	1.1	1.3	15	1.6	180	2.0	15	12	150	50
60	1.1	1.3	15	1.6	180	2.0	15	12	150	55
60	1.0	1.2	13	1.6	180	2.0	10	12	150	55
70	1.5	1.6	17	2.2	400	2.2	30	15	175	65
95	1.6	1.8	20	2.1	280	2.6	15	19	200	75
90	1.6	1.7	20	2.1	260	2.6	15	16	200	75

(see Dietary Reference Intakes for Calcium, Phosphorus, Magnesium, Vitamin D, and Fluoride, 1997).

among most normal persons as they live in the United States under usual environmental stresses. Diets have been less well defined.

age, as reported by NHANES II. The median weights and heights of those under 19 years of age were taken

Terms and Definitions

Amaranth   Amaranth is an ancient grain that was a staple food of the Aztecs of Central America.

Amenorrhea   Amenorrhea is the cessation of regular menstrual cycles.

Amino acids   Amino acids are the building blocks of proteins and have other functions in the body as well.

Antioxidants   Antioxidants are phytochemicals that are present in abundance in plant products and help rid the body of free radicals.

Athlete   For the purposes of this book, the term athlete refers to anyone who is vigorously physically active most days of the week for extended periods of time.

Beta-carotene   Beta-carotene is a substance found in abundance in deep yellow or deep orange and red fruits and vegetables. It may protect against cancer and coronary artery disease.

Cholesterol   Cholesterol is a waxy substance that is a major component of the plaques that form in diseased arteries. It is found only in animal products; there is none in foods of plant origin.

Complementary proteins   The term complementary proteins refers to a practice whereby foods were combined in order to optimize their amino acid profiles. Eaten together, the foods formed a "complete protein." This practice is no longer considered necessary.

Creutzfeldt-Jakob Disease   *See* Mad Cow Disease.

Cruciferous   Cruciferous vegetables are those in the cabbage family, including broccoli, bok choy, Brussels sprouts, kale, collard greens, turnip greens, and many others.

Cyanocobalamin   Cyanocobalamin is the form of vitamin B12 that is physiologically active for humans.

Debeaking   Debeaking is the practice of snapping off the end of a chicken's beak with a machine.

Desertification   Desertification is the slow death of the land caused by the overgrazing of cattle. The topsoil erodes and the land dries out, preventing it from supporting the growth of plant life.

Diplomacy   Diplomacy is skill in handling affairs without arousing hostility.

Empty calorie foods   Empty calorie foods are foods that provide little in the way of nutrition in exchange for the calories they contribute to the diet.

Essential amino acids   Essential amino acids are amino acids that cannot be manufactured by the body and must be obtained from food.

Free radicals   Free radicals are molecules that damage the body's cells.

Fruitarian diet   A fruitarian diet consists of only fruits, vegetables that are classified as fruits, and seeds and nuts.

Gerontology   Gerontology is the study of normal aging.

Gluten   Gluten is the protein portion of wheat.

Hemachromatosis   Hemachromatosis is a condition in which the body stores excessive amounts of iron.

Heme iron   Heme iron is the form of iron found in meat, poultry, and fish. It's more readily absorbed by the body than iron that comes from plant sources. *See also* Nonheme iron.

Hydrogenated fats   Hydrogenated fats are often used in commercial baked goods and other food products. Hydrogenated fats stimulate your body to produce more cholesterol. *See also* Hydrogenation.

Hydrogenation   The process of hydrogenation changes the chemical configuration of a vegetable oil in such a way that the oil is hardened.

Iron deficiency anemia   Iron deficiency anemia is a condition that results when the iron stores in your blood are depleted and you can't get enough oxygen to the cells of your body.

Kamut   Kamut is a type of grain that has been popular in Europe for generations.

Lactase   Lactase is an enzyme produced by infants and very young children. It allows babies to digest lactose, the form of sugar found in milk. After infancy, lactase production diminishes or stops, except in most people of Northern European descent.

Lactose intolerance   Lactose intolerance is the normal condition of most of the adults in the world. They can't digest the milk sugar lactose because their mature bodies no longer produce the enzyme lactase.

Lacto vegetarian   A lacto vegetarian is a person whose diet excludes meat, fish, poultry, and eggs but includes dairy products.

Lacto ovo vegetarian   A lacto ovo vegetarian is a person whose diet excludes meat, fish, and poultry but includes dairy products and eggs.

Leavening   Leavening agents in recipes provide lift to baked goods and help them to be lighter in texture.

Legumes   Legumes are dried beans and peas such as pinto beans, black beans, kidney beans, garbanzo beans, lentils, split peas, and others.

Listeria   Listeria is a type of bacteria found on meats and in other animal products. It can cause severe illness and/or death.

Macrobiotic diet   A macrobiotic diet is sometimes classified as a type of vegetarian diet, even though it may include seafood. With the exception of seafood, a macrobiotic diet excludes all other animal products as well as refined sugars, tropical fruits, and "nightshade vegetables" (potatoes, eggplant, and peppers). The diet is based on the Chinese principles of yin and yang.

Mad Cow Disease   Mad Cow Disease is the popular term for Creutzfeldt-Jakob Disease or CJD. Mad Cow Disease is characterized by a progressive and fatal deterioration of the brain tissue, literally causing the animal or person to lose their mind.

Natural foods   There is no legal definition of the term natural foods, but within the natural foods industry it is generally understood to mean foods that have been minimally processed and are as close to their natural state as possible.

Neural tube defect   A neural tube defect is a type of birth defect that involves an incomplete closure of the spinal cord.

Nonheme iron   Nonheme iron is the form of iron found in plant foods. Nonheme sources of iron are not as available to the body as are heme sources of iron. *See also* Heme iron.

Organic   Federal guidelines are pending that will give a legal definition to the term organic. As of this writing, the term is generally understood to mean that the food has been grown without the use of synthetic fertilizers and pesticides, using farming methods that are ecologically sound. To be certified as organic, foods must be grown in soil that has been free of prohibited substances for at least three years.

Osteomalacia   Osteomalacia is a condition of the bones in which a lack of vitamin D causes the bones to demineralize and soften.

Osteoporosis   Osteoporosis is the condition that results when the bones begin to waste away and become porous and brittle, which can lead to fractures and often life-threatening consequences.

Oxalates   Oxalates or oxalic acid are substances naturally found in certain plant foods (such as spinach, Swiss chard, and beet greens) that diminish the body's absorption of certain minerals.

Pesco pollo vegetarian   A pesco pollo vegetarian is a person who avoids red meat but eats seafood and poultry. Most vegetarians don't consider this a true vegetarian diet.

Pesco vegetarian   A pesco vegetarian is a semi-vegetarian who avoids red meat and poultry but eats seafood occasionally.

Phytates   Phytates are substances naturally found in plant foods (such as wheat bran, cereals, and nuts) that diminish the body's ability to absorb certain minerals.

Pollo vegetarian   A pollo vegetarian is a semi-vegetarian who avoids red meat and seafood but eats poultry occasionally.

Protein   Protein is a vital part of all living tissues. Proteins are nitrogen-containing compounds that break down into amino acids during digestion.

Quinoa   Quinoa is a high-protein grain that was used by the Incas in Peru and is becoming popular again today.

Raw foods diet   A raw foods diet consists primarily of uncooked foods.

Riboflavin   Riboflavin is also known as vitamin B2. It has multiple functions in the body, many related to enzyme activity. Our requirements for riboflavin are related to our energy intake, so the recommended intakes vary according to calorie needs.

Rickets   Rickets is a disease that causes deformity of the bones. It's prevalent in children who do not have access to adequate amounts of vitamin D.

Salmonella   Salmonella is a bacteria found on meats and in other animal products. Salmonella poisoning may be passed off as the "24-hour flu," though some cases can be serious and may result in death.

Saturated fat   Saturated fat is found in large amounts in foods of animal origin such as red meats, the skin on poultry, and in dairy products. They raise your body's blood cholesterol level.

Seitan   Seitan is an Asian food made from wheat gluten.

Semi-vegetarian   A semi-vegetarian is someone who is cutting back on his or her intake of meat in general.

Spelt   Spelt is a type of wheat that has been popular in Europe for generations.

Strict vegetarian   A strict vegetarian is someone who eats no meat, fish, poultry, eggs, or dairy products but who doesn't necessarily avoid other animal products, such as wool, silk, leather, or nonfood items made with animal by-products.

Teff   Teff is one of the oldest cultivated grains. It is used in Ethiopia today to make injera, a traditional bread.

Tempeh   Tempeh is a traditional Indonesian soyfood made from whole soybeans and sometimes mixed with a grain such as rice. It is fermented and pressed into a flat, rectangular block.

Textured vegetable protein   Textured vegetable protein (TVP) is made from soy flour that has been denatured by compressing the soy fibers. It's usually sold in granules that resemble ground beef when they are rehydrated. It may also be sold in chunks.

Tofu   Tofu is a traditional Asian soyfood. It's white, nearly odorless, and bland, and it picks up the flavor of the foods with which it is cooked.

Trans fatty acids   Trans fatty acids are vegetable fats that have had their chemical compositions changed through a method of processing that hardens the vegetable oil. Trans fats are associated with an increased risk for coronary artery disease.

Transition foods   Transition foods are foods that take the place of meat and serve as a crutch or "training wheels" to help people gradually adopt a vegetarian eating style. Examples include veggie burgers and vegetarian hotdogs.

Vegan   A vegan is a person who eats no meat, fish, poultry, eggs, or dairy products and who also avoids the use of other animal products, including wool, silk, leather, and any nonfood items made with animal by-products.

Vegetarian   A vegetarian is a person who eats no meat, fish, or poultry.

Whole foods   Whole foods are foods that are as close to their natural state as possible, or the least processed as compared to other foods in the same category.

Index

Q-R

vitamins
  adult requirements,
    121-125
  for athletes, 135
  for babies, 98
  supplementing or
    not, 79-81
  supplements, National
    Academy of
    Sciences, 80
VN DPG (Vegetarian
  Nutrition Dietetic Practice
  Group), 304
VRG (Vegetarian Resource
  Group), 272, 296,
  299, 307
  free booklet, 112
  Roper Poll (1994), 4
  Web site, 110, 128, 304

W-X

washing fruits, 216
waste materials,
  eliminating, 15
water
  intake during
    exercise, 137
  pollution, 20
Web sites
  American Dietetic
    Association, 303
  CSPI (Center for Science
    in the Public
    Interest), 302
  Dr. Andrew Weil, 80
  NCND (National Center
    for Nutrition and
    Dietetics), 303
  PCRM (Physicians
    Committee for
    Responsible
    Medicine), 303

PETA (People for the
  Ethical Treatment of
  Animals), 23
USDA (United States
  Department of
  Agriculture), 52, 60, 69,
  74, 79
VRG (Vegetarian
  Resource Group), 110,
  128, 304
weight
  of children, obesity, 105
  controlling with dietary
    fiber, 15
  losing, 211
  during pregnancy,
    controlling, 87-88
  special diets, 125
  of teens, 116-117
Weil, Andrew, 80
wheat
  bulgur, meat
    substitution, 248
  gluten, seitan, 248
  kamut, 188-189
  spelt, 188-189
whole foods, 17-18
whole-grains
  daily food guide,
    211, 213
  mixes, 194
women, amenorrhea, 135
workplace, handling
  vegetarianism, 268
world hunger, 21-22

Y-Z

yeast, nutritional,
  as cheese substitute, 245
  Red Star T-6635+, 68
YMCAs (Young Men's
  Christian
  Association), 298

yogurt in recipes,
  substituting, 244-245
zinc
  absorption of, 77-78
  calcium supplements,
    time to take, 78
  and phytates, 78
  RDA (Recommended
    Dietary Allowance), 77
  vegetarian foods,
    content in, 78-79